LIFE
A USER'S
MANUAL

LIFE

A USER'S MANUAL

*Life Advice from
the Great Philosophers
to Get You Through*

JULIAN BAGGINI
& ANTONIA MACARO

1

Ebury Press an imprint of Ebury Publishing,
20 Vauxhall Bridge Road,
London SW1V 2SA

Ebury Press is part of the Penguin Random House group of companies
whose addresses can be found at global.penguinrandomhouse.com

Penguin
Random House
UK

First published by Ebury Press in 2020
This edition published in 2021

www.penguin.co.uk

A CIP catalogue record for this book is available from the British Library

ISBN 9781529104530

Typeset in 9.24/12 pt Bembo Infant MT Std
by Integra Software Services Pvt. Ltd, Pondicherry

Printed and bound in Great Britain by Clays Ltd, Elcograf S.p.A.

The authorised representative in the EEA is Penguin Random House
Ireland, Morrison Chambers, 32 Nassau Street, Dublin D02 YH68

Penguin Random House is committed to a sustainable
future for our business, our readers and our planet.
This book is made from Forest Stewardship
Council® certified paper.

Contents

Introduction

'Life doesn't come with an instruction manual,' so the old saying goes, and with good reason. The makers of phones, chairs, soufflés and other created objects have a clear idea of what kinds of things these are, what function they serve and how they should be made or used. And they can draw on all this knowledge to create manuals for users.

It's different for human beings. We were not created with a predetermined purpose. We find ourselves 'thrown' into the world, to use Heidegger's evocative expression. Or, as Jean-Paul Sartre put it, for human beings, 'Existence precedes essence.' We are, before we know *what* exactly we are and how we ought to live. We have to work out our purpose for ourselves: it's not a given.

There is, however, one kind of user's manual we can resort to, one that requires a small but significant change in punctuation. Strictly speaking, it is a *users'* manual – a manual *for* users written *by* users. These user-authors are the philosophers who have been grappling with the human condition for millennia, from the ancient worlds of China, India and Greece to the present day.

The words of dead philosophers speak to us across the centuries because human beings have a great deal in common with each other. There are universal human needs and common life situations. Each person, like a snowflake, is unique, just like every situation and every society is different. But we can draw on what we know about humanity more generally to illuminate particular cases.

Of course many believe we are created with a purpose by a designer God who gave us an instruction manual in the form of the sacred texts of their religion. Even they, however, would surely accept that they can learn from other traditions of thought and that the world's great philosophers have a great deal to offer.

This manual is a compendium of their wisdom. Unlike traditional philosophy reference books, it is not organised by the names of philosophers, schools or abstract concepts but by life situations. When people face problems in life they do not go looking for what the great thinkers have said about deontological duties, *a priori* principles or the difference between substance and attribute (even though all of these might actually be of use to them) – they want to know what philosophers have to say about relationships, work, illness, despair.

The relevance of philosophy to these questions has varied. For the ancient schools, questions of how to live were central. Most modern philosophers, in contrast, have had little or nothing to say about the art of living. However, in the last couple of decades or so, philosophy's public image seems to have changed from impenetrable scholasticism to something that could be useful to everyone. Stoicism in particular has grown enormously in popularity, and with its wealth of practical advice on how to live, it is easy to understand why. The Stoics excel in perceptiveness and clarity, and many of their words feature in these pages.

Many who have helped to create this shift have argued that it marks a return to philosophy's historic mission and that ancient philosophy was a form of psychotherapy. Supporting evidence includes the fact that both Albert Ellis, founder of rational-emotive behaviour therapy, and Aaron Beck, founder of cognitive behavioural therapy, were influenced by Stoicism. In particular, they acknowledge a debt to Epictetus' saying that 'People are disturbed not by things, but by the views they take of things.' The idea is that how we think affects how we feel, so we can change our feelings by changing our thinking.

According to Richard Sorabji, the idea of philosophy as therapy can be traced back to the fifth century BCE, when Democritus said, 'Medicine cures diseases of the body, wisdom frees the soul from emotions.' This view seems to have been retained by the later Stoics, Sceptics and Epicureans. 'Vain is the word of a philosopher which does not heal any [human] suffering,' wrote Epicurus. 'For just as there is no profit in medicine if it does not expel the diseases of the body, so there is no profit in philosophy either, if it does not expel the suffering of the mind.' Stoic philosophers also clearly stated that philosophy should be seen as a 'medical art for the soul'.

But the relationship between philosophy and therapy is not as clear-cut as it might seem. Apart from the point, already made, that some philosophical schools are much more relevant to daily life than others, there is also the issue that meanings can be lost over the eras, as well as in translation. When the ancients spoke of 'therapy', they did not mean exactly the same as we do. In particular, they did not believe that studying philosophy was a technique for feeling better. They thought that through philosophy we could come to see things more clearly and, most importantly, more truthfully. We would be 'cured' of the false beliefs and values that cause suffering, like attachment to the things of the world. This *would* make us feel better. But that was not the purpose.

If we take the Stoics, for instance, it's easy enough to agree that coming to see things truthfully means realising that many things we ordinarily pursue – wealth, popularity, success – have only limited value. But accepting the Stoics' specific views about what beliefs and values we should embrace is a bigger ask. To achieve Stoic calm and tranquillity we'd need to accept that virtue is the only true good and that almost all our emotions, urges, desires and attachments are misguided. Even if we were prepared to do that, 'curing' ourselves of our delusions would require a lot of hard work and training: reading, memorisation, repetition, self-examination.

This conception of philosophy is far removed from the current academic ethos as well as the usual understanding of therapy, in which the goal is primarily symptom reduction (for instance in anxiety or depression) and improved functioning. The range of current psychotherapies is wide, and some are more interested than others in self-exploration and development. But, generally speaking, instigating a radical overhaul of people's value system is not part of the remit.

Nonetheless, there is a sense in which even the more detached contemporary kind of philosophy can be therapeutic in the broad sense of the term. Much of our confusion in life is self-inflicted and our thinking can lead us astray. This is why philosophy can help us to make sense of things and give us insight into our predicaments. This book draws on philosophy's capacity to provide the tools for a better understanding of issues and dilemmas. A grasp of ethical theories, for instance, can help us to clarify how to handle a moral dilemma; a more sophisticated view of free will can enable us to get to grips with the extent of our responsibility; and even apparently dry logic is useful to help us to spot fallacies in our reasoning that result in false beliefs. People can resort to philosophical counselling to take this process further and examine values, assumptions and ideas about the good life. This kind of therapy may or may not lead to changes in mood, but it will have done its work so long as it has helped us 'to show the fly the way out of the fly bottle', as Wittgenstein put it.

A wide range of perspectives is presented in this book, but we have unashamedly drawn more on the philosophers we think are the most insightful guides to everyday life – Aristotle and Hume in particular. Of course, we don't agree with everything that any of the chosen philosophers said, and we have selected aspects of their thought that we believe to be most relevant to today's world.

It is up to you to decide what is worth adopting. However, like the dishes in a buffet, not all combinations work equally well: ideas fit together into more or less coherent wholes. You'll get some sense of the kind of package we favour from the recurrence of certain key ideas. We haven't hidden our own views or tried to smuggle them in as though they were The Truth. Our biases are open so you can question them.

Our users' manual is not a set of instructions. A traditional manual tells you how things work and what you have to do to fix them when they don't. It is really a set of algorithms: linear, rule-based processes for solving problems. No such algorithms exist for human life. If they did, someone would have come up with them long ago and we'd all be getting on just fine.

A philosophical manual is therefore a set of tools to help you to live better, rather than a list of rules and instructions. Philosophy is as much about asking better questions as it is about finding answers. The wisdom it offers is best thought of not as a body of knowledge that directs each step we take in life, but as a way of thinking and reasoning about ourselves and the world that helps us to take those steps for ourselves.

Reading
Pierre Hadot, *Philosophy as a Way of Life* (Wiley-Blackwell, 1995)

A

'It is bad today, and it will be worse tomorrow; and so on till the worst of all.'
Arthur Schopenhauer

Acceptance *see* Contentment

Achievement

Achievement has become one of the things we most worry about. Is our career stellar enough? Are we on a high enough rung of the housing ladder? Do our qualifications adequately reflect our abilities? The sense that we 'should' have achieved this, that or the other by a certain life stage can be tormenting.

Achievement regularly appears in theories of human needs and of motivation. It is also included in some philosophers' lists of requirements for a good life. John Cottingham writes that 'some degree of achievement is necessary for everyone'. Spending our days in a drug-fuelled stupor is no way to live. We need to develop our talents. Cottingham is realistic: people have different abilities and not everyone will become a top-level musician or athlete. But, he says, the 'truly happy life must be one where we are *stretched*'.

But there's another side to achievement. The Stoics illustrated this through the analogy of the archer. If we're trying to hit a target, all we can do is practise our archery skills as best we can. Once the arrow has left the bow, it is no longer in our control, and any gust of wind can divert it from the target. It is the same with goals: to achieve them we need a certain amount of luck. It's better, therefore, to concentrate on what is in our control, which is our mindset and actions. The final outcome is not up to us.

Another reason to be suspicious of achievement is that ultimately everything will crumble to dust. We might call this the 'Ozymandias' perspective, after Shelley's poem of the same name. The inscription on the pedestal of a shattered statue in the desert warns, 'My name is Ozymandias, King of Kings; Look on my Works, ye Mighty, and despair! Nothing beside remains.' This vividly captures the vanity and folly of seeking achievement for the sake of elevating one's status or leaving a legacy.

So is achievement essential for everyone's flourishing or is it a false value, a vain temptation that we should resist? Shelley and the Stoics make a persuasive case that too much focus on it is unhelpful. But Cottingham is surely right that the sense of achievement that comes from developing our capacities can help to give life value.

One way to keep achievement in its place is to make it more ordinary. Montaigne casts doubt on the idea that it's necessary to achieve great things:'We are great fools.''He has spent his life in idleness," we say, and "I have done nothing today." What! have you not lived? That is not only the fundamental, but the most noble of your occupations.' If we look at it in this light, we can discover little daily achievements that had completely passed us by. Sometimes even surviving is achievement enough.

A complementary approach is to focus more on process than on outcome. Kieran Setiya recommends maintaining a balance between what he calls 'telic' and 'atelic' activities. Telic activities have a clear endpoint that, once reached, exhausts their meaning or value – building a model boat or walking the Camino de Santiago, for instance. Drawing on the work of Schopenhauer, Setiya argues that the problem with focusing too much on telic activities is that in a way it means constantly losing the very things that make our life worthwhile. (*See* **Boredom**.)

Atelic activities have no such point of completion. For example, any given walk or album will come to an end, but that doesn't mean you're done with walking or listening to music. It might be beneficial to reflect on the balance of activities in your life and, if appropriate, introduce more atelic ones, which Setiya says 'are not exhaustible'.

Zen Buddhism brings together the idea of focusing on the activity rather than the result and that of appreciating smaller achievements. This is captured in the old saying, 'Before enlightenment: chop wood, carry water. After enlightenment: chop wood, carry water.' If enlightenment is a kind of achievement, what is achieved is not something exceptional but a transformation of the unexceptional.

So by all means set yourself a goal, such as writing a book. But focus more on the *process* than on any rewards you imagine will follow its completion. That is certainly achievable.

See also: Boredom, Carpe Diem, Competition, Contentment, Cosmic Insignificance, Envy, Failure, Leisure, Meaning, Needs, Reputation

Reading
John Cottingham, *On the Meaning of Life* (Routledge, 2002)

Addiction *see* **Self-Control**

Afterlife

Death is both the most undeniable fact of life and one of the most difficult things to truly believe in. Sometimes it seems impossible that people who shared our joys and sorrows, who were so alive, have simply gone for ever. We may have intimations of mortality after near misses, illnesses or the death of other people, but in the normal run of things it's hard to connect with the idea that we too will one day simply cease to be. One way people commonly heal this fracture between how things seem and how they know they are is to believe in a life to come.

There are certainly plenty of philosophers who can bolster this belief, most obviously Plato's Socrates. 'When death comes to a man, the mortal part of him dies, but the immortal part retires at the approach of death and escapes unharmed and indestructible,' he told his assembled followers before his execution. 'It is as certain as anything can be . . . that soul is immortal and imperishable, and that our souls will really exist in the next world.'

Nearly two millennia later, René Descartes expressed almost exactly the same view, arguing that the mind is 'really distinct from my body, and can exist without it'.

In essence, their argument for the immortality and indestructibility of the soul was that since thought and consciousness constitute our essential nature, and thoughts are not physical, the essence of human beings must be immaterial. Few people today would find this logic persuasive, as we now have overwhelming reason to believe that thought emerges from, and depends on, brain processes. All the evidence suggests that when the brain dies, so does the mind, and with it, the self.

Another source of potential hope for a life to come is found in Indic philosophies, almost all of which believe in rebirth. This is little comfort, alas, since they also believe that as long as we continue to be reborn we are condemned to the trials and tribulations of life – what the Buddhists call *dukkha*, or unsatisfactoriness. (*See* **Suffering**.) The true prize is not being born again, but breaking the cycle of rebirth. In these systems, it is not the personal day-to-day self that is reborn anyway. When we 'come back' in future lives we do not remember previous ones, which is why we don't know we had them. What returns is something thinner, a kind of bare locus of experience.

Those who seek the comfort of a life to come won't find it in philosophy today. If it can help at all, it is by persuading us that perhaps what we long for is not only impossible, but also not to be desired. The neuroscientist David Eagleman has written forty brilliant short stories, collectively showing that the idea of an afterlife is not as clear as it seems, and suggesting that many possible versions of it might be more of a curse than a blessing. In one you only ever see people you already know and are doomed to an eternity of tedium. In another, the well-worn question of how old you are in heaven is solved by there being multiple versions of you, each frustrated by the immaturity or decrepitude of the others. In yet another you see what might have been if you'd made different choices and are envious of your more successful selves. (*See* **What If**.)

Instead of hankering for an afterlife, we could learn to see it as a quixotic impossibility. This may seem too demanding, but Chinese philosophy shows that one of the oldest and largest civilisations on earth got along just fine without it. The classics of Confucius and Mencius are largely silent on what happens after death. They do have a concept of heaven (*tian*), but this refers to the guiding principles of the universe rather than a place we go to. Their philosophy is centred on the here and now and their morality on the duties and responsibilities we have to each other, showing us that living for what is valuable in this life does not have to leave an afterlife-shaped hole.

The only truthful way in which we can soften the full stop of death and turn it into an ellipsis is to think about how we live on in the lives, hearts and minds of others. After the end of every biography, there is an epilogue in the biographies of others. Perhaps the aspiration to live for ever could be replaced by the common Chinese ambition to 'leave behind a fragrance lasting for millennia'.

See also: Bereavement, Death, Meaning of Life, Mortality, Suffering

Reading

David Eagleman, *Sum* (Canongate, 2009)

Ageing

The terror of ageing is so strong that many feel it even when they are still very young. People turning 18 or 21 are often heard moaning that they are now 'so old!', much to the amusement of those who really are ancient. Even turning 30 or 40 is traumatic for many.

Given how old age is often represented, it's not surprising that we dread it. The horizons of T.S. Eliot's J. Alfred Prufrock have shrunk so much that the most weighty decisions he has to ponder are whether he should part his hair behind or dare to eat a peach. Shakespeare's famous 'seven ages of man' speech in *As You Like It* pictures a 'lean and slipper'd panta-loon' with a 'shrunk shank' by the sixth age, while the seventh and last looks forward to 'second childishness and mere oblivion, Sans teeth, sans eyes, sans taste, sans everything.' Schopenhauer was hardly challenging received wisdom when he wrote, 'It is bad today, and it will be worse tomorrow; and so on till the worst of all.'

Ah, *the worst of all*. Added to our gradual corporeal entropy is the awareness that each day brings us closer to the grave. But cheer up – it's not all bad! For instance, in our libidinous times we have somehow come to believe that it is good, natural and desirable to have the sex drive of a hormonal teenager for as long as possible. But for Plato's Socrates, the calming of the libido was one of the advantages of growing older. Quoting Sophocles, he says, 'I feel as if I had escaped from a frantic and savage master.' It's not just sex. 'Unquestionably old age brings us profound repose and freedom from this and other passions,' he says. Slowing down has its advantages, and many older people report feeling a kind of liberation from striving and ambition, which enables them to savour the present more.

In Confucian philosophy, the old are more revered than pitied. There are various reasons for this. One is that Confucius did not fetishise novelty, believing that all the greatest wisdom came from the ancients, and that the old are its best repositories. Another is that, like many other Chinese thinkers, he believed that experience was essential for wisdom. One of his most famous sayings is 'At fifteen my heart was set on learning; at thirty I stood firm; at forty I was unperturbed; at fifty I knew the mandate of heaven; at sixty my ear was obedient; at seventy I could follow my heart's desire without transgressing the norm.' The young can learn facts, but wisdom cannot be hurried. Finally, Confucian ethics is hierarchical, and so elders always have some authority. Globally and historically, this view is much more common than those that see old age negatively.

Some philosophers are good adverts for old age by their example rather than by explicit teaching. Three months before his impending death, David Hume wrote, 'were I to name a period of my life, which I should most choose to pass over again, I might be tempted to point to this later period'. This was despite suffering from a 'disorder in my bowels' that was 'mortal and incurable'. Hume's cheerfulness came in part from his natural disposition, but also from an acceptance of mortality and an appreciation that the best things in life are simple and require no youthful exuberance to enjoy them. 'Never think,' he wrote, 'that as long as you are master of your own fireside and your own time, you can be unhappy, or that any other circumstance can make an addition to your enjoyment.'

Given his health problems, Hume might have endorsed the view that Seneca expressed in a letter to a friend: 'But come, did you not know, when you prayed for long life, that this was what you were praying for?' A long life brings many problems, but it is better than the alternative.

See also: Death, Gratitude, Health and Illness, Midlife Crisis,
Mortality, Retirement, Slowing Down

Reading
David Hume, *My Own Life* (1777)
Seneca, 'Letter 96'

Aloneness *see* Solitude

Alternative Medicine *see* Evidence

Altruism

If you live in a decent-sized town or city, a walk down any main street quickly becomes a guilt trip. You pass homeless people begging for money or selling street papers, the destitute sleeping in doorways and, worst of all, 'chuggers' (charity muggers) with clipboards, flashing you a friendly smile and asking if you have time for a chat, when all you want them to do is *go away*. Turn on the television or open a newspaper and there will be more stories about people in need and charity appeals. You need to be either unusually altruistic already or happily selfish not to feel bad at these constant reminders of how much more we could be doing to help others.

When we experience this kind of dissonance, we tend to rely on mental gymnastics to make ourselves feel better. In this case, one way to ease our guilt is to persuade ourselves that no one is *really* altruistic and that every apparent work of charity is actually self-interest in disguise. (*See* **Selfishness**.) Do-gooders are simply making sure everyone, including themselves, thinks they are great.

Apparent altruism can certainly harbour selfish motives, in which case there is little to admire in it. 'When people sit by the bedsides of their sick friends, we honour their motives,' wrote Seneca. 'But when people do this for the purpose of attaining a legacy, they are like vultures waiting for carrion.'

But just because we often get some personal gain from altruistic actions, it doesn't mean we *always and only* act out of self-interest. It would be very odd if we praised people for doing good only if they didn't like doing it.

In reality, hardly anyone is an out-and-out egoist. Few people need persuading that we should think of others, as we tell our children to do. But the injunction leaves out the most difficult thing about putting it into practice: just *how much* should we think of others? Is it enough not to do them harm, or should we be actively altruistic and act for the best interests of other people?

There are philosophers who give us a pass on this by suggesting that all we need to do is pursue our own self-interest, as that is also in the best interest of everyone else. The eighteenth-century British philosopher Bernard Mandeville was one of the first to propose this, in *The Fable of the Bees*. Mandeville compared a society to a hive, in which every bee serves the interest of the whole simply by doing what it is born to do. Bees don't think of others, but their activity helps others nonetheless. Humans, he argued, are the same: the best way for everyone to be taken care of is for everyone to take care of themselves.

Mandeville's near contemporary Adam Smith is often taken to be suggesting something similar when he talked about the 'invisible hand' of the market. 'It is not from the benevolence of the butcher, the brewer, or the baker that we expect our dinner, but from their regard to their own interest,' he wrote. However, this argument against excessive state regulation was never meant to suggest that all we ever need to do is look after ourselves.

In fact, Smith was a believer in 'moral sympathy', a basic human response to the distress of others that moves us to do something to relieve it. Mandeville's optimism that self- and other-interest are always in harmony was too optimistic for Smith, as it was for most other thinkers.

At the other end of the spectrum from Mandeville are the utilitarians, who argue that we ought to consider the welfare of everyone equally and never put our own interests, or those of our families, first. If you spend thousands of pounds a year on frivolous pleasures that add little (or nothing at all) to your overall welfare, when that money could have transformed the lives of the really needy, you've failed in your moral duty.

Peter Singer is currently the most famous advocate of this position. He argues that it is our duty to give away everything in excess of what we need for a moderately comfortable life. This is no more than the rigorous application of the apparently unarguable principle that 'if it is in our power to prevent something bad from happening, without thereby sacrificing anything of comparable moral importance, we ought, morally, to do it'.

This is a very high-minded philosophy. Few, if any, measure up to these demanding standards, including professed utilitarians. But for many it is a standard to aspire to. The only way to escape its logic, apart from ignoring it, is to deny either that everyone's interests count equally or that morality requires us to consider everyone's interests impartially. The first option seems indefensible. How could we justify the second?

The late Bernard Williams did so by appealing to what he called the 'separateness of persons'. Williams argued that we cannot treat our fellow human beings as though they were interchangeable bearers of well-being. A good life requires having special relationships with some people, therefore our duties and responsibilities will vary depending on the relationship. Sure, from a God's-eye perspective the life of your brother and a stranger a thousand miles away are equal. But we are not gods, looking down on all creation. We are human beings occupying particular parts of it.

The 'role ethics' of Confucius recognises this. In his system, moral obligations depend on your social role: the particular duties a father has to a son differ from those a ruler has to a subject or a teacher has to a student. Hence his version of the Golden Rule states only that we should not impose upon others what we ourselves do not desire. (*See* **Duty**.) This is a principle of non-interference that doesn't oblige us to help strangers as much as we would help ourselves or our family.

The Confucian Golden Rule contrasts with the stronger version held by Jesus, who said, 'Do to others what you would have them do to you.' Like later utilitarians, Jesus advocated a radical impartiality, which is why he told his disciples that if they wanted to follow him, they had to be willing to leave their families.

If we reject the demands of absolute impartiality, we still have reasons to try to be more altruistic. We don't need to beat ourselves up for being less than completely self-denying saints. But that doesn't mean we shouldn't try to find the good will to go that extra mile to help others, motivated by nothing more than human sympathy.

See also: Charity, Duty, Empathy, Selfishness

Reading
Bernard Mandeville, *The Fable of the Bees* (1714)
J.J.C. Smart and Bernard Williams, *Utilitarianism: For and Against* (Cambridge University Press, 1973)
Adam Smith, *The Theory of Moral Sentiments* (1759)

Ambition *see* Achievement

Ambivalence

Think back to a time when you were so torn between competing options that you felt completely paralysed. It could be a big issue, with lots of possible repercussions – whether to give up your job, get married, sell your house – or a small one, like where to go on holiday, or which of two coats to buy. Not a good feeling, is it?

You don't have to be a chronic sufferer of ambivalence to appreciate what an essentially human experience it is. We value lots of things in life and would ideally like to secure all of them: we want the expensive coat but also to keep our hard-earned cash; we want the freedom of being single or self-employed but also the security of being in a relationship or a job. Unfortunately, real life doesn't often allow us to have our cake and eat it. It forces us to choose. We may try to avoid choosing, but that can be just another way of choosing, like when we wait so long that the situation is taken out of our hands.

Being stuck between competing goods is the plight of Buridan's ass, a legendary donkey that died of hunger while unable to decide which of two equal and equidistant bales of hay to go for. (In some versions, the choice is between a bale of hay and a pail of water.) It was named after the fourteenth-century French philosopher Jean Buridan, but the issue had been discussed in ancient times by the likes of Aristotle and the twelfth-century Persian thinker al-Ghazali.

The main question they were all grappling with is whether the impasse could be broken by the assertion of human will. Buridan argued that it couldn't, and that all will can do is 'to suspend judgement until the circumstances change, and the right course of action is clear'. Al-Ghazali was more positive, reckoning that we can will our way out of the predicament.

A modern philosopher worth consulting in relation to this is Isaiah Berlin. He argued that human values are plural and often incompatible. 'Values may easily clash within the breast of a single individual,' he writes, 'and it does not follow that, if they do, some must be true and others false.' Freedom and security, for instance, are both sound values. It just so happens that it is not always possible to realise both at the same time.

Therefore, Berlin says, 'We are doomed to choose, and every choice may entail an irreparable loss.' Or, as Kierkegaard sardonically put it, 'Marry, and you will regret it. Do not marry, and you will also regret it.'

At the very least, this should reassure us that ambivalence is a natural response to the complexity of the world. It may also hint at a way to overcome it. 'Priorities,' Berlin continues, 'must be established.' If we believe that certain conflicting values are genuinely important, we need to deeply reflect on ourselves and the situation and identify the value that is most worth affirming. If after thinking about it we still don't know, then all we can do is flip a coin, perhaps literally. Better a random choice than none at all.

Whatever way out of the impasse we choose, we have to accept that to make any choice means closing others down. Every gain has a corresponding loss, and this is why ambivalence is such a human experience.

See also: Anxiety, Choice, Commitment, Dilemmas, Indecision, Regret, Uncertainty, What If

Reading
Isaiah Berlin, *The Crooked Timber of Humanity* (Princeton University Press, 2013)

Anger

The consequences of excessive anger, or anger expressed badly, are many and potentially catastrophic: violent fights, falling out with people, careers and relationships ruined, harm to our physical or mental health. Anger is clearly problematic, but is it always wrong?

There was a longstanding dispute in ancient Greece between followers of Aristotle, who thought that anger could be useful if properly managed, and the Stoics, who had a zero-tolerance policy towards it.

Aristotle writes that anger – like feelings of fear, confidence, appetite, pity, pleasure and pain – can be experienced too much or too little, and the trick is 'to have them at the right time, about the right things, towards the right people, for the right end, and in the right way'. (*See* **Balance**.) This is rightly one of his most famous quotations – and quite a tall order.

For Aristotle, appropriate anger is an acceptable part of the human repertoire only when it is tamed by reason. If you took his advice seriously, you'd never shout at a shop assistant for something that is not their fault, or at your children when you've had a stressful day at work. You probably wouldn't shout very much at all, you'd just take the appropriate action to deal with the situation.

Seneca is more uncompromising: for him, anger is never acceptable. It creates its own momentum and can't really be controlled. Giving in to anger is like jumping off a cliff. He says that those who do it 'retain no independent judgement and cannot offer resistance or slow the descent of their bodies in freefall'. What he advises, therefore, is 'to reject straightaway the initial prickings of anger, to fight against its first sparks, and to struggle not to succumb to it'.

How do we achieve this? Mainly by challenging our thinking. We should remind ourselves that bad behaviour is endemic to human nature, says Seneca, so expect and tolerate it. After all, we are as prone to it as anyone else. Given 'the murkiness of our minds', we are all bound to make mistakes. 'To keep from becoming angry with individuals, you must forgive all at once: the human race should be granted a pardon.' Also, deep down we know that the kinds of things we get angry about are often trivial and inconsequential, and that it's wrong to waste our energies on them.

Next we must take issue with any sense that revenge is appropriate. Instead, the relevant question should be: what must be done for the best? Sometimes this might mean letting things go, sometimes calmly confronting someone about some bad or thoughtless deed they've done.

Seneca also recommends using delay as a strategy. If we don't rush into anything, our anger will probably begin to back off of its own accord. And if we could only get ourselves in front of a mirror, we'd be put off anger by seeing how ugly we look when we're angry (although Seneca admits that by the time we made it to the mirror to check this, our outlook and demeanour would already have changed).

You might be thinking that a complete lack of anger can also be problematic, like when we can't find it in us to address some wrongdoing because we're too easily cowered or scared of rocking the boat. Sometimes those who are behaving badly need to know that they've gone too far or hurt people, and that there may be consequences for what they've done.

Seneca would agree that wrongdoing should be confronted. He just believes that anger is not the right tool for the job. Any action that needs to be taken – correcting someone's behaviour, for instance – can be taken calmly. This might seem to be in agreement with Aristotle's view about bringing anger in line with reason. But for Seneca, if anger responds to reason it is no longer anger.

The advice common to both philosophers is to act from a place of reason rather than agitation. In order to do this, we need to catch the first signs of anger. This is doable, says Seneca: 'Just as signs of a rainstorm arrive before the storm itself, so there are certain signs that announce the coming of anger, love, and all those storm gusts that vex our minds.' We just have to learn what they are.

A contemporary philosopher bridging the two positions is Martha Nussbaum. She writes that it is not wrong to feel outrage about an injustice, for instance, but that we can disentangle this from any desire for retribution. She calls this 'Transition-Anger', which is the response she character-ises as 'How outrageous! Something must be done about this.' For Nussbaum, anger must be channelled towards constructive thoughts of what can be done, not useless grievance at what can't be undone. Political anger is a good example of this, when it is used as a powerful force for social change.

So if you're angry, take a few deep breaths. Remind yourself that bad behaviour is normal; you often do it yourself. Ask yourself how serious the issue is. If it isn't, let it go. If it is, think through what should be done to manage it in the best possible way. All good advice – if you're not already in a rage. The trick is to remember this the next time you feel the first twinges of anger.

See also: Balance, Calm, Emotions, Forgiveness, Protest, Self-Control

Reading
Seneca, *On Anger*
Martha Nussbaum, *Anger and Forgiveness* (Oxford University Press, 2016)

Anxiety

If you've got any anxiety in your life, the chances are that the only thing you want to know is how to get rid of it. You might be able to tolerate the occasional bouts of anxiety that are part and parcel of life but don't interfere with it too much, like butterflies in your stomach if you're about to give a speech, have a job interview or go on a date. It would be more difficult to live with the pervasive kinds of anxiety that can interfere with even simple daily tasks like getting on a bus or paying the bills.

But there is an alternative, philosophical perspective on anxiety that sees it as much more than a problem to be eliminated. This school of thought started with Kierkegaard. Anxiety for him was tied up with the Christian concept of sin and the possibility of faith, but the core of his thinking is universal. The theme was taken up by Heidegger and then by Sartre. Although they each developed it in their own distinctive ways, there is a lot of overlap.

The general picture is that anxiety inevitably arises from the human condition. Unlike inanimate objects and other animals, we are free and responsible for choosing what we do. This awareness of the future and its possibilities evokes anxiety. Kierkegaard likened it to the kind of vertigo we feel when we are on the edge of a cliff, aware that we could jump, and called it 'the dizziness of freedom'.

This anxiety is not the same as fear, as it does not have a concrete object. It is deeply unsettling, so we consciously and unconsciously try to suppress it, or avoid it by diving into everyday busyness or conventional social roles.

In Sartre's analysis, our main ploy for escaping anxiety is denying our freedom. He calls this denial 'bad faith'. We are in bad faith every time we make excuses and claim to be more passive and determined than we are. We may say we can't help it, or that we're bound to act in a certain way because of our star sign.

This denial of freedom has a positive side, in that it helps to keep life manageable. But, according to the existential philosophers, the strategy backfires and we end up living inauthentically, out of touch with who we really are. From this point of view, the bursting through of anxiety is positive, because it can jolt us out of our delusions and fake securities. It is a wake-up call to grapple with our authentic being.

This may not sound like the kind of anxiety you'd see a therapist about. But 'ordinary' anxiety and even apparently specific worries could well turn out to be unconscious attempts to conceal a deeper, more disturbing existential anxiety. While we're busy fretting about our career or financial position, deeper concerns are kept at bay.

The existentialist view is a challenge to the idea that anxiety is something to get rid of. From this perspective, a better strategy is to accept our anxiety and use it construc- tively, as a reminder that we can choose our own path. It is the price we pay for taking responsibility for our life. Kierkegaard wrote about learning to be anxious 'in the right way'. Perhaps that – rather than eliminating anxiety – could be our aim.

See also: Authenticity, Choice, Death, Fear, Free Will, Meaning

Reading
Jean-Paul Sartre, *Basic Writings,* edited by Stephen Priest (Routledge, 2000)

Appreciation *see* Gratitude

Argument

In a fractious world and in fractious homes, we might feel that the last thing we need is more argument. But if we want to cool tempers and understand each other, we actually need to learn to argue more, only better.

If that sounds odd, it's because the meaning of 'argument' has shifted over the centuries. Today it refers primarily to heated rows or disputes, but its Latin root, *argumentum,* meant a logical argument, coming from the verb *arguere*, to make clear or prove. To argue is not to start a fight but to make a case, rationally and, preferably, calmly.

Philosophy is (arguably) all about argument. What we now call philosophy emerged in ancient Greece, China and India, when people stopped founding their worldviews on myths and proclamations of authority and started looking seriously at the reasons and evidence for what they believed. Some of the earliest philosophical texts, such as Aristotle's *Organon*, were about the nature of argument itself.

One of the most remarkable of such works is the *Nyaya Sutras*, written some time between the sixth century BCE and the second century CE and attributed to Akshapada Gautama. In it Gautama describes the principles of proper argumentation in great detail. For instance, he distinguishes three kinds of inference by which we establish one fact on the basis of another. In the first we derive knowledge of an effect from knowledge of its cause: for example, we see the approaching rain clouds and know it will rain. In the second we infer the cause by observing its effects: we see the wet roads and know it has rained. Finally, we infer the existence of one thing from knowledge of what usually accompanies it: you see a corner shop and infer it will sell snacks.

None of these inferences is infallible: rain clouds dissipate, hosepipes spray roads and corner shops are idiosyncratic in their stock. But that is the nature of all 'inductive' arguments about the real world, that is to say ones based on our experience of how things are. Certainty is possible only in deductive arguments, which rely solely on the meaning of concepts – such as the mathematical argument that two plus two equals four, or the truth that anyone who is married has a spouse. But there are no irrefutable principles of logic that tell us that one thing can cause another. And as David Hume pointed out, we don't even observe causation – all we see is one thing following another. When the succession is regular we assume a causal link, but we neither observe nor deduce its existence. This leaves us on shaky ground. Bertrand Russell compared our plight to that of a chicken who sees that every morning the sun shines and it gets fed, and expects each new day to be the same. Only one of those regularities is because of a reliable rule of nature, however, as it discovers one day when instead of being fed it has its neck wrung.

The 'problem of induction' was also formulated by the fourteenth-century Indian Charvaka thinker Madhvacharya. It has never been satisfactorily solved. It's a reminder to be careful about assuming that because things have been a certain way in the past, they are bound to be so in the future. A good inductive argument can provide reasons to accept a conclusion, but not proof beyond any doubt.

Gautama goes into some detail about what makes for a good argument or for a bad one. For example, he defines *discussion* as adopting two or more sides of an argument in order to ascertain the truth. To *wrangle*, however, is to take part in an argument with the aim of winning, whether one is correct or not. To *cavil* is not even to want to win but simply to find fault in your opponent.

It is fair to say that much of what passes for discussion is really just wrangling or cavilling, but that's not necessarily because the discussants are insincere. We often don't even notice ourselves that the desire to win or to show why others are wrong motivates us more than establishing the truth.

However skilled we are in the process of argumentation, we can't get anywhere unless we start from true premises: the statements we base our arguments on. That is why even Gautama made the odd dodgy argument. For example, he identified a form of argument he called *confutation*, which is summed up in Sherlock Holmes's principle that 'When you have eliminated all which is impossible, then whatever remains, however improbable, must be the truth.' It's a good principle, as long as you remember that finite human minds can never be completely sure they have eliminated everything that is impossible.

However, Gautama's example of this is not persuasive for anyone who does not already buy into some fundamental tenets of orthodox Indian thought. He asked if the soul is eternal or non-eternal, arguing that if we assumed it were non-eternal, it would not be able 'to undergo transmigration, and to attain final release'. He thought that was absurd and so 'we must admit that the soul is eternal'. However, if you don't accept the premise that souls exist, the argument doesn't get off the ground.

Argument of the philosophical variety is the best prophylactic against the shriller, combative variety. It encourages us to offer reasons for our beliefs rather than simply assert them. It makes the quest for truth rather than victory paramount. Perhaps most importantly, it commends humility, because anyone who knows how to argue properly also knows that certainty is rarely merited in this uncertain world. Sincere arguers are always open to new perspectives and to changing their minds. In a world of cavillers and wranglers, we need them more than ever.

See also: Evidence, Intuition, Knowledge, Rationality, Truth

Reading
Akshapada Gautama, *Nyaya Sutras*

Asceticism

Sometimes the over-consumption we see around us, or our own overindulgence, leads us to crave a leaner lifestyle. We don't quite imagine ourselves in a monastic cell, but we feel the need to counter the excess with some proper austerity. So we go for dry January, or start fasting or even having cold showers.

Nowadays we tend to dabble in this kind of 'clean living' for health reasons. In so doing we're dipping our toes in the waters of an ascetic tradition that has been around for over two thousand years. (Interestingly, the Greek term *askesis*, from which the English word 'ascetic' derives, was originally used in relation to the physical training of athletes and only later came to refer to intellectual and ethical development.)

A great flurry of ascetic movements occurred in India at the time of the Buddha. Some of the practices embraced by these renunciants were extreme, including remaining motionless and giving up food or even breathing, with obvious consequences. The Buddha himself joined one of these groups at first, but later concluded that a more moderate approach was a better road to awakening.

Then there were the Christian hermits – mostly men, some women – who around the third century started going into the Egyptian deserts in search of purification through self-mortification: celibacy, fasting, poverty, silence, solitude, humility, prayer.

The lives of these Desert Fathers and Mothers were consumed by their effort to resist the temptations they believed Satan was constantly putting their way. One hermit ate while wandering around to avoid getting pleasure from eating. Another, named Agatho, kept a stone in his mouth for three years to help himself to be silent. Yet another wrapped his cloak around his hands when carrying his mother across a river, because touching a woman's body might awaken his desire for other women.

Why would anyone embrace such an austere life? Ascetics have tended to believe that the lowly body creates suffering and is an obstacle to spiritual realisation – whatever we may take that to mean. It follows that to achieve spiritual liberation we have to curb bodily pleasures and desires.

Philosophers of a less spiritual bent had little time for asceticism. For instance, it is telling that there is little of it in the Confucian or Daoist traditions. That is because neither is at all other-worldly. Confucian ethics aims to create a harmonious society, while Daoism seeks life in accordance with nature.

Aristotle likewise appreciated that our embodiment was an essential part of us, and wrote that 'human nature is not self-sufficient for contemplation, but the body must be healthy and provided with food and other care'. He allowed a *moderate* (this is important) amount of bodily pleasures – like 'fine food and wine and sexual intercourse' – in the good life. It is only excessive indulgence that is harmful.

Montaigne also advised savouring the pleasures of the body in moderation, neither seeking to deny them (as this means denying our embodied nature) or maximise them (as excess only brings pain). Among other things, he wrote that the 'genital activities of mankind' are natural and necessary. He concludes that we are inescapably a mix of the mental and the physical: nothing in us is 'either purely corporeal or purely spiritual and . . . it is injurious to tear a living man apart'.

The most uncompromising in this respect was Hume, who wrote against what he called the 'monkish virtues' of 'celibacy, fasting, penance, mortification, self-denial'. Hume believed they 'serve to no manner of purpose' and are vices rather than virtues. They 'stupify the understanding and harden the heart, obscure the fancy and sour the temper'. In a dig at ascetic saints, he said: 'A gloomy, hair-brained enthusiast, after his death, may have a place in the calendar; but will scarcely ever be admitted, when alive, into intimacy and society, except by those who are as delirious and dismal as himself.'

Small quantities of 'monkish virtues' like self-discipline and restraint can act as a valuable check on the indulgence of modern life. But when moderation tips over into the mortification of the flesh, we deny our physicality and so what we essentially are.

See also: The Body, Carpe Diem, Consumerism, Desires, Food, Pleasure, Self-Control, Silence, Simplicity, Slowing Down, Solitude

Reading
David Hume, *An Enquiry concerning the Principles of Morals* (1751), Section IX, Part 1
Michel de Montaigne, *Essays* (1580). See especially 'On Some Lines of Virgil' and 'On Experience'

Assisted Dying

There are people who genuinely mean it when they claim they don't fear death. Fear of *dying*, however, may be a tougher nut to crack. The exit from life's stage can be tortuous, torturous, or both. In such cases we may wish to get help in speeding up the process, though most don't have that legal option. Even if we did, should we take it?

The debate on the morality of assisted dying (or voluntary euthanasia) is in some ways a settled one. Almost every moral philosopher believes that a person has a right to decide to end their suffering by choosing death, and that it is morally permissible for someone else to help them to do so. In his seminal *Causing Death and Saving Lives*, Jonathan Glover takes just four pages to conclude that voluntary euthanasia is justified when the decision is evidently a serious and reasonable one that has been properly thought out and is 'not merely the result of a temporary emotional state'.

The main objections to assisted dying are usually religious. One is that it is wrong to kill. However, most religions do not uphold this as an absolute principle, since they permit killing in just wars and in self-defence. Another argument is that the gift of life is only for God to give or take away. But few religious people have any problem thwarting God's plans by trying to save premature babies and the very ill.

If the moral argument is so clear, why is assisted dying still illegal in most jurisdictions? Religion is a major factor in many countries. But there are also concerns about what Glover calls 'side effects'. Many worry that if it becomes more common for the terminally ill to end their lives, society could become less sympathetic to those who need and want help to keep living. This is a particular concern for some disability rights activists.

Another worry is that where voluntary euthanasia is legally available, people might feel under pressure to end their lives earlier than they would like to, or be fearful of entering a hospital or hospice. Doctors have tended to be reluctant to change the law on assisted dying because of the potential damage to the bond of trust with patients. So although a majority of the public in the UK has backed the 'right to die' for a couple of decades, the Royal College of Physicians only dropped its opposition in 2019, adopting a policy of neutrality.

The objections based on side effects are not about principles, but about what actually happens when assisted suicide is legalised. These are empirical questions, and since it is already legal in places like the Benelux countries and Oregon, it should be possible to see if people's fears are well-grounded. Unfortunately, maybe because investigators find it hard to be neutral, studies have reached very different conclusions.

In any case, legal and moral issues are separate, as illustrated by the case of the ethicist Mary Warnock. When her husband Geoffrey was terminally ill, his doctor Nick Maurice eased him on his way on the old 'nod and a wink' principle. 'We all knew my husband was going to die and Nick told me he was going to make him better,' the baroness said in the House of Lords. 'When he said "make him better" we all knew what this meant . . . end his suffering and end his life.'

Most people believe the doctor involved acted morally and compassionately, even though what he did was technically illegal. Warnock's view at the time was that this worked well enough, and no change of the law was needed. She later changed her mind, but her story shows that it's possible to combine the beliefs that assisted dying is not always wrong, and that the law should not make it too easy.

One of the most lamentable features of the debate is that people considering assisted dying are sometimes criticised for being cowardly, or not valuing their own lives. The best riposte to this comes from Schopenhauer, who strongly argued that choosing to end one's life does not mean failing to appreciate its value. One remark of his is particularly poignant in the context of many assisted suicides: 'The suicide wills life, and is only dissatisfied with the conditions under which it has presented itself to him.'

See also: Bereavement, Consent, Courage, Death, Love of Life, Mortality, Pain, Suffering, Suicide

Reading

Jonathan Glover, *Causing Death and Saving Lives* (Penguin, 1977)

Mary Warnock and Elisabeth Macdonald, *Easeful Death: Is There a Case for Assisted Dying?* (Oxford University Press, 2009)

Authenticity

Modern Western culture values authenticity and 'keeping it real'. Electorates sometimes even choose bigoted politicians who come across as 'genuine' over evidently more competent ones who seem too polished and professional. But while it's clear enough to say that a painting is, say, an authentic Vermeer, what does it mean for a *person* to be authentic?

The obvious answer is something like 'being true to oneself'. Authenticity in this sense is getting to know who we really, deeply are, and acting accordingly. This reflects the common-sense assumption that there is an authentic self to discover and be true to.

Nietzsche had a different view. For him, being authentic was not about *finding* a true self waiting to be discovered but rather meant *creating* a self. We have to *choose* who we are and make ourselves the heroes of our own life. We create ourselves just as we might create a work of art or write a novel. The sign of authenticity is that the signature of the author of our being is ourselves.

There is certainly a lot of truth in the idea that we are always in the process of becoming and that there is no permanent essence of self that defines who we are. (*See* **Identity**.) If we are to undertake the project of becoming who we want to be, we need to reflect on what we value. Nietzsche invited us to do this with the question: 'What have you up to now truly loved, what attracted your soul, what dominated it while simultaneously making it happy? Place this series of revered objects before you, and perhaps their nature and their sequence will reveal to you a law, the fundamental law of your authentic self.'

However, there are two serious dangers of getting too carried away with the possibilities of self-creation. One is of ignoring ethical constraints and potentially creating oneself in ways that are morally objectionable. This is the mistake made by the students in Patrick Hamilton's play *Rope*. Their crude reading of Nietzsche leads them to a gratuitous murder, as a way of proving that they are not constrained by conventional morality. Murder is extreme, but there are risks with any view that puts self-expression first, without tethering it to ethical concerns.

The other danger is of ignoring the constraints of reality. We have talents, strengths and weaknesses, and we rightly take these into consideration when we decide to turn one way rather than another. If we become too intoxicated with the idea that we can be the authors of our own lives, we can easily ignore these and succumb to delusions of grandeur.

One such constraint is that none of us emerges from a vacuum. Charles Taylor argues that our ideals of authenticity have become corrupted through excessive individualism. He agrees that 'There is a certain way of being human that is *my* way. I am called upon to live my life in this way, and not in imitation of anyone else's life.' However, he thinks that the ideal of authenticity makes sense only if we recognise that our own values can't be completely torn away from shared notions of the good. We are all products of our times and cultures, hence authenticity has a social as well as a personal dimension. As he says, 'My discovering my own identity doesn't mean that I work it out in isolation, but that I negotiate it through dialogue, partly overt, partly internal, with others.'

The trick to this 'working out' of who we are is to be neither too individualistic nor too passively shaped by society. This seems to be a core message of Heidegger's changeable and obscure views about authenticity. He argued that most people are inauthentic because they let their lives be moulded by the social norms of the group, what he calls 'the They'. By doing this, they avoid facing up to their mortality and taking responsibility for choosing what to do with their lives.

Sometimes, however, the spell of complacency gets broken, and the reality, inevitability and suddenness of death burst into our consciousness. This allows us to leave behind the distractions and obfuscations of everydayness and focus on what really matters: that is when we become authentic, our own person.

However, for Heidegger this authenticity is rooted in historical traditions. It is not a question of creating our own morality, but of drawing on the genuine values of our community. When we do this consciously, for ourselves, we avoid the inauthenticity of simply following these values unthinkingly.

What this suggests is that authenticity is best thought of not as an outcome but as a way of being. We live authentically when we think through the values we want to live by, in dialogue with all that has come before and formed us. We are realistic about our inclinations, capacities and limitations, but avoid letting them completely dictate who we are. We neither unquestioningly accept the norms that we absorbed as children nor discard them just to make a point. This process of self-development inevitably has ethical implications: the values we embrace are part and parcel of how we act in the world and with others.

See also: Character, Death, Free Will, Identity, Integrity, Self-Actualisation, Self-Deception, Self-Knowledge

Reading
Charles Guignon, *On Being Authentic* (Routledge, 2004)

Authority

There is more than one way to have a problem with authority, whether it is difficulty accepting the authority of others, not having as much of it as you would like, or not feeling confident to exert the authority you have. It doesn't help that authority has become something of a dirty word: there's no such thing as a good authoritarian.

For some, authority is a necessary evil. Thomas Hobbes believed that the state needed an all-powerful sovereign because only that could stop society falling into an anarchic struggle, a 'war of every man against every man'. In such a state, 'notions of right and wrong, justice and injustice have . . . no place. Where there is no common power, there is no law.' There would be 'no arts; no letters; no society; and which is worst of all, continual fear, and danger of violent death, and the life of man, solitary, poor, nasty, brutish and short'.

A gentler vision of authority can be found in Confucian thought. For Confucius, authority is not about one person or class dominating another. It is about a division of social and political labour, in which each individual plays his or her appropriate role. Parents have authority not in order to subjugate children, but to enable them to grow up safely and well. Rulers have authority not to tyrannise their subjects but to enable them to flourish in a peaceful, orderly society. (*See* **Duty**.)

In this view, authority is a necessary good rather than a necessary evil. It is not simply a matter of power but of responsibility. Furthermore, the more authority a leader has, the less they have to resort to force. People follow a good leader the way the grass follows the wind, bending easily and naturally. Leaders can achieve this only if they are exemplary persons. Only tyrants need to bully, cajole or terrorise others into submission, thereby showing not authority but a lack of it. When it is exercised well, authority suits everyone.

Confucius offers us a way of thinking about our problems with authority. If our issue is with those who have it, we might ask whether they are abusing it or whether we are too proud to accept their rightful exercise of it. If we don't feel we have enough, is it because we are being stopped from using it or because we want to wield a power we have not earned? And if we feel uncomfortable exercising it, we should ask whether we are simply shirking the proper responsibilities of our role.

See also: Duty, Impostor Syndrome, Office Politics, Politics, Parenthood

Reading
Confucius, *The Analects*

B

'Because we cannot be sure how long we will have our friends, let us eagerly enjoy them now.'
Seneca

Bad Faith *see* **Self-Deception**

Balance

Are you working too hard and not having enough time to unwind? Or are you spending too much time surfing the Internet instead of getting out and doing things? Are you doing too much or too little exercise? Are you too indulgent or too austere in your dietary habits?

The idea that there is a point of equilibrium between opposite extremes, which wise people are able to find, has an illustrious history in philosophy across the globe. In the Buddhist tradition, balance is implicit in the doctrine of 'the middle way'. For instance, the Buddha advises against the two extremes of excessive sensual gratification and excessive asceticism, saying that there is 'devotion to indulgence of pleasure in the objects of sensual desire, which is inferior, low, vulgar, ignoble, and leads to no good; and there is devotion to self-torment, which is painful, ignoble and leads to no good'.

In Western philosophy, the classic exposition of this principle comes from Aristotle, who says that things like 'fear, confidence, appetite, anger, pity, and in general pleasure and pain can be experienced too much or too little, and in both ways not well'. The challenge is 'to have them at the right time, about the right things, towards the right people, for the right end, and in the right way'.

Aristotle calls the ideal point between these two extremes 'the mean', saying, 'There is an excess, a deficiency and a mean' in most aspects of daily life. Rare exceptions include 'spite, shamelessness, envy, and, among actions, adultery, theft, homicide'. There is no such thing as an appropriate degree of these vices. Confucius had a remarkably similar view, and there is even a Confucian text called *The Doctrine of the Mean*.

The mean is a very practical principle that applies to all sorts of situations. If we are too impatient, for instance, we need to develop patience, but not to the extent that we become passive procrastinators. If we are not assertive enough and let people get away with too much, we have to become more forceful without tipping over into aggression.

The mean is not about bland moderation. Aristotle explicitly says that what he's talking about is not the arithmetic mean, in the way that five is the mean between nought and ten. Sometimes the mean is closer to one end of the spectrum than the other.

Nor is the mean the same for everyone: it is relative to each particular person and situation. For example, 'if ten pounds of food is a lot for someone to eat, and two pounds a little, the trainer will not necessarily prescribe six; for this may be a lot or a little for the person about to eat it – for Milo [a well-known athlete] a little, for a beginner at gymnastics, a lot'.

This is important. There is no generic mean between recklessness and timidity, generosity and meanness, laziness and overexertion. What we need to do is work out where we tend to sit on the relevant spectrum and what the mean might look like for us in any given situation. To do that, we need self-knowledge and reflection.

So how can we apply this understanding to daily life? Aristotle has some tips. First, he offers two useful rules of thumb for when we are unsure where the mean is. One is to move away from the extreme that is more harmful. For example, being reckless generally carries greater risks than being cautious, so in such cases erring on the side of caution is good Aristotelian advice.

The other is to move away from the extreme towards which we naturally tend. For instance, if we suspect we're not generous enough, we should make an effort to be more giving, even if it feels like overcompensating or it pains us to round our tips up rather than down.

A key piece of advice is that hitting the mean requires developing the right habits. We can't expect to change radically on the strength of understanding and insight alone. So if we need to be less assertive, say, we should watch ourselves in small daily encounters and try to soften up our approach. Getting the right balance in life is as difficult as walking a tightrope and requires at least as much practice.

See also: Character, Habits, Emotions, Self-Love, Virtue, Wisdom

Reading
Aristotle, *Nicomachean Ethics*

Beautification *see* **Objectification**

Bereavement

Grief is both a universal human experience and different in each particular case, as unique as any relationship between two human beings. Our inability to comfort people as much as we would like is partly due to the fact that, despite what we may say, we can never truly understand exactly how they feel. Hence the mantra 'there is no right or wrong way to grieve'.

That has not stopped a number of philosophers suggesting better ways to do so. The calm, rational detachment of their advice makes it of limited use at a time of loss, when a sympathetic ear or even someone making a cup of tea is probably more welcome. Who at such a time would like to receive a letter saying, 'I am sorry your friend has passed away, but I want you not to grieve excessively'? The writer, Seneca, was not a man to encourage you to have a good old cry. 'You should not be dry-eyed, but neither should you drown in weeping,' he sternly instructed.

Seneca tells his friend Lucilius that he cannot ask him not to grieve at all. He is sure that would be better, but 'such firmness of mind belongs only to the person who has risen high above misfortune'. For Seneca, in an ideal world we would know that grieving for the loss of a friend is as foolish as weeping over a lost tunic.

But Seneca was aware of how difficult it was to follow his advice, so when he talks about human beings as they really are – weak and emotional – his guidance is more useful. His reflections, like those of other philosophers, are worth dwelling on in death's absence, to help us better prepare for grief when it comes.

Seneca is brutally open about something we find it difficult to be honest about: the extent to which our grieving behaviour is influenced by how we want to be perceived by others. He writes, 'We are trying by our tears to prove our loss; it is not that grief forces us but that we are exhibiting grief to others.' *Surely not*, you may be thinking. But it's not so much about deliberate play-acting – it's more that we feel the pressure to conform to expectations. We may internalise these and berate ourselves for not grieving as much as we – or others – think we should. Freeing ourselves from this way of thinking would remove an unnecessary and distressing complication to grief.

Seneca also points out that even the deepest grief does not purge us of ordinary needs and desires. He reminds Lucilius that even Niobe, whose grief for her twelve children was famously deep, got hungry after ten days. We shouldn't feel guilty if we fancy a sandwich while we are mourning, or if when biting into it we find ourselves noticing how tasty it is. In fact, there is something fitting about appreciating the delight of life when we are most aware of how tenuous our grip on it is. 'Because we cannot be sure how long we will have our friends, let us eagerly enjoy them now,' says Seneca – one piece of advice that we can all agree with.

If Seneca's approach to death seems hard, the Daoist Zhuangzi appears downright callous. After his wife died, a friend who had come to mourn saw him singing and beating a drum. Zhuangzi explained that at first he mourned the same as everyone else, but then he thought about the nature of the universe and being. As a Daoist, he believed that the world is in perpetual flux, a never-ending process of things taking and losing form. So when his wife was born, 'The form changed and she had life. Today there was another change and she died. It's just like the round of four seasons: spring, summer, autumn, and winter.'

Whether or not accepting this idea should make us able to sing just days after losing a loved one is moot, but the picture Zhuangzi paints rings true for everyone and not just Daoists. The more we accept that nothing is permanent but change, the more we can accept that death does not so much rob people of life as take back from them what they had merely borrowed.

Both Seneca and Zhuangzi urge us to put our grief in perspective. The British philosopher Derek Parfit goes further, questioning whether our loss is as absolute as we think. Parfit believes that a person is no more than the sum of all their thoughts, feelings and experiences, connected as on a thread over time. If we accept this, there is a surprising bonus: since we are also psychologically connected with other people across time, we are not entirely separate from those we are closest to. 'There is still a difference between my life and the lives of other people,' says Parfit. 'But the difference is less.'

This is why in grief we often feel that a part of ourselves has died. The flip side of this is the more positive thought that part of the person we have lost still lives on in us. This may not provide the comfort of a fully-fledged life after death, but it does something more credible: it allows us to keep something of the deceased deep inside our own hearts and minds.

See also: Afterlife, Death, Loss, Mortality, Suicide

Reading
Seneca, 'Letter 163'
Derek Parfit, *Reasons and Persons* (Oxford University Press, 1984) §95
Zhuangzi, Chapter 18

Betrayal

It's difficult enough when something bad happens to us, but when the person causing it is someone we expected to help us through hard times rather than create them, insult is added to injury. Betrayal can sometimes seem trivial to outsiders, especially in the case of something common like infidelity. But for the person who has been betrayed, the experience can be one of the hardest to cope with, which is why even breaking a minor confidence can ruin a friendship.

Understanding why betrayal hurts so much can be the first step towards working through it. Trusting someone means placing intimate aspects of ourselves in their hands, a big deal that does not come easily to many people. So when that trust is broken, we are left feeling vulnerable and exposed. We are angry at the person who betrayed us, and at ourselves for having trusted them. The world seems a harsher place, in which we are wary of ever putting ourselves in the same position again. We retreat into ourselves, feeling alone.

Before thinking about how to handle betrayal, it is worth sounding the warning that not everyone who feels betrayed really has been. Jean-Jacques Rousseau is the worst philosophical example of this. In 1766 Hume took the Swiss philosopher, who was destitute and persecuted, to England and helped to find him a home and people who could support him. But for reasons that have never been adequately explained, Rousseau became convinced that Hume had been out to get him all along. 'I threw myself into your arms; you brought me to England, apparently to procure me an asylum, but in fact to bring me to dishonour,' he wrote to Hume. 'The public love to be deceived, and you were formed to deceive them.'

Rousseau's paranoia was pathological, but we are all capable of seeing treachery where there is none, or of interpreting understandable carelessness as malicious intent. Before trying to cope with a betrayal, it's worth asking whether it really was one.

If we do find ourselves seriously betrayed, we can draw on Martha Nussbaum's valuable insights. She rightly says that we have to accept the depth of our hurt, as 'grief and mourning are legitimate, and indeed required, when one loses something of such great value'. However, she cautions against anger, which unhelpfully keeps our focus on the wrongdoer and stops us moving forward. (*See* **Anger**.)

Interestingly, Nussbaum is also unpersuaded that forgiveness is essential in this process. One problem, she thinks, is that the forgiver can come to feel smugly superior. What we need instead, she says, is a 'gentle and non-resentful response to a loved one's wrongful act'. This means understanding their weakness, as well as accepting their apologies and attempts to make up for things. We can do all this without absolving them.

For Nussbaum, the most important thing is moving forward. With betrayal can come a loss of a central relationship and a gaping hole in our life. The best we can do is try to fill it. One way of doing this is building new bonds and strengthening existing ones. Others are learning how to enjoy being alone and cultivating valued activities. This isn't easy, so we should not berate ourselves for finding it hard.

An essential part of the process is the realisation that we must be willing to leave ourselves open to new betrayals if we are to have any close relationships again. (*See* **Vulnerability**.) Permanently retreating into a protective shell is sure to get in the way of a well-rounded life. But we can use our wounds as reminders not to expect too much of our fellow human beings. As the much-wronged Hume put it, 'to a Philosopher & Historian the Madness and Imbecility & Wickedness of Mankind ought to appear ordinary Events'.

See also: Anger, Forgiveness, Friendship, Loyalty, Lying, Relationships, Vulnerability

Reading
Martha C. Nussbaum, *Anger and Forgiveness* (Oxford University Press, 2016)

Blame *see* **Responsibility**

The Body

Anything you have to live with 24/7 is probably going to become somewhat problematic. Take our bodies. You may not be sick of the sight of yours, but according to a survey by *Psychology Today*, 56 per cent of women and 43 per cent of men are dissatisfied with their overall appearance. Our abdomens, weight and muscle tone bother us the most, and many dislike a particular body part or feature, such as their noses, eyebrows, ears or knees.

We might say that we have a difficult relationship with our bodies. But that expression itself suggests one source of the problem. We have become used to thinking of 'our bodies' as though they were not the same as 'us', regarding them instead like vehicles we inhabit, necessary for getting around but not integral parts of what we really are.

In many philosophical traditions, this way of thinking is given intellectual support by theories that see the real self as a kind of non-physical soul 'within'. Both Plato and Descartes promoted this 'dualist' idea, which became prominent in Western philosophy. (*See* **Afterlife**.)

It is obvious even to many dualists that this picture struggles to do justice to the evident inseparability of mind and body. Descartes explicitly accepted this, saying, 'I am not merely in my body as a sailor is in a ship. Rather, I am closely joined to it – intermingled with it, so to speak – so that it and I form a unit.' His philosophy, however, could not account for how this was possible.

Many Indian thinkers have also advocated the essential difference of soul and body. One major difference with the Western tradition is that most Indian schools believe that practices involving the body, such as yoga, are necessary to liberate the soul from its mortal shell. The *Kaushitaki Upanishad*, for instance, teaches the 'sixfold yoga', which includes mental and physical exercises of 'restraint of the breath, withdrawal of the senses, meditation, concentration, contemplation, absorption'.

There have been plenty of thinkers who have resisted this cleavage of the human being into two radically different parts. For instance, Aristotle did not see the soul as a non-material substance but rather as the organising principle that gives life to the organism. This is essentially the contemporary scientific view: that however mysterious mind and consciousness are, they are the product of organic, material things and nothing more.

Perhaps the most thorough attempts to put the body at the heart of the human experience were made by the twentieth-century French and German phenomenologists, for whom the body is not just another object in the world but the subject of lived experience. We need to be reminded of this, because when our bodies are working as they should, they almost disappear from our consciousness, which is instead turned towards our environment. As Drew Leder puts it, when the body is functioning well, it is 'a transparency through which we engage with the world'. Paradoxically, because our bodies are ever-present, they seem to be absent. They only become present to us in consciousness when we find they are unable to do what we want them to do, or when we have acute bodily sensations like sexual arousal.

Awareness of our embodiment is most acute when our bodies play up. Havi Carel writes that while we usually take it for granted that the body is 'a healthy functioning element contributing silently to the execution of projects, in illness the body comes to the fore'. When we are ill, it 'is not just a body function that is disrupted. Rather, one's entire way of being in the world is altered.' This experience is so different from the ordinary invisibility of the body that it feels uncanny. When the body, says Leder, 'is rendered opaque through loss of function, we become aware of it as an alien presence'.

What does this mean for our experience of the body in daily life? It's more than just something to think about the next time you're ailing with flu – it is a reminder that the body is 'our general medium for having a world', as Maurice Merleau-Ponty put it. Instead of thinking about the body – what we look like, or what may or may not be wrong with us – it may be more illuminating to attend closely to our *embodied experience*. By paying attention to our bodies, we can become more aware of the astonishing process through which our world comes into being.

It does not require the sight of an amazing sunset or a remarkable physical feat to evoke this. It could be ordinary things, like the sensation of one hand on another, or feeling the cold air on the tip of our nose. The magic is that it is through the body that we encounter the world.

See also: Afterlife, Asceticism, Food, Health and Illness, Mortality

Reading
Havi Carel, *Illness* (3rd edition, Routledge, 2018)

Boredom

Ordinary boredom isn't very interesting – it's just a sign that we need to change what we're doing or look harder for what might be absorbing in whatever is driving us to tedium. However, chronic feelings of global boredom, which can stop us fully engaging with the world, are more of a problem.

Deep and all-pervasive forms of boredom have historically been seen as sicknesses of the soul and given special names such as ennui and accidie. Kierkegaard, for example, thought that 'Boredom is the root of evil.' For him, it is not an absence of stimulation or of things to do but an absence of meaning, a sense of emptiness. 'How dreadful boredom is – how dreadfully boring.' You can't break this kind of boredom by simply doing things – you have to understand why life has become drained of meaning and how you might recover it. (*See* **Meaning**.)

The Portuguese writer and poet Fernando Pessoa identified another source of profound boredom, which he described as 'nothing but the monotony of myself'. His 'heteronym' (an aspect of himself that he turned into a fully-formed character) Bernardo Soares knows full well that 'since today is not yesterday', every moment of life is unique. But still he cannot escape the wearying sameness of his own self.

Schopenhauer was even gloomier, taking the view that profound boredom is the inevitable result of the human condition. For him, life consists in constant striving after something that we think will remove our dissatisfaction and make us happy. But as soon as we reach a goal, instead of being elated we are overcome with boredom, which 'hovers over every secure life like a bird of prey'. Then we set new goals, and so it goes on. We can't win: if we're not bored we're dissatisfied; if we're satisfied we're bored. (*See* **Suffering**.)

Schopenhauer may have been too pessimistic, but he was on to something. Setting ever more ambitious goals to stave off boredom is indeed something of a trap. It will never get us where we think it will. We might not agree with his take on the pervasiveness and intractability of boredom. Nonetheless, we are undeniably often more energised when we are working towards a goal than when we've finally attained it, which can bring feelings of emptiness.

The analyses of boredom offered by Kierkegaard, Pessoa and Schopenhauer are all different but have something important in common. Boredom is not a simple problem of being unoccupied but is rather rooted in an attitude to the world or ourselves that sees either or both as dull and lacking in meaning or value. Trying to cope with this by keeping ourselves busy is just a form of distraction.

That is why Bertrand Russell thought that a happy life required tolerating a certain amount of boredom. 'A life too full of excitement,' he wrote, 'is an exhausting life, in which continually stronger stimuli are needed to give the thrill that has come to be thought an essential part of pleasure.' To him, activity was like an addictive drug that dulls the pain of dealing with the world as it is and ourselves as we are.

A happy life, in Russell's view, is therefore to a large extent a quiet life, in which we have reduced our need for novelty and excitement. In their place he advises us to cultivate the kinds of pleasures that are not so liable to lingering dissatisfaction. Chief among these, he thought, are the things that bring us into contact with the natural world. We are 'creatures of the Earth,' he writes, and 'we draw our nourishment from it just as the plants and the animals do'.

To avoid the wrong kinds of boredom, we do not need frenetic activity or a constant stream of new experiences. All we require is a life that honours what we most value and is sensitive to the textures and rhythms of the world around us.

See also: Achievement, Busyness, Carpe Diem, Leisure, Purpose, Routine, Suffering

Reading
Fernando Pessoa, *The Book of Disquiet* (Serpent's Tail, 2010)
Arthur Schopenhauer, *Essays and Aphorisms* (Penguin, 1976)

Busyness

If you're wrestling with a busy schedule, unable to find the time to stop and smell the roses, play with the children or even just relax with a gin and tonic, the answer does not lie in a new time management app. Believe it or not, you need a dose of Heidegger.

Heidegger argues that our experience of time is not chiefly determined by the nature of time itself: it is more a matter of the attitude we have towards things. In his view, the normal 'everydayness' of experience is characterised by working and *doing* (as opposed to just being). In this mode, we experience the world primarily as a resource and fill our minds with material concerns.

Heidegger suggests a radical overhaul of this. We need to understand that focusing on *doing* filters out *being*. The more we obsess about getting things done, the less mental space we have to take in the world for what it is, rather than how it is useful. The good news is that we have some control over what we pay attention to. When we switch from doing to being, we appreciate the subtle changing of the seasons, say, or the patterns in the mud in a riverbed at low tide. Instead of focusing on *how things are*, we marvel *that things are* at all – that we are conscious beings who perceive colours and sounds, here on this planet in a mysterious universe.

The demands of life mean that everydayness is inevitably, well, an everyday experience. But it is worth making the effort to create at least some space in our routine to suspend instrumental thinking and connect more deeply with what it is to be alive.

See also: Gratitude, Inner Life, Mindfulness, Simplicity, Slowing Down

Reading
Martin Heidegger, *Being and Time* (1927)

C

'Most of what we say and do is not essential. If you can eliminate it, you'll have more time, and more tranquillity.'
Marcus Aurelius

Calm

For those of us who would like to feel a bit calmer and less flustered more of the time, the ability to keep our cool in challenging circumstances is both admirable and enviable. Is this just a matter of being blessed with a happy-go-lucky disposition, or is it something we can cultivate?

Many people looking for calm try yoga. In its original form this is a spiritual and philosophical practice, defined in the *Yoga Sutras* as 'the cessation of the functioning of ordinary awareness'. That certainly sounds calming, but the aim wasn't to relax – it was to enable practitioners to see things as they really are by stopping the constant barrage of sense perceptions and thoughts that distract us.

There are similarities here with Stoics and Epicureans, who valued states like tranquillity and equanimity not because they were pleasant but because they were by-products of a clear understanding of what matters in life and what doesn't. If we genuinely realise that the things of the world are of limited value, for instance, we will not be upset if they're damaged or lost. As Epictetus puts it, 'If you are fond of a jug, say, "It is a jug that I am fond of"'; then, if it is broken, you will not be disturbed.' However, his view was much more radical than it sounds, applying not only to possessions but also to relationships and people.

Neither of these traditions aimed for calm for its own sake. But there is something more down to earth we can take away from them if we wish to be calmer. The key point is perspective. Most of us frequently lose this, worrying ourselves sick or getting irate about things that with a bit of distance reveal themselves to be trivial. If we sincerely applied Epictetus' views to cars, clothes and homes, if not to more fundamental issues, we'd be much calmer as a result. And finding ways of stilling the mind can help us to remember what really matters but gets easily lost in the blur of daily life.

Marcus Aurelius was fond of space and time meditations to put things in perspective. He writes, 'The infinity of past and future gapes before us – a chasm whose depths we cannot see. So it would take an idiot to feel self-importance or distress. Or any indignation, either. As if the things that irritate us lasted.'

A similar effect can be achieved by pondering the big philosophical questions. According to Bertrand Russell, this is a good antidote against a life in which our narrow aims and interests always take centre stage: 'In such a life there is something feverish and confined, in comparison with which the philosophic life is calm and free.' Contemplating something bigger than ourselves can make our own self-centred concerns shrink, as we come to recognise that in the grand scheme they are not that significant.

Marcus Aurelius also suggests that 'most of what we say and do is not essential. If you can eliminate it, you'll have more time, and more tranquillity.' He recommends asking ourselves at regular intervals, 'Is this necessary?' (*See* **Needs**.)

So the key to developing a calmer frame of mind is getting a sense of perspective by questioning the value and importance of things, stilling our minds and thinking about what's greater than ourselves. Slowing down our frantic pace can also help. However, we should avoid having unrealistic expectations about how chilled we can become. According to the ancient Greeks, calm is in principle possible for all of us if we vigorously challenge the faulty thinking that leads us to value and be attached to things that are not worth it. But it is an open question whether everyone can achieve this. Individual temperament can be impervious to change. If you are by nature easily ruffled and start demanding that you should be able to transform yourself into someone quite placid, you may be creating more agitation instead of more calm.

That is not to say that changing how we think can't alter our life experience. It can, as long as we accept that it is more likely to bring incremental gains than complete transformation.

See also: Anger, Anxiety, Contentment, Cosmic Insignificance, Frustration, Mindfulness, Slowing Down, Worrying

Reading
Marcus Aurelius, *Meditations*

Career

Once upon a time, it was widely believed that if you wanted to get on in life, you needed to choose a career. This was something of a historical anomaly. For centuries people used to have a trade that was generally handed down, or were mothers, or wealthy landowners who could do as they pleased. Careers as we know them are the product of mass education and an expanding middle class.

We are already past the heyday of the career. A rapidly changing world means that people are expected to have at least two 'careers' in their lives. Even those that require years of training, such as medicine or law, are no longer necessarily for life, especially now that retirement is for many people only a hypothetical possibility.

Philosophers have provided many encouraging examples for people who nonetheless feel uncomfortable about their lack of clear career success or who are uncertain about what career, if any, they want to pursue. Nietzsche started out as a university professor but gave it up in his thirties in order to be more independent. From then on, clashes of principle made his working life problematic. When he tried to get back into academia a few years later he was deemed too controversial. Soon after, he dumped his publisher Ernst Schmeitzner in disgust at his anti-Semitic views, which meant he had to self-publish his next book, *Beyond Good and*

Evil. Nietszche is an example of how a smooth career is usually incompatible with counter-cultural idiosyncrasy. It is not quite like trying to fit a square peg into a round hole. Rather, there are people of such interesting and complex shapes that there is no financially viable hole for them to fit into. That is something a person might both regret and be proud of at the same time.

The young David Hume, lacking a large family fortune, decided that his ambition to be a man of letters was not realistic and that he needed a more sensible career. He tried working for a merchant in Bristol but 'in a few months found that scene totally unsuitable to me'. As a good empiricist, he learned quickly from experience and decided to live by his pen after all. To do so he 'resolved to make a very rigid frugality supply my deficiency of fortune, to maintain unimpaired my independency, and to regard every object as contemptible, except the improvement of my talents in literature'.

That Hume did, though it took him a long time to earn a decent living and the reputation he has today. He also had other career misses along the way, twice being rejected by Scottish universities for professorships that he was clearly best qualified to occupy. He is a wonderful example for anyone who has ambitions that others tell them are not practical. You have a choice: give them up, or make whatever sacrifices are needed to pursue your passion. If you are not prepared to earn less as a result or, like Hume, to refrain from starting a family, then maybe your 'passion' is more of an idle fantasy.

Perhaps the most notorious career move in the history of philosophy was Descartes' landing of a prestigious job with Queen Christina of Sweden. She was an unusually intelligent and reflective monarch, who had corresponded with Descartes and in a different age might have become a philosopher herself. She employed him in Stockholm as her tutor and the head of a proposed new scientific academy. The legend is that the 5 a.m. lessons in her cold castle led to him catching pneumonia. Whether or not that was the cause of his illness, it killed him anyway.

Descartes provides a warning: beware of seductive, lucrative, prestigious jobs – sometimes they're the ones that kill you. Nietzsche and Hume for their part remind us that good careers may require us to give up what we most want to do in life. The lack of a career is sometimes a sign not of failure but of success at resisting convention.

See also: Authenticity, Midlife Crisis, Retirement, Unemployment, Wealth, Work

Reading
Sue Prideaux, *I Am Dynamite! A Life of Friedrich Nietzsche* (Faber & Faber, 2018)

Carpe Diem

Although 'seize the day' is the standard translation of the poet Horace's phrase *carpe diem,* the alternative 'pluck the day' is much nicer: it has delightful associations of picking a ripe fruit rather than suggesting a potentially violent act of appropriation. However you translate it, many have adopted *carpe diem* as a motto – it's even one of the most popular motifs for tattoos. Its urgent call tends to pop to the front of our minds when something goes wrong – when a crisis or near miss draws our attention to the fact that the future we normally take for granted is by no means guaranteed. *Quam minimum credula postero*, continues Horace's quotation: 'trust tomorrow as little as possible'.

But what does seizing the day *really* mean? Should we just 'eat, drink and be merry' and not give the future a second thought? That's pretty much what the Cyrenaics, an ancient Greek school, advocated. They believed we should seek whatever brings pleasure in the present moment without worrying about the future, as we don't know whether it will ever come. They also thought the past has gone, so we shouldn't concern ourselves with it. (*See* **Pleasure**.)

Epicurus might also appear to endorse an entirely present-orientated position, according to which it's important to find pleasure in the present and remove anxiety about the future. Seneca reports the Epicurean saying, 'The foolish life is ungrateful and fearful; it looks wholly to the future.' But Epicurus was also aware that while many of the indulgent pleasures – eating and drinking to excess, having affairs – may be enjoyable at the time, they almost inevitably lead to future problems. Just following our fancies in life is a recipe for more pain than pleasure.

For Plato, a life devoted solely to pleasure would not be human. In his dialogue *Philebus*, Protarchus claims that pleasure is all we need in life. Socrates challenges this, arguing that without 'intellect, memory, knowledge and true judgement' you would not even know or be able to remember you were feeling pleasure. You would have 'not the life of a human being, but of a jellyfish or some sea creature which is merely a body endowed with life, a companion of oysters'.

Kierkegaard also criticised a life dedicated to the immediacy of present pleasures by describing a fictional banquet in which even the wine glasses are smashed at the end, symbolising the lack of concern for anything enduring. But the hedonistic guests are empty and live for moments that are forever passing, which makes satisfaction of any kind impossible. No matter how good a moment is, as soon as it has passed all you can do is reach for the next one.

That is not to say that letting go every now and again is a bad idea. Even Seneca, an advocate of sobriety and restraint, wrote that sometimes the mind 'must be stretched in joyful liberty', and that occasionally we should allow a drink to take us 'close to tipsiness'.

The overall message, however, is that *carpe diem* is best understood not as an incitement to focus on what feels good in the present moment but as a call to get on with what we value most. If things like travelling or spending time with friends are important, we need to make them a priority *now* and not wait until we retire, our career is on track or whatever it is we think we are waiting for.

Carpe diem can also be an invitation to enjoy the little everyday pleasures that are all around us rather than seek new horizons. Sometimes we are so absorbed in striding towards the future that we barely notice the flavours of the food we eat or the beauty of the architecture we walk past. 'Extract all the joy you can without delay,' says Seneca. 'No promise has been made about the coming night; I have granted too long an extension – no promise has been made about the next hour.'

One important qualification to *carpe diem* is that although we don't know what tomorrow will bring, or even whether it will come, our lives extend beyond the moment. Too much focus on enjoying the present could detract from what often gives most meaning to our lives, such as long-term relationships, setting and achieving goals, pursuing valued projects. We need to both savour the present moment and keep an eye on the well-being of our future self. As Epicurus said, remember that 'the future is neither entirely ours nor entirely lost to us: we may not take its coming for certain, nor must we despair of it as quite certain not to come'.

Live only for today and you risk messing up tomorrow; live only for tomorrow and you risk missing out on today. Schopenhauer seemed to capture this dilemma when he pointed out that it could be said 'that the greatest *wisdom* consists in enjoying the present and making this enjoyment the goal of life, because the present is all that is real and everything else merely imaginary. But you could just as well call this mode of life the greatest *folly*: for that which in a moment ceases to exist, which vanishes as completely as a dream, cannot be worth any serious effort.'

We should not seize today so violently that we break tomorrow. But because we so easily miss the present while our mind is set on the future, what we most often need to do is balance this mindset with more of a present orientation. 'Give yourself a gift: the present moment,' says Marcus Aurelius. Just make sure you don't have to pay for it later, with interest.

See also: Achievement, Busyness, Calm, Contentment, Gratitude, Love of Life, Midlife Crisis, Pleasure

Reading
Søren Kierkegaard, *Stages on Life's Way* (1845)

Change

Change can be exciting, terrifying or merely inconvenient. Which of these it is depends on a number of things. One of these is the degree of uncertainty surrounding it. Sometimes it's clear enough what a change involves in the short-term, while at other times what's coming next is less transparent. Either way, we can't know what a change will involve in the longer term, and whether it will turn out to be good or bad. A divorce might be a short-term trauma and a long-term liberation; a wedding could be the opposite.

Another factor is how we relate to uncertainty. Many people find they're more able to deal with change if they feel in control of it. (*See* **Control, Uncertainty**.) Unfortunately a lot of change is involuntary, and you can do little or nothing to guide it. At those times, trying to take charge can be a recipe for frustration, and accepting uncertainty is ultimately a better policy.

It helps if we are in the habit of appreciating the impermanence of all things. This is something that the Western philosophical tradition has found difficult. This has roots in Plato, who argued against placing importance on the material world because it was too unstable. In contrast, ultimate reality was 'the realm of the pure and everlasting and immortal and changeless'. Similar ideas are common in the philosophy of the Islamic world. For instance, the medieval Islamic philosopher al-Ghazali wrote, 'Know that true demonstration is what provides necessary, perpetual and eternal certainty that cannot change.'

There have always been dissenters in both traditions. One of the most notable was the early twentieth-century British philosopher Alfred North Whitehead. He advocated a 'process' philosophy that understood the natural world in terms of the interrelations between things and their change over time. This fluid dynamic model contrasts with the mechanistic, atomistic one that had characterised the scientific revolution. One of the catchier slogans in this dense, difficult philosophy is that we should reject the 'continuity of becoming' in favour of the 'becoming of continuity'. Anyone from a non-Western background will wonder why Whitehead was considered so radical. One of China's foundational philosophical texts is the *I Ching*, the book of changes. Chinese thought makes great use of the concept of *qi*, which refers to the flows of energy that permeate the world. This captures the idea that everything is in flux and that energy is constantly moving.

Daoist thought in particular embraces the central importance of change, and this is embedded in the concept of *yinyang*. One of the most important things about *yin* and *yang* is that they are not static, permanent properties of a thing. Whether something is *yin* or *yang* depends on the context and what it is being related to. The very origin of the words testifies to this: they literally mean the sunny (*yang*) and shady (*yin*) sides of a hill. As the sun moves across the sky, *yang* becomes *yin* and *yin* becomes *yang*.

In India, change is also central, especially in Buddhist philosophy. This is perhaps most evident in the ideas of the second to third century philosopher Nagarjuna, who developed the idea of 'dependent origination'. This means that nothing has any fixed, permanent essence and so everything is what it is only by virtue of what it is related to. The best-known example of this is the self, which in Buddhism is not an unchanging core but a series of experiences, thoughts and sensations.

We're often told that change is inevitable and so we have to embrace it. Non-Western philosophies go further: change is not only inevitable but omnipresent. Change is not the exception to the rule: it *is* the rule. To resist it is to resist the world, even yourself. And would the alternative really be preferable? Without change, there is no movement, no dynamism, no life.

Best then to take the advice of Daoism's founder, Lao-Tzu, whose most famous poem describes the constant changes of nature before asking, 'Do man's visions last? Do man's illusions?' The conclusion is unarguable: 'Take things as they come. All things pass.'

See also: Identity, Midlife Crisis, Routine, Uncertainty

Reading
Daodejing
Nagarjuna, *The Mulamadhyamakakarika* (or Fundamental Verses on the Middle Way)

Character

From time to time, we have to ask others to vouch for us. If someone had to do that for you, what do you think they would honestly be able to say? They might point out your skills and achievements, but they would primarily talk about the kind of person you are. Have you made it easy for them to give you a glowing reference?

We don't often think about our character, and when we do we tend to confuse it with personality. When we talk about personality we refer to our natural inclinations to react in certain ways to events, situations and other people. Personality traits include being optimistic or pessimistic, neurotic or calm, sensuous or intellectual, adventurous or timid, and so on. Although these are malleable – you can try to turn down your neuroticism or challenge your timidity, if you think they are excessive – they are not easy to change. Aspects of our personality may be problematic for us, but they don't make us good or bad.

Character, on the other hand, is a matter of being a better or a worse person. Honesty is a commendable character trait, dishonesty a deplorable one. A caring person is praiseworthy, while a callous one is blameworthy.

Character and personality interact but they are not the same. The philosophy of character predates the modern psychology of personality (which often lumps the two together) by millennia. There is remarkable agreement among several giants of philosophy that character is more important than rules regarding personal virtue and a good society. They also agree that it can and should be cultivated. Any liar or cheat who says 'that's just how I am' deserves the response that Confucius gave to a disciple who claimed he wanted to follow the master's way but didn't have the strength: 'Someone whose strength is genuinely insufficient collapses somewhere along the Way. As for you, you deliberately draw the line.'

The Confucian classic *The Great Learning* says: 'From the emperor down to the common people, all, without exception, must consider cultivation of the individual's character as the root.' In the *Dhammapada*, the Buddha says, 'Engineers who build canals and aqueducts lead the water, fletchers make the arrow straight, carpenters carve the wood; wise people fashion themselves.'

As for how to cultivate character, Aristotle was clear that the best way was to work on our habits. He wrote that the virtues 'are engendered in us neither *by* nor *contrary to* nature;

we are constituted by nature to receive them, but their full development in us is due to habit.' Confucius would have been in complete agreement with this. (*See* **Habits**, **Virtue**.)

If you want to build your character, just reading self-help books won't do it – you have to push yourself to *act* in the way you think is right, until it becomes second nature. Make sure you wait for your partner to finish speaking and in time you'll become a more sympathetic listener. Find the courage to stand up to a bullying boss and the next time it will be easier. As David Hume said, 'Where one is thoroughly convinced that the virtuous course of life is preferable; if he have but resolution enough, for some time, to impose a violence on himself; his reformation needs not be despaired of.'

See also: Habits, Human Nature, Integrity, Values, Virtue

Reading
Aristotle, *Nicomachean Ethics*
The Great Learning

Charity

Charities always want your money, and the people they help usually need it. The obvious question to ask is: do you give them enough? However, perhaps the more important one is: do you give to the right ones?

That we should give *something* is almost universally agreed. For instance, Islam has the requirement of *zakat*, whereby believers pay a proportion of their wealth per year to help the poor, and Judaism and Christianity have long traditions of tithing to the church or the community. In most societies today some contribution towards the common good, especially to the poor, is mandated through taxation. Charitable giving is what we voluntarily give over and above this. This is usually seen as *supererogatory*, meaning that while it is good if we do it, we have not failed morally if we don't. That's probably how most people think about charity.

Nonetheless, many of us feel guilty that we don't give enough. Feeding this guilt are the utilitarians, who believe that we behave morally when our actions produce the greatest welfare for the greatest number. (*See* **Altruism**.) If that's right, almost all of us fail to contribute as much as we could to this desirable outcome.

Whether we are utilitarian or not, we could all learn something from one of its recent byproducts, the 'effective altruism' movement. Since utilitarians are concerned with doing whatever achieves the most good, many of them are now encouraging us to direct our funds to the charities that are most effective. Websites such as givingwhatwecan.org turn this into practical advice. They tend to recommend giving to projects such as women's education and cheap but effective treatment of unfashionable health problems such as obstetric fistula, which causes incontinence and carries a social stigma.

Effective altruism is not without controversy. For instance, its advocates often advise against giving to guide dog charities, because the improvements they bring to quality of life cost far more than alternatives that can save hundreds of lives. But being encouraged to think twice about who we give to is a useful exercise in itself. Often we lazily think 'it's for charity' as though that automatically makes it good. But the good that charities do varies enormously, and some of them unintentionally cause harm. Most of us could probably give more, but almost all of us could certainly give better.

See also: Altruism, Duty, Pleasure, Selfishness, Wealth

Reading
William MacAskill, *Doing Good Better: How Effective Altruism Can Help You Make a Difference* (Avery, 2015)

Peter Singer, *The Most Good You Can Do* (Yale University Press, 2015)

Children *see* **Parenthood**

Choice

In principle, having options seems like an entirely good thing. In reality, choosing between them is often difficult and time-consuming, especially when the stakes are high. It's stressful to feel we can't afford to make a mistake, like when we're changing jobs, moving to a new country or ending a relationship. Philosophy won't make these decisions any easier, but it can help us to better understand why they are so hard.

The problem is that many choices involve a clash of values. (*See* **Ambivalence**.) Jean-Paul Sartre tells the story of a student who sought his advice during the Second World War. His father was a collaborator and his brother had been killed. He lived with his mother, who had been badly affected by her husband's actions and the death of her other son, and was much consoled by his presence. The student badly wanted to go to England to join the Free French Forces but he also felt responsible for his mother's well-being, and was reluctant to leave her. He realised that if he stayed he could be helpful to his mother in concrete ways, whereas the effects of joining the fight against fascism were far more uncertain. He valued both options but could choose only one.

If the student was looking for a clear answer, he was asking the wrong person. Sartre reports saying to him, 'You are free, therefore choose.' We don't know whether the student appreciated this, but on the face of it the response seems remarkably unhelpful.

There is more to the advice than meets the eye, however. According to Sartre, freedom is a fundamental human capacity, and with it comes choice. We constantly mould and remould ourselves through the decisions we make. We're nothing but the sum of our actions. It's no good comforting ourselves by thinking of what we could have been, as that person is not real. We are what we make of ourselves, and we are responsible for what we become.

In this we have no guidance from human nature (as there is no such thing) or from God (who does not exist). We can't *not* choose, as this is itself a choice. There is no escaping the necessity of choosing and thereby fashioning ourselves. This is inevitably a cause of anxiety, so we often attempt to deny our freedom by casting ourselves in a fixed mould, seeing ourselves as determined by our past, our social role or our genes.

Of course, Sartre is not saying that we never find ourselves in situations that are not of our choosing. But whatever situation we happen to be in, it is incumbent on us to choose what to do about it, commit ourselves and act. His is an 'ethic of action and self-commitment'.

Because our choices of action are also choices of values, Sartre believed that every choice we make is endorsing a value for all of humankind. If we choose to get married, for instance, we are affirming the value of marriage for anyone else. His account of freedom helps to explain why some choices are not just practically difficult but emotionally agonising. As his student found, knowing this does not break the impasse. But it can clarify the situation we face, why it feels so hard and what we have to do about it.

Thankfully there are plenty of choices where the stakes are lower. Even Sartre admitted that some choices shouldn't cause too much anxiety, like that between eating a mille-feuille or a chocolate eclair. When we get stuck on these we're usually simply overwhelmed by the options. In our consumer society, this is common. It might help if we reduced the number of trivial choices we have to make each day, as Barack Obama advocated: he wore only grey or blue suits, saying, 'I'm trying to pare down decisions.'

It might also help to remind ourselves that it doesn't matter much either way – few choices are genuinely life-changing and irrevocable. Bertrand Russell wrote: 'Our doings are not so important as we naturally suppose; our successes and failures do not after all matter very much.'

Choosing is unavoidable, but agonising over small matters is pointless. If we remember this we can stop sweating the small stuff, especially when we realise that a lot of stuff is much smaller than we think. But Sartre was right to make it clear that there are no easy rules for making choosing easier. Even more reason to save our concern for the choices that really matter.

See also: Ambivalence, Anxiety, Authenticity, Commitment, Dilemmas, Free Will, Indecision, Mistakes, Risk, Self-Deception

Reading
Jean-Paul Sartre, *Existentialism and Humanism* (1946)

Commitment

If you have problems with commitment, rest assured that this is in part because commitment is something of a problem itself.

Sometimes our failure to commit is a species of weakness of will. (*See* **Self-Control**.) But more often it is rooted in uncertainty. Is this really the right choice? Are the risks too high? What if I change my mind? Philosophers of many stripes have argued that it is precisely in such situations that commitment is needed most. We're mistaken if we think that we have to resolve our uncertainties in order to commit.

Rather, we need to commit in order to deal with the uncertainties.

According to both William James and Søren Kierkegaard, there are times in life when reason cannot determine the right choice – whether to believe in God or uphold a moral principle, for instance. (*See* **Faith**.) Since we *have* to believe something, in those cases we have to commit to a 'leap of faith'. Kierkegaard was critical of philosophers like Hegel, who thought that knowledge always advances by a rational process. In Kierkegaard's view rationality is not so powerful. Passion or commitment, not reason, is what enables us to move beyond the contradictions we confront in life.

These and other philosophers have tended to focus on the big issues of life, death and God, but their conclusions apply equally to more mundane matters. Sometimes, like when we feel clear about the best course of action, commitment is so easy that there is no need to commit as such at all – we just do it. But often in life we just cannot know what the best choice is. We can weigh up the pros and cons, but there are too many unknowns. It is at those times that commitment is most necessary.

Take a house purchase, for example. You don't know how much you'll like living somewhere until you live there, and you can't assess how much of a financial burden the mortgage will be unless you assume that your earnings will remain the same. Wait for certainty and you'll never move – at some point you have to commit one way or the other.

The same is true of everything, from phones and cars to relationships and jobs. Of course, no one should commit to anything major without having thought about it as much as possible. But rational deliberation can only take you so far: you need commitment to take you over the line.

Commitment can also help us to live with the consequences of our choices, for better or for worse. Knowing that we have made our decisions without any guarantees should make it easier for us to accept our plight when things don't turn out well. We can do without the extra problem of berating ourselves for the mistake. *C'est la vie.*

To commit is to embrace uncertainty; to avoid commitment is to allow uncertainty to embrace you. The choice is not between risk and safety, but between which risks to take for ourselves and which to leave to chance.

See also: Choice, Dilemmas, Faith, Indecision, Mistakes, Regret, Risk, Uncertainty, Vulnerability

Reading
The Living Thoughts of Kierkegaard, edited by W.H. Auden (New York Review Books, 1999)
William James, *The Will to Believe* (1896)

Community

If you live somewhere that has a real sense of community, you will almost certainly think that's a good thing. If you don't, you'll just as surely think that a loss. Then again many of us have had experiences of stifling communities, such as small towns where those with any aspiration feel they have to leave; or intolerant societies where anyone with a different sexuality, religion or even hairstyle is marginalised or persecuted. Online communities can give people the sense of belonging they crave but they tend to be even more insular than flesh-and-blood groups.

Our ambiguous attitude towards community reflects a tension between seemingly opposite yearnings for individuality and belonging. The reason it is now more common to hear people bemoan the lack of community than complain about its oppressiveness is that individuality has been on the rise. The world is waking up to the fact that autonomy's gain is belonging's loss.

The tension is real, because we are both individuals and parts of a wider society. Like trees in a forest, our uniqueness is rooted in the environment in which we were born and live. Western thought has emphasised the individual side of this equation, focusing on our solitary minds and souls; Eastern thought has emphasised the relational side, the ways in which our identities depend on our role in the family and society.

The Western correction to this has been led by a number of philosophers broadly characterised as communitarians, such as Alasdair MacIntyre, Michael Sandel, Charles Taylor and Michael Walzer. They have criticised the liberal emphasis on the individual, arguing that no one exists in a vacuum and that even to know who you are requires knowing the community (or communities) that shaped you. As Taylor puts it, 'To know who I am is a species of knowing where I stand.'

It might look as though the communitarianism vs. liberalism dispute is indicative of a more general conflict between community and individualism. But most of us want both. Are we asking to square a circle? Perhaps not. It's important to remember that the Eastern alternative to individualism is not collectivism, but a greater sense of how people relate to and depend on one another. This doesn't require us to give up our unique identities, merely to acknowledge how they exist only in relation to the individualities of others.

One of the most famous philosophical communities is the one established by Epicurus in his house and garden near Athens, where his followers lived and studied together. But it seems that in this community individuality could thrive. Epicurus himself wrote in a distinctive, individual voice. Diogenes Laertius observes that he was prolific, writing over three hundred rolls (few of which, sadly, have survived): 'They do not include any quotations from other authors, but contain only his words.'

Maybe the opposition between community and individuality is not inevitable, but the two can coexist in harmony and even facilitate each other.

See also: Identity, Loyalty, Politics, Relationships, Tolerance

Reading
Diogenes Laertius, *Lives of the Eminent Philosophers*
Charles Taylor, *Sources of the Self* (Harvard University Press, 1989)

Companion Animals *see* Pets

Compassion *see* Empathy, Love

Competition

Does life often seem like a series of competitions, most of which you lose? Our world has become a hypercompetitive place. Things like getting a job or a place at university were always competitive, but now we also compete for attention and validation on social media, business networking hubs, dating sites. You even have to be careful when travelling – guests and passengers get online ratings, as well as hotels and taxi drivers.

But perhaps this is not so new. Back in 1920, Bertrand Russell was complaining of 'the generally received philosophy of life, according to which life is a contest, a competition, in which respect is to be accorded to the victor'.

Russell worried that once 'the competitive habit of mind' becomes established, it 'easily invades regions to which it does not belong'. Cooking for friends, for instance, becomes a kind of contest, in which everyone feels the need to go one better than their guests did when they were hosting. Philosophy itself can be infected by this competitive spirit: the desire to win the argument often becomes more important than the desire to find the truth.

Russell believed there was 'too much emphasis upon competitive success as the main source of happiness'. It isn't enough to do well; you have to do better than your peers. The poison of this mindset leads to Somerset Maugham's principle that 'it is not enough to have achieved personal success. One's best friend must also have failed.'

The cure for this is simple: don't make a competition out of anything that isn't one. Life is not always a zero-sum game, and for you to do well it is usually not necessary for anyone else to do badly. Focus on what is good in your life rather than on what is better or worse than anyone else's and you will be free of what Russell describes as the 'too grim, too tenacious' life of relentless competition.

See also: Achievement, Envy, Failure, Reputation

Reading
Bertrand Russell, 'Competition' in *The Conquest of Happiness* (George Allen & Unwin, 1930)

Consent

Tick the box. Sign here. We're given such instructions on an almost daily basis. No one is doing it for fun. It's all about getting our legal consent: to share information, to have medical treatment that carries risks, to accept the terms and conditions of a contract. Consent is also important in personal matters. People don't usually sign contracts before having sex (although there are some apps that in effect facilitate this), but without consent it would be rape.

Consent clearly matters. But it is not always clear that we've truly given or got it. What does it really mean to give consent, and can we realistically hope to live in such a way that everything we do is consensual?

Start by thinking about why consent is important. Ethicists generally offer two types of explanation. The negative reason is protection: the requirement for consent protects us against exploitation and abuse. The positive reasons are connected with autonomy: we believe that we should make all important decisions for ourselves, so no one should be able to make any on our behalf without our agreement.

If autonomy is critical, then it follows that consent is meaningless unless it is *informed*. If I agree to a medical procedure having been told it is much safer than it really is, I have not truly consented to undergo what is, in fact, a risky operation.

In general terms, the requirement for informed consent seems clear and essential. In practice, however, it soon becomes messy. For instance, our competence can be limited by circumstances. Think of medical consent. If I am in severe pain, I can't calmly assess the options to deal with it, and if I'm unconscious I can't consider anything. There are times when we might even be grateful that doctors undercut our autonomy. In her practical and lucid discussion of consent in the medical sphere, Onora O'Neill points out that 'well-directed coercion and deception by professionals can sometimes benefit patients and contribute positively to their health'.

Our judgements when giving consent can also be distorted, especially when emotions are strong. The fact that some informed parents still deny their children vaccines on the basis of unfounded claims shows how hard it can be to think clearly when feelings are running high. Many contracts are signed following subtle emotional manipulation by skilled salespeople.

Then there is the question of how informed I have to be. If I'm not an expert in investing or medicine, there is a sense in which any consent I give in such domains is less than fully informed. As O'Neill says, 'full disclosure of information is neither definable nor achievable; and even if it could be provided, there is little chance of its comprehensive assimilation.' Too much information can actually be a way of bypassing meaningful consent. If you tick a box on a web form that says 'We will send you marketing information', that's clear enough. Ticking one to confirm you have read the terms and conditions, which may run to several pages and no one ever reads, is hardly an informed choice.

Another complication is that consent is not always explicit. This is obvious in the case of sex, where people usually express their willingness by their actions rather than their words. Of course, in almost all cases it should be obvious whether a partner is genuinely consenting or not. But the implicit nature of agreement opens up the possibility of genuine misunderstanding (possibly rooted in self-deception) or of using the ambiguity as an excuse for 'date rape'.

So we would appear to be in a bit of a bind: we believe informed consent is essential but don't always explicitly give it, we can't provide it in every single case, and we are rarely both fully informed and able to assess the relevant information.

What is needed to bridge the gap between full, informed consent and the more limited reality is trust. Trust allows us to consent to medical treatments we don't fully understand, to make ourselves vulnerable in sex without fear of exploitation, and to allow others to make decisions on our behalf when we are unable to do so. O'Neill argues that attempts to make consent full and explicit can actually undermine trust, replacing it with something more formal and legalistic.

Our reliance on trust might seem unsatisfactory. In many cases of consent, we rightly don't trust those to whom we give it. Do you trust the tech giants and multinationals whose

C

terms and conditions you have no choice but to accept? In these cases, trust is indirect: we have to assume that the laws of the land will protect us against being tricked. Because we cannot trust the law to always be right, experts to be correct or friends and family to act in our best interests, we would do well to get into the habit of pausing before we put our fate in their hands.

Informed consent is important, but it is an ideal we can only get close to, and rarely something we can entirely give or receive. We have to accept that informed consent is not a secure replacement for trust but depends on it. And where consent matters and trust is absent, we have to be very careful before we grant it.

See also: Assisted Dying, Health and Illness, Objectification, Pornography, Sex, Trust

Reading
Onora O'Neill, *Autonomy and Trust in Bioethics* (Cambridge University Press, 2002)

Consumerism

If we were to walk around your house looking for brands, what would we find? Think of the makes of your clothes, shoes, watch, car, fridge, kettle, furniture. Unless you are exceptionally idiosyncratic, the list you came up with would allow a market researcher to make some pretty accurate predictions about all sorts of things, such as the kind of area in which you live, your level of education and your political, social and moral values.

Shopping has become much more than a simple matter of buying things you need. It has come to be part of the construction of identity. In today's world, you are what you buy. This is true whether you think you are a victim of consumerism or not.

As an economic theory, consumerism is simply the idea that spending fuels economic growth. But consumerism is also used to describe a mindset in which we are driven to buy, buy, buy, as though shopping were the route to salvation. When we casually quip about 'retail therapy', we're revealing just how pervasive this idea is. At its extreme, it engenders the belief that without consumption we'd be nothing. As Barbara Kruger's 1987 artwork put it, 'I shop therefore I am.'

It is a paradox of modern life that you'd be hard-pressed to find someone who believes consumerism is a good thing, but it's just as difficult to find people who *act* as though it isn't. We live in what we might call a 'consumogenic' environment of ubiquitous logos and adverts, encouraging us to shop our way to health and happiness. And it's not just *stuff* – shows, yoga retreats and off-the-beaten-track holidays are also packaged and sold as must-buy experiences.

If we want to resist this, Harry Frankfurt's analysis of desire is a powerful resource. He makes a distinction between first- and second-order desires. First-order desires are the ones we simply find ourselves having: we see the jacket in the shop window, the cake on the counter or the car winding down the photogenic mountain road in an advert, and we just want them.

Second-order desires, on the other hand, are the ones that emerge when we step back and ask ourselves what we *want to want*. Sometimes these match our first-order desires. After reflection, you are reassured that you do want nice, affordable, ethically made clothes, just like the ones you are trying on. But often first- and second-order desires are out of joint. Maybe you're a bit overweight and you don't want to want cake so much. Or you see your fantasies about buying a sports car for what they are, and realise this is not the best way to boost your morale.

Unaware of this distinction, many of us assume that first-order desires tell us all we need to know about what we really want. Businesses take advantage of this, constantly drawing us into spending, often for spurious reasons. Algorithms and artificial intelligence track our online activity to make sure that what most tempts us pops up on our screens.

Frankfurt's thesis is that our choices are only really free when first- and second-order desires are in harmony. When they're not, and we act on first-order desires, we are simply slaves to our impulses. In order to be more autonomous, therefore, we need to realise that sometimes our desires have to be challenged rather than satisfied, and put this awareness into practice.

From this point of view, resisting consumerism means spending only on things that, on reflection, we *want* to want, aligning our choices with our deeply-held values. This would ideally result in reducing consumption, but at the very least it should lead to becoming more reflective about the reasons for our shopping choices and giving more weight to ethical considerations. Such 'ethical consumerism' need not be the naive idea that we can shop our way to a just and sustainable world. It is simply the acknowledgement that our buying choices can either support good, ethical companies or rapacious, amoral ones.

There is a sense in which we are what we buy. If we shop with a conscience, questioning our immediate desires, we are at least trying to think of more than ourselves and take some responsibility for where our money ends up. Slavishly buying whatever we find ourselves wanting, on the other hand, is not therapy but a malaise that needs to be cured.

See also: Asceticism, Desires, Free Will, Needs, Self-Control, Simplicity, Wealth

Reading
Harry Frankfurt, *The Importance of What We Care About: Philosophical Essays* (Cambridge University Press, 1988)

Contentment

Not every moment can be pleasurable. Not every day can be a happy one. But isn't it possible to reach a stage when we are content with life, at least most of the time? To be content is to be sanguine about the possibility that this is as good as it gets. Is such contentment desirable and achievable?

Most advice on achieving contentment is based on accepting things as they are rather than striving to improve them. (*See* **Control**.) As the Stoic Epictetus pithily put it, 'Do not ask things to happen as you wish, but wish them to happen as they do happen, and your life will go smoothly.'

So if we find ourselves in a situation we dislike, we ought to reframe the way we understand it. For example, 'you ought, when you live alone, to call that peace and freedom, and compare yourself to the gods; and when you are in company, not to call it a crowd and a tumult and a vexation, but a feast and a festival, and thus accept all things with contentment'.

It might be challenging to implement this if you feel you've made a big mistake, or even if your neighbours' dog is keeping you awake at night. But if we can accept things just as they are, whether good or bad, contentment should follow. We may not be happy, if by that we mean a zingy, upbeat frame of mind. We may not even be completely satisfied with our life. We may not have been blessed with something we wanted – a loving relationship, for instance – or we may be aware that for whatever reason we haven't fulfilled our potential. All that can be true and yet we may be content.

Some philosophers have been suspicious of contentment, on the grounds that it implies passive acceptance rather than active engagement with the world. John Stuart Mill believed that to be content showed you were too easily pleased. It is 'better to be Socrates dissatisfied than a fool satisfied', he wrote. He thought happiness was more worthwhile, since to become happy in a fully human way you have to partake of higher pleasures, such as art, music and conversation. (*See* **Pleasure**.)

Nietzsche was even more forceful in his contempt for the content, whom he lumped together with the happy. In his view, we should not 'strive after happiness', because this would lead us to avoid the hard work of becoming the best possible versions of ourselves. The goal is '*Not* contentment, but more power', he says, by which he does not mean power over others but self-mastery and the full development of our potential.

Nietzsche and Mill had a point. If acceptance is taken to extremes, the result may indeed be passivity, which is not the most helpful attitude. While it is sensible to have low expectations of the world and what we can achieve, in order to do our best we have to aim high and ask a lot of ourselves.

However, we do need to question the assumption that changing unsatisfactory situations will necessarily make us happy. Since there will always be things that would be different in an ideal world, the feeling that our lives won't be right until certain changes have happened could easily end up becoming a permanent state of mind. Also, the greater our expectations, and the more we focus our attention on potential improvements, the less content we become. Instead, it is often acceptance that brings relief and tranquillity.

So we need the right kind of contentment, which avoids excessive acquiescence. In practice this means balancing our efforts to make things better with a genuine acceptance of how things actually are. Above all, it means not allowing life's imperfections to obscure what we can appreciate and enjoy every day.

See also: Achievement, Calm, Control, Desires, Gratitude, Happiness, Perfectionism, Simplicity

Reading

Friedrich Nietzsche, *Twilight of the Idols* (1889)

Control

It is not uncommon to get upset about all sorts of things we can't do anything about – things that have happened in the past, other people's attitudes and behaviours, or simply facts of life, like that we get old and die. We may know perfectly well that we can't or are very unlikely to change these, but it's still hard to let them go.

The Stoics had some seemingly straightforward advice to deal with this: bear in mind at all times the difference between what is in your control and what isn't, and when it comes to anything in the latter category, just accept it as it is. Epictetus returns to this point again and again: 'Some things are up to us and others are not. Up to us are opinion, impulse, desire, aversion, and, in a word, whatever is our own action. Not up to us are body, property, reputation, office, and, in a word, whatever is not our own action.' Given this, he advises to 'make the best of what is in our power, and take the rest as it naturally happens'.

Epictetus makes it sound as though there is an unmistakable line between what is up to us and what isn't, but in practice it is not always so transparent. It is clear enough that we can't change the past, or bring dead people back to life. When it comes to changing other things – our health, other people, unsatisfactory situations – we have a degree of influence, but it can be hard to work out just how much.

As for changing our own thoughts and actions, this can be trickier than Epictetus suggested. We are a tangle of unconscious processes and engrained habits, which many years of therapy can only begin to untangle, and which are surely impossible to unravel completely. It may be easier to change ourselves than other people, but our control over ourselves is still partial and limited.

It would certainly be sensible to practise full acceptance of things that are completely outside our influence. For everything else, it's a question of putting some effort into changing things while remaining aware that the outcome depends not only on what we do but also on the world's cooperation, and that the world doesn't always oblige. There may come a point where effort to change has to turn into acceptance.

Paradoxically, sometimes accepting how limited our control is can produce change more fruitfully than tense striving. Daoism tells us that 'It is the Way of Heaven not to strive, and yet it skilfully overcomes.' Life is difficult only because we are not in tune with the natural order of things – the 'Way of Heaven'. Once we let this natural order dictate how we act, and 'go with the flow', everything is easy. The snag is that it takes experience and practice to learn how to go with the grain of the world, like an experienced carpenter developing a feel for the wood. Still, even being aware that this is the goal can be helpful. If the cause of our frustration is trying to go against the grain, maybe by changing direction we will finally be able to move forward.

See also: Contentment, Frustration, Regret, Uncertainty

Reading
Epictetus, *Discourses* and *Handbook*

Cosmic Insignificance

Every now and then we are hit by the disturbing thought of how small and insignificant our life is in the vastness of space and time. When we become aware that in the blink of an eye the human race will be gone, goals like completing a degree or securing a promotion can lose their shine.

There is no shortage of philosophers who have pursued this line of thinking. One is Schopenhauer, for whom 'the infiniteness of time and space contrasted with the finiteness of the individual' reveals what he calls 'the vanity of existence'.

We can't get our head around the fact that 'we suddenly exist, after having for countless millennia not existed; in a short while we will again not exist, also for countless millennia'.

Thomas Nagel has sought to pinpoint the mechanism behind this sense of disorientation. Normally, our daily activities fill our horizon relatively unproblematically. We get up and go to work, see friends, play with the cat, read a book, plan our holidays. But this flow can be disrupted by the fact that 'humans have the special capacity to step back and survey themselves, and the lives to which they are committed, with that detached amazement which comes from watching an ant struggle up a heap of sand'. We peep at our lives from the outside and the solid everyday perspective dissolves.

Albert Camus also wrote about this 'outside' perspective, comparing it to seeing a man 'talking on the telephone behind a glass partition; you cannot hear him, but you see his incomprehensible dumb show: you wonder why he is alive'. In his view, the clash between our need for meaning and the universe's refusal to provide it creates a sense of absurdity.

For Nagel, the source of the absurd is a clash not between us and the world, but between two viewpoints within ourselves. It is a 'collision between the seriousness with which we take our lives' and 'a point of view outside the particular form of our lives, from which the seriousness appears gratuitous'.

But the outside point of view needn't rob our daily life of significance, says Nagel. We are able to hold the two perspectives without one undermining the other because we cannot sustain the detached attitude. 'We cannot do very much as pure spectators of our own lives, so we continue to lead them.' It is enough to find value from within our lives, whether or not they matter from a cosmic viewpoint. After all, if nothing matters from the standpoint of the universe, mattering can only be something that occurs on a smaller scale anyway.

There is another side to the cosmic perspective: although it sometimes seems to drain meaning from our daily activities, it can also have the comforting effect of making our worries seem smaller and less menacing.

Marcus Aurelius' *Meditations* are full of reminders of our insignificance. For him, this was a way of putting things in perspective, of remembering that the things we stress about are irrelevant when we look at them from a wider vantage point. He invites us to 'discard most of the junk that clutters your mind' by 'comprehending the scale of the world', 'contemplating infinite time' and 'thinking of the speed with which things change'.

Nagel is right to suggest that we can manage the dual perspective. We can celebrate and engage with everyday life just as it is, with no need of further justification. But it is also helpful to entertain the sobering thought that in the greater scheme of things we are not that important. The trick is to downgrade our worries without downgrading what is of value in life.

See also: Anxiety, Fate, God, Meaning, Purpose

Reading
Arthur Schopenhauer, 'On the Vanity of Existence' in *Essays and Aphorisms* (Penguin, 1970)
Thomas Nagel, 'The Absurd' in *Mortal Questions* (Cambridge University Press, 1991)

Courage

Few virtues are praised more than bravery. We are regularly told that 'fortune favours the brave', that we should 'search for the heroes inside ourselves' and 'just do it'. So why don't we?

For very good reasons. Aristotle made it clear that there are different problems we can have with courage, and not having enough of it is only one of them – we can also have too much. What we praise as courage is actually a sweet spot between a deficiency we call cowardice and an excess we call recklessness. People who habitually 'just do it' without due thought are rash and foolish, not paragons of valour.

So to assess whether we need to work on building our courage, we have to start by auditing where we are on the spectrum. If we tend to be too cautious we would do well to push ourselves to be bolder; if we tend to rush in headlong, the best advice might be to stop listening so much to the hero inside ourselves and pay more attention to our gentle inner grandparent.

Whatever we conclude, we also need to remember that whether we are being genuinely courageous depends on what we are being courageous about. After all, it would take a kind of bravery to conduct an armed robbery or a carjacking, but no one should be praised for doing either. Confucius put this well when he said, 'A person in a superior situation, having courage without righteousness, will be guilty of insubordination; one of the lower people having bravery without righteousness, will commit robbery.'

Courage is best mustered for the most valuable actions. Sometimes this is personal. There is nothing inherently good or bad about quitting a job, for example, but sometimes that is what we need to do, despite it being scary.

Other things worth being brave about are more universal. 'To see what is right and not to do it is want of courage,' said Confucius. When we are confronted with injustice in life, we should try to have the courage to do something about it rather than treat it as somebody else's problem. The experience of the #MeToo movement and the uncovering of numerous child sex-abuse scandals show how easy it is for people to witness grave wrongdoing yet do nothing about it. Having the courage to stand up to such wrongs is worth any number of skydives.

Kant highlighted a less-appreciated form of bravery. In his essay 'What Is Enlightenment?' he said humankind had been living in 'self-imposed childhood'. We do not remain in this state because of a lack of understanding but a 'lack of courage to use one's own mind without another's guidance'. Kant urged us: 'Dare to know!' (*Sapere aude*) The courage to act for yourself is rooted in the courage to think for yourself.

See also: Commitment, Fear, Insecurity, Risk

Craft *see* Leisure

Reading
Confucius, *Analects*
Immanuel Kant, *Answering the Question: What is Enlightenment?* (1784)

D

> 'One should bring this question to bear on all one's desires: what will happen to me if what is sought by desire is achieved, and what will happen if it is not?' Epicurus

Dating

The great philosophers of the past had little to say about dating, for the simple reason that it is a modern invention. For example, Brits of a certain age never 'dated' in their youth. They simply 'asked someone out' (or were asked out themselves), or were 'seeing someone'.

Of course, people have been getting together since time immemorial, but dating is something much more specific: it is a formalisation of the pairing process that strips out ambiguity and leaves all parties in no doubt that they are checking each other out as potential partners.

Online dating has a lot in common with shopping. We browse the products (or profiles) available, select the ones we'd like to try, and if they are in stock (willing to meet us) we take them for a risk-free trial, with no obligation to proceed to purchase as long as we return them within the guarantee period (three dates is usually considered the maximum). Many people believe we are even entitled to try out different competitors at the same time.

The system has become popular because it seems to work. In many countries, online dating is now the most common way for couples to meet. Many long-term relationships have started in the virtual equivalent of the supermarket aisle. However, many dislike the process, largely because of the need to sell yourself.

Michael Sandel has written about how 'market values . . . have come to govern our lives as never before', with corrosive effects. The value of almost everything is now judged by the criteria of the market: it's all about what people are willing to pay for something (whether with cash or other resources) and the forces of supply and demand. Sandel cites the influential Chicago School economist Gary Becker as evidence that this marketisation even affects our most intimate relationships. You may think people marry for love, but according to Becker, 'a person decides to marry when the utility expected from marriage exceeds that expected from remaining single or from additional search for a more suitable mate'. Who said romance was dead?

Becker's description of marriage might strike you as cold. But apply it to dating and it sounds eerily accurate: 'a person decides to go on a second date when the utility expected from it exceeds that expected from remaining single or from additional search for a more suitable date'. In the dating game, market logic rules the roost.

Maybe that's not such a bad thing. Dating has become the dominant way to meet a mate precisely because it seems the most effective option. We may bristle at its transactional aspects, but on balance most people judge it better than going to evening classes or pubs and waiting to bump into Mr or Ms Right.

We are therefore faced with two options. One is to reject dating. Just as some people refuse to shop at supermarkets, even though the alternatives are less convenient and more expensive, we might decide that our relationship values don't fit well with dating and that we'll take our chances elsewhere.

The other option is to try to take the best features of dating without taking the worst. We date, but try to make sure we do not succumb to the selling and buying mindset. We remind ourselves when we're on a date that we are two people who may or may not be attracted to each other. We respect ourselves and our dates as people, not products. We can do this, but only if we are aware of how the dating etiquette insidiously makes it more difficult. In dating, as in so much else, we must, as Sandel advises, 'rethink the role and reach of markets in our social practices, human relationships and everyday lives'.

See also: Consumerism, Love, Objectification, Relationships, Sex, Solitude

Reading
Michael Sandel, *What Money Can't Buy: The Moral Limits of Markets* (Penguin, 2012)

Death

''Tis impossible to be sure of any thing but Death and Taxes,' wrote the English playwright Christopher Bullock in 1716, seventy-three years before Benjamin Franklin's more famous spin on the phrase. Like taxes, the certainty of the grave does not stop many of us seeking evasion. Although we can't ultimately avoid it, we usually do a pretty good job of at least avoiding *thinking* about it. But few of us are untouched by the thought of death to some degree or other. Whether it is an intermittent awareness flickering at the edges of consciousness, or a looming presence we're constantly struggling with, it is there.

Ancient Greece bequeathed us the idea that philosophy can help us to face death with equanimity, an ideal embodied in the figure of Socrates, who is reported to have been imperturbable before death. In fact, he fully embraced it, arguing in Plato's *Phaedo* that philosophers should welcome death. His reason for this was that he believed that his true self – his soul – was immortal and would live on in another realm. (*See* **Afterlife**.) It was in this context that the concept of philosophy as a preparation for death arose, as it involved the well-being of the soul in advance of its liberation from the body.

The Stoics shared the belief that philosophers were in training for death. Students should nurture reason, the truly valuable part of a human being, and combat their mistaken perceptions about the value of worldly things. Thinking about death frequently was part of the training, which is why the Stoic literature contains so many reminders of it.

Take this example from Epictetus: 'Day by day you must keep before your eyes death and exile, and everything that seems terrible, but death above all; and then you will never have any abject thought, or desire anything beyond due measure.' And from Seneca: 'There's no way to know the point where death lies waiting for you, so you must wait for death at every point.'

Dealing with the prospect of death was also a cornerstone of Epicurus' philosophy. He believed that in order to live a good life we should free ourselves of the fears plaguing us, especially the fear of death. His main argument is that there is no point in worrying about something we won't be aware of. 'Death is nothing to us,' he says, 'for the body, when it has been resolved into its elements, has no feeling, and that which has no feeling is nothing to us.' One of the best-known Epicurean slogans is: 'While we are, death is not; when death is come, we are not.' The Epicurean poet Lucretius made the related point that just as we don't worry about the time before we were born, we shouldn't worry about the state of being dead.

But the idea that philosophy is a preparation for death has its detractors. When one of Confucius' disciples asked, 'I venture to ask about death', he received the answer, 'While you do not know life, how can you know about death?' When our focus is on how best to live, death is an almost uninteresting irrelevance.

Montaigne had reservations about the whole idea of preparing for death and counselled, 'If you do not know how to die, never mind. Nature will tell you how to do it on the spot, plainly and adequately.'

Often it is not so much that we fear death, or even the process of dying, but that we object to losing the good things in life. Some philosophers have considered it perfectly reasonable to dislike the idea of dying if you have a rich life and don't wish it to stop. Aristotle, for instance, believed that since death entails 'losing the greatest goods', the more flourishing one's life is, the more painful the thought of it will be.

Simone de Beauvoir adds flesh to the bones of this sentiment in her autobiography, when she writes, 'I think with sadness of all the books I've read, all the places I've seen, all the knowledge I've amassed and that will be no more. All the music, all the paintings, all the culture, so many places: and suddenly nothing.' Her partner Jean-Paul Sartre lamented the loss of the future, describing death as 'the possibility that there are for me no longer any possibilities'.

So, what advice can there be, if we believe that death is the end and we are still quite attached to life? What can preparing for death possibly mean then? What is left is a need to cultivate an understanding of death as 'nothing but a process of nature', as Marcus Aurelius wrote. 'It too is one of the things required by nature. Like youth and old age. Like growth and maturity . . . Like all the other physical changes at each stage of life, our dissolution is not different.'

This might seem like a minor point, but it has the potential to make a big difference: a genuine acceptance of finitude, some sense that birth and death are part of the natural rhythm of things, and the awareness that we should use our brief time on Earth as fully as we can.

See also: Afterlife, Ageing, Authenticity, Bereavement, Carpe Diem, Love of Life, Mortality

Reading
Simon Critchley, *The Book of Dead Philosophers* (Granta, 2009)

Decision-Making *see* Choice, Indecision

Depression *see* Melancholy

Desires

It is often assumed that our well-being depends on our desires being fulfilled, and it is certainly frustrating when they are not. But should we be more questioning of our desires and what we do about them?

Philosophers have generally been wary of the power of desire. Plato likened it to an unruly horse that drove the chariot of the soul in harness with the more disciplined reason. Where philosophers have differed is in their views about how best to tackle this troublesome beast. Should we tame it or slay it?

Plato was ambiguous. Although his chariot metaphor suggests we should tame it, elsewhere he says that a philosopher 'secures immunity from . . . desires by following Reason and abiding always in her company'. The Stoics were more clearly in the renunciation camp. Musonius Rufus succinctly sums up their view when he says, 'one man and one man only is truly wealthy – he who learns to want nothing in every circumstance'. Similarly, the neo-Confucian Zhou Dunyi says of the sage: 'Having no desire, he will be tranquil.'

But why should we try to purge ourselves of all desires? Different thinkers give different answers, but they generally agree on two points. One is that most desires are for things that are not truly valuable, like money, fame, power. We want these because we believe them to be good, but they are not. In theory this is encouraging, since once we realise our error we should cease to desire them. But it takes effort, and the most common human desires are difficult to eliminate. Stories about 'spiritual' leaders falling prey to their lure are a constant warning.

The second reason for trying to eradicate desire is that even having 'good' desires can be bad for us. As Epictetus says, 'Remember that it is not only a desire for riches and power that makes you abject and subservient to others but also a desire for quiet and leisure, and travel and learning. For the value you place on an external object, whatever it may be, makes you subservient to another.' We are slaves to our desires, even when they are for good things.

Epicurus distinguished between three kinds of desires: natural and necessary; natural but not necessary; and vain and empty. Natural and necessary ones are easy to satisfy, and include things like food, drink and shelter. Natural but not necessary ones are optional pleasurable treats, like nice food. Finally there are vain desires for such things as fame and power, which are neither natural nor necessary, take effort and conflict to attain, and have endless capacity to expand. Both these vain desires and the natural but not necessary ones, says Epicurus, 'are due to illusory opinion' and are therefore misguided. Instead of trying to fulfil these, we would do better to eliminate them. We can enjoy occasional luxuries that happen to come our way, but we should not depend on them.

The problem with all this advice is that most of us do not wish to reduce our desires so dramatically. The approach of the Confucian Mencius seems a little more accommodating of this: 'Here is a man whose desires are few: in some things he may not be able to keep his heart, but they will be few. Here is a man whose desires are many: in some things he may be able to keep his heart, but they will be few.' You don't have to reduce your desires to zero but it would be good to make them few.

Confucius suggests that if our desires are fulfilled as a consequence of us living a good life, that's a good thing: 'Wealth and social eminence are things that all people desire, and yet if they are not acquired in the proper way I will not abide them,' he said. 'Poverty and disgrace are things that all people hate, and yet unless they are avoided in the proper way I will not despise them.' As long as we are not greedy, ruthless, shallow and materialistic, it is good and natural to take pleasure in the things we desire. The key is not making the fulfilment of our desires our main life goal.

Although most of us would rather moderate and control our desires than eliminate them, we can learn a little about how to do this from those who take a harder line. Epicurus' distinction between necessary and unnecessary desires is particularly useful, with some adaptation. The concept of 'need' is complex and slippery, (*see* **Needs**) so the question 'Do I really need this?' is often inconclusive. But it is still worth asking ourselves some hard questions as prompts for reflection. In what way is what you desire necessary? What will it bring you that is truly worth having? On this point, another of Epicurus' formulations might also come in handy: 'One should bring this question to bear on all one's desires: what will happen to me if what is sought by desire is achieved, and what will happen if it is not?'

See also: Asceticism, Contentment, Needs, Pleasure, Self-Control, Simplicity, Wealth

Reading
Musonius Rufus, *Lectures and Sayings*

Dieting *see* **Self-Control**

Dilemmas

Most dilemmas are thorny but philosophically uninteresting. Should you take a job that is better paid or one that is nearer home? Should you leave your dependable partner for someone who seems exciting but is an unknown quantity? Answers can be hard to find, but that is only because you can't know how things will turn out, and so whatever you do will always entail a risk.

More interesting are *moral* dilemmas. These are not about what might work better for you, but about what is morally right. If you have a moral dilemma, you have moral reasons to do two things that are incompatible and so are torn between competing moral considerations. For instance, if you discover that a friend's partner has been having an affair, you might be torn between being truthful and being kind, feeling that you owe your friend honesty but also wanting to protect them from hurt. These things are not *intrinsically* incompatible. It's just that, in this case, you can't both be honest and shield them from pain at the same time. You have to choose which value is going to be your priority.

In some dilemmas, one moral requirement will clearly trump the other, as in the case of having to decide whether or not to return a weapon to someone who is not in their right mind, which Plato discusses in the *Republic*. Sure, repaying debts has moral significance, says Socrates, but protecting others from harm counts for more. In a way this is not a real dilemma.

The really intractable dilemmas are those in which there is no overriding factor that makes one option clearly better. Take the novel and film *Sophie's Choice*, in which a mother is forced to choose which of her two children would go to the gas chamber and which would be saved. This is a case of 'moral tragedy': there is no right way to act, and whatever we do will be 'wrong'.

The predicament in *Sophie's Choice* is extreme and exceptional, but there are more mundane situations in which no moral consideration is decisive enough to deliver a clear answer. Take the question of whether it is better to continue to work with an ethically flawed company to try to improve it or to wash your hands of it and leave.

So how can you resolve a moral dilemma? The first step is to check that the moral obligations we perceive are real. Sometimes we feel burdened by a responsibility that is not really justified. For example, people may feel obliged to visit relatives who expect it but have never shown themselves deserving of such attention. Realising that you don't have to go out of your way to see people who don't give a damn about you can be a huge relief.

If we decide that a dilemma is real, we should clarify the moral reasons to act one way or the other. There are different kinds of obligations, and they can clash – a conflict between professional confidentiality and a duty to disclose something to the authorities, for instance. If that is the case, we will have to try to work out which, if any, is the weightier consideration.

If we really can't settle it, we have to accept that we can't avoid doing something we justifiably think is wrong. Imagine a doctor having to choose between treating the potentially fatal injuries of other people's children in the aftermath of an explosion or going to look for their own child, who is unaccounted for in the confusion. The choice is morally impossible: it would be wrong to abandon your special duty of care to your own child but also wrong to sacrifice other children for yours.

When we make such choices, we are likely to be left with some kind of guilt or regret. This is not just understandable but to be expected. However, we have to remind ourselves that we would have felt bad either way. (*See* **Responsibility**.) Our unease is the necessary consequence of an impossible situation, not a sign of moral culpability. Some moral dilemmas cannot be solved. They can only be dealt with by making a choice and accepting the consequences, with regret but without blame.

See also: Ambivalence, Choice, Guilt and Shame, Indecision, Regret, Responsibility, Uncertainty, What If

Reading
Lisa Tessman, *When Doing the Right Thing Is Impossible* (Oxford University Press, 2017)

Disappointment *see* **Frustration**

Divorce *see* **Love**

Doubt *see* **Uncertainty**

Duty

The idea of 'doing one's duty' has an old-fashioned ring to it. It is difficult to imagine a government today using the Second World War poster slogan 'Britain expects that you too, this day, will do your duty'. Google's Ngram, which tracks the prevalence of words since 1800, shows 'duty' peaking in the 1830s and now being used only a quarter as often.

We do still find ourselves wondering whether we are failing in our duties, although more often to friends and family than to country or employer. But we are increasingly likely to question whether any supposed duty is genuine. To answer that, we have to ask where duties come from.

One view is that duties (and rights) are rooted in contracts, whether formal or informal, written or unwritten, and are taken on in return for certain benefits. For instance, a job might come with certain duties, as does becoming a parent. Signing a contract or making a promise also places a duty on us to honour it. Duties on this contractarian account are mostly assumed voluntarily.

When duties are based on voluntary contracts, they are usually clear enough. There may be no universal duty of monogamy, for example, but if you've agreed to a monogamous relationship there is no shirking your duty to act accordingly. Similarly, you can't become a parent without taking on a lot of duties.

The duties of citizenship are a little different. These are based on a kind of 'social contract' that no one actually signs but that we all have to assume in order to live in a peaceful, lawful society. As Thomas Hobbes, one of the first social contract theorists put it, a person must be willing, when others also are, 'to lay down this right to all things; and be contented with so much liberty against other men, as he would allow other men against himself'. This, argued Hobbes, was no more than the duty laid down in the Gospels that 'Whatsoever you require that others should do to you, that do ye to them.' (Hobbes quotes the Latin *Quod tibi fieri non vis, alteri ne feceris*, for no other apparent reason than it sounds good.)

For Immanuel Kant, however, duties have a more robust source than any kind of contract: we have duties because reason demands it. This idea springs from what Kant calls the categorical imperative: 'Always act in such a way that you can also will that the maxim of your action should become a universal law.' To put it another way, do only what would be acceptable for everyone to do; never do anything that would be disastrous if everyone did it. Kant gave lying as an example. If everyone lied, we would never be able to trust anything anyone said, therefore communication itself demands that we don't lie.

Kant's ethics of duty is very demanding. It requires us to consider much more than what we have agreed to do, explicitly or implicitly. It says we have a duty to behave as we would have others behave. It is, in other words, like Hobbes's principle, a version of the Golden Rule to treat others as we would be treated ourselves.

Kant also places an important limit on duties: 'The action to which the "ought" applies must indeed be possible under natural conditions.' This is the principle that 'ought implies can' – you cannot be under any duty to perform an action if you can't possibly do it. This is important to remember. Often we feel guilty that we have failed in our duties when the truth is that we couldn't have done any better. There is a limit to how much time we can devote to caring for a sick or elderly relative, or how much we can relieve the depression of another person. Although 'I did all I could' is often just an excuse for inaction, it can be a genuine description of the limits of our powers.

Confucius located duties in a third place, neither in the universal, objective moral law nor in contracts. Confucian 'role ethics' says that we all have duties specific to our social roles, which are neither chosen nor universal. They apply specifically to certain people according to their place in society and are not the result of any kind of contract. A parent has duties, for example, simply because all parents have duties, which is why it makes no difference whether parenthood is planned or accidental. Children also have duties towards their parents, even though (as they often tell them) they didn't choose to be born.

Interestingly, Confucius, like Hobbes and Kant, advocated a version of the Golden Rule: 'Do not impose upon others what you yourself do not desire.' All three thinkers thought that duty was rooted in an obligation to apply the same rules to ourselves as we do to others. In a sense, to perform your duty is simply not to be a hypocrite.

Duty is far from an outmoded concept. If it seems old-fashioned it's because we valorise individual choice and are therefore reluctant to accept any obligations that we do not voluntarily take on. But if we think about it, we can see that some duties impose themselves on us, and it is irresponsible to neglect them. The danger of a misplaced sense of duty is still real, but the risk of an equally misplaced sense of being free from duty is even greater.

See also: Family, Integrity, Loyalty, Parenthood, Responsibility, Trust

Reading
Confucius, *Analects*, Books 12 and 15
Immanuel Kant, *Groundwork of the Metaphysic of Morals* (1785)
Thomas Hobbes, *Leviathan* (1651), Chapter XIV

E

'One kind of missing the mark is to fear the wrong thing, another to fear in the wrong way, another to fear at the wrong time, and so on.'
Aristotle

Education

There is no disputing the value of a good education. There is, however, plenty of dispute about what a good education is. That can make it difficult to decide how to teach our children, as well as how to continue our own lifelong education. One way to think this through is to consider what education is for. Only when that is clear can we assess the different options for how to educate ourselves.

Many philosophers have offered their answers to this question, usually focusing on the education of children. For Plato, the main function of education was to produce good citizens, and so it was the responsibility of the state. In his proposed system, everyone would enter education on an equal footing, but as the differing abilities of the children became apparent, some would be educated as warriors, others as craftspeople, and the best as rulers.

To many of us today, Plato's republic sounds less like the ideal it was supposed to be and more like an authoritarian nightmare. Few would deny that one role of education is to prepare children for working life, but the idea of schools selecting their students' destinies goes much further than this. Unfortunately, this is indirectly what many schools do. In the UK, only 7 per cent of the population goes to fee-paying private schools, but this minority ends up comprising 71 per cent of the top military officers, 74 per cent of the top judges and 51 per cent of the leading print journalists. As parents, we have to decide whether to play this game of privilege (if we can afford to do so); as citizens, we ought to think about whether we should allow it to continue.

One reason why Plato's education system jars today is that we believe in nurturing individuality and autonomy. The educational theories of Jean-Jacques Rousseau are more in tune with this. Rousseau believed that 'civilisation' corrupted what was naturally good in human beings. 'Everything is good as it leaves the hands of the Author of things,' he wrote, 'everything degenerates in the hands of man'. Society, however, is a necessity, and so the role of education is to prepare children to enter it while preserving as much of their natural goodness as possible. So he placed the emphasis on children learning for themselves by experience and experiment, interacting more with the world than with books. He also believed in toughening up the body, training in crafts, and learning about the ways of the heart.

The American pragmatist John Dewey shared Rousseau's belief that children should be active in their learning. He also thought that 'Any education given by a group tends to socialise its members, but the quality and value of the socialisation depends on the habits and aims of the group.' Confucian philosophy similarly stresses the socialising role of education, especially in building good character. Only people of education, Mencius thought, 'are able to maintain a fixed heart'.

Although Dewey and Rousseau believed in nurturing the natural curiosity of children, neither favoured the kind of ultra-liberal approach that leaves more or less everything to the child. Bertrand Russell took that extra step. Believing that 'obedience is the counterpart of authority', he set up his own school, Beacon Hill in Sussex, in which children could do pretty much what they wanted. Like other such schools, it was neither as much of a success as its advocates believed it would be nor as disastrous as its critics predicted. Russell accepted its failings and later concluded that 'children cannot be happy without a certain amount of order and routine'.

Taking all these views together, something resembling a consensus emerges. First, education is socialisation, so when deciding how to educate children we are also choosing how their characters are going to be built and what sorts of citizens they are to become. Second, a good education balances order and routine with freedom and creativity – the best environment is neither too rigid nor too chaotic. Third, no matter what high ideals we may have for education, no responsible parent can ignore the fact that the schooling children receive is important in determining their employment prospects.

Our tendency to focus on children's education can lead us to think too much about its role in preparing us for adult life. Education, however, is not just a preparation for something else. At its best, it is valuable in itself. Russell wrote, 'I regard disinterested learning as a matter of great importance'. Learning for learning's sake is something many of us find deeply rewarding. 'Lifelong learning' is not just about keeping our skill sets up to date in a changing labour market, it is also about keeping our minds active and using the intellectual capacities that make human life uniquely wonderful.

See also: Authority, Knowledge, Parenthood

Reading
John Dewey, *Democracy and Education* (1916)
Jean-Jacques Rousseau, *Emile, or On Education* (1762)
Bertrand Russell, *On Education* (George Allen & Unwin, 1926)

Embarrassment

How would you feel if you were reading this book in public and realised your flies were undone? Or if you were telling someone about it and were picked up on your wrong pronunciation of a Greek philosopher's name? Or if you were sitting on one of those train toilets with an electric door and it opened?

Many of us are far too easily embarrassed, constantly worrying about whether we've made a faux pas, what people think of us, whether we'll be rejected. Even if we know it doesn't really matter, our sense of discomfort can be surprisingly resistant to reason.

We could spare some of our blushes by listening to the ancient Greek school of the Cynics. Its founder is thought to have been Antisthenes, but one of the best-known figures is Diogenes of Sinope, who is said to have lived in a wine barrel. Most of the information we have about the Cynics comes not from their own writings but from sayings and anecdotes recounting their colourful lives. This is appropriate, as the Cynics viewed ethics as lived daily practice rather than theory.

One of their most important principles was to live a simple life in agreement with nature. According to Diogenes Laertius, some 'are vegetarians and drink cold water only and are content with any kind of shelter or tubs, like Diogenes the Cynic, who used to say that it was the privilege of the gods to need nothing and of god-like men to want but little'.

This vision of the good life crucially required disregarding social conventions, which get in the way of self-sufficiency by obliging us to do unnecessary things to meet others' expectations. In place of conformity they adopted an ethos of shamelessness. It seems they were not averse to performing acts in public that are usually done in private, such as having sex. This was not particularly appreciated, and reportedly Plato's view of Diogenes the Cynic was that he was like a 'Socrates gone mad'.

Like other Hellenistic schools, the Cynics believed that their chosen lifestyle required practice. Their training in shamelessness brings to mind the American psychotherapist and founder of rational-emotive behaviour therapy Albert Ellis. He advocated what he called 'shame-attacking exercises', ranging from going out wearing something silly to taking a banana for a walk as if it were a dog on a leash. The rationale for this is in line with the Cynics' values: to prove to ourselves that nothing terrible is going to happen and ultimately become less dependent on other people's opinions.

All this can be challenging. You might not go as far as Diogenes of Sinope and masturbate in public (in fact, we urge you not to), but there are less extreme ways of learning not to be so easily embarrassed. So you could watch out for small opportunities to practise, like stepping up to the karaoke mic, not covering up parts of your body you dislike, or admitting your ignorance about a topic of conversation. Feeling uncomfortable is to be expected: it's the price you pay for freeing yourself from excessive embarrassment.

See also: Authenticity, Guilt and Shame, Reputation

Reading
Diogenes Laertius, 'Diogenes of Sinope' in *Lives of the Eminent Philosophers*

Emotions

Some of the peak moments in life are ones of intense emotion: holding your newborn baby for the first time, watching the climax of an incredible sporting contest, reaching the top of a mountain. Life would be far duller without these.

But feelings and emotions (the terms are used interchangeably here) don't make life easy for us sometimes. We often feel in the grip of unpleasant emotions that we don't know how to change, such as jealousy or regret. Or we act hastily on the basis of a feeling that we should have been more wary of, like when we get married to someone we hardly know, or pour our wrath on a person we presume to be guilty but who turns out to be innocent.

In a way it's strange that it turned out this way. Emotions are believed to have evolved to make life easier, as they alert us to things that could affect us – and our reproductive prospects – for better or for worse. Pleasant emotions draw us towards potentially good things like energy-rich food and potential mates, while unpleasant ones keep us away from what can cause harm, like rotten food and rotten mates.

But human evolution has come a long way and emotions are far from reliable now. Is it a good idea to trust the lust that pushes us to start an affair, or the fear that compels us to withdraw from a challenge? Despite the popular belief that we should 'trust our feelings', our emotions have fuelled many foolish actions.

It can be hard to know when to trust emotions and when to keep them at arm's length. To learn how to best manage them, it helps to be clearer about what they are. The simple, single word 'emotion' might trick us into thinking it refers to a simple, single thing. In fact, it is more like a set of overlapping phenomena, which typically include a physiological reaction (such as changes to heart rate, tightening of the chest, loosening of the bowels), a cognitive evaluation (judgements like good or bad, safe or dangerous), a 'feel', and a behaviour, or at least the propensity to act in some way (run away, cry, throw your arms around someone). Not all of these are present in every emotion, and they may occur in different degrees. Some have a strong bodily feel, some lack it altogether, and they may or may not have a behavioural expression. When emotions are quite diffuse they overlap with moods, which are generally vaguer. Moreover, emotions, especially those with a social dimension, such as shame, can be more or less culturally variable.

Some philosophers have emphasised the cognitive side of emotions. The Stoics, for instance, saw them as value judgements. They rightly saw one that a pleasant emotion contains a judgement that something in the world is good and worth having, an unpleasant one that something is bad and should be avoided. But the judgement underscoring an emotion is not necessarily a fully-fledged and articulated belief: it could simply be an initial, inchoate appraisal of what an event means for us and our well-being.

Others have stressed the physiological side of emotions. William James counter-intuitively held that an emotion is our perception of a bodily reaction. For example, coming across a bear in the woods, it is not the case that we are frightened and then break into a sweat. Rather, perceiving the bear leads to certain bodily changes: the amygdala triggers the hypothalamus to activate the pituitary gland, which secretes the adrenocorticotropic hormone into the blood. Our breathing rate increases, blood vessels in the skin constrict and muscles become tighter, giving us goosebumps and making our hair stand on end. It is our perception of these changes that we call fear. The body moves first, subjective experience follows. We don't cry because we're sad, we feel sad because we're crying.

Both these theories have problems but they also contain kernels of truth that we can learn from. First, since an emotion has a cognitive component, we can try to work out whether this is truthful or distorting, whether we should trust it or not. Here we can refer to Aristotle, who knew we can get emotions wrong. Writing about courage, he explains: 'One kind of missing the mark is to fear the wrong thing, another to fear in the wrong way, another to fear at the wrong time, and so on.'

This suggests the kind of questions that we can ask ourselves: are we feeling this emotion about the right thing, in the right way, at the right time? Realising that an emotion is misdirected doesn't automatically correct it, but it can make it more understandable and easier to deal with.

Because emotions also have bodily and behavioural components, it is sometimes better to address these first. For instance, at moments of high anxiety, calming ourselves down through breathing techniques can be more effective than asking ourselves if we really need to be so anxious. Different emotions may need different approaches. But Aristotle got the general principle right: we should neither suppress nor celebrate them unquestioningly. Rather we should interrogate them and the value system they spring from, and if necessary take action to modify how we respond to them. Not that it's easy. But it is important, because if we are too quick to 'trust our feelings' we might end up acting in ways that go against the values that on calmer reflection we most endorse.

See also: Balance, Habits, Intuition, Moods, Rationality, Self-Control, Values

Reading
William James, *The Principles of Psychology* (1890)

Empathy

If you want to become a better person, what is the one thing you should focus on most? Many today would tell you that it's empathy: your capacity to understand and share the feelings of others. When he was president, Barack Obama underlined this when he said that society's 'empathy deficit' was a greater problem than the federal deficit – the national debt. What we all need more of, he said, is 'the ability to put ourselves in someone else's shoes; to see the world through those who are different from us'.

The idea that fellow feeling is of paramount importance is not new. The leading Scottish Enlightenment thinkers, Adam Smith and David Hume, both endorsed versions of the view that ethics is built not on logic or God's commands but on what Smith called 'moral sympathy'. 'That we often derive sorrow from the sorrows of others, is a matter of fact too obvious to require any instances to prove it,' he wrote.

Sympathy and empathy have slightly different connotations nowadays, which vary according to context. But it is clear that when Smith and Hume used the word 'sympathy' they were often referring to what we would today call empathy.

For these philosophers, the idea that empathy is all you need is far too simple – it is the starting point of ethics, not the whole of it. For one thing, our moral decisions often vary depending on which emotional buttons are being pushed.

This has been shown by Joshua Greene and others, working on the border between psychology and philosophy. When we are thinking coolly and rationally, we tend to prefer moral choices that have the best consequences for the greatest number of people. For instance, we are more likely to say that it is right to sacrifice one innocent life to avoid ten innocent deaths. But when we are asked to get up close and personal to a singular victim and put them in harm's way to save others, we tend to decide that it is wrong and choose to let the ten die. In Greene's view, this is a case of empathy distorting moral judgement. If we believe that it is wrong to kill one person in order to save ten others, we will disagree with him. But at the very least this example problematises the equation of empathy with morality.

Another type of situation where empathy might distort moral judgement is charitable giving. It is well known that people give more to charities when they see images of suffering, especially those of young children or cute, furry animals. Moral philosophers promoting 'effective altruism' argue that we need to resist acting on the pull of our heartstrings and be more rational. (*See* **Charity**.) A dollar given to a charity treating intestinal worms does much more good than yet another dollar given to a famous and well-funded children's hospital.

Finally, empathy would be a fine thing if we felt it reliably. In fact, we often merely *feel* that we are feeling the same as others, when what we are really doing is falsely imagining how they feel. Telling someone 'I know exactly how you feel' is often patronising, arrogant and false. Also, because our empathy is unreliable, we tend to feel more sympathy for people who make a show of being distressed and less for those who exercise self-control.

Empathy is important. We need to be sensitive and responsive to the feelings of others. But philosophy warns us not to trust our instinctive reactions too easily. As well as emotional empathy we need *cognitive* empathy, which is the conscious effort to recognise and understand another's emotional state, checking whether our assumptions are correct and whether our responses are the most helpful or simply the ones that come most naturally. Without feeling there can be no morality at all. Without thinking, however, there can only be a naive morality.

See also: Altruism, Charity, Emotions, Intuition, Love, Other People

Reading
Joshua Greene, *Moral Tribes: Emotion, Reason, and the Gap Between Us and Them* (Penguin, 2013)
Adam Smith, *The Theory of Moral Sentiments* (1759)

The Environment *see* Nature

Envy

Many so-called negative emotions have a plus side. Anger can stir us to protest for change, grief is a necessary part of coming to terms with bereavement, fear alerts us to danger. It is not clear, however, that envy has any positives. Even Aristotle, who thought that most feelings had a purpose if felt in the right amount and expressed appropriately, thought that envy (alongside spite and shamelessness) was always bad.

The most that can be said for envy is that we can put it to good use by seeing it as an informative snapshot of what we value. If we envy someone's holidays, maybe we need to go away more often. If we covet someone's career, perhaps we need to make changes to our own.

According to Robert Solomon, much envy is not like this. 'The typical object of envy' is 'something that is not transferable' – something like a talent. For him, envy is a kind of frustration born of constantly wanting what another has without being able to do anything about it.

The nub of the problem is the unfortunate but pervasive human habit of comparing ourselves with others. Bertrand Russell writes that envy 'consists in seeing things never in themselves, but only in their relations'. So although we may be earning enough to cover our needs, learning that someone else (who we might not rate) earns twice as much as us might make our own salary seem inadequate.

Russell was not the first to notice this. Hume said that envy 'is excited by some present enjoyment of another, which by comparison diminishes our idea of our own'. And Seneca wrote, 'No matter how much you own, the mere fact that someone has more will make you think that your resources are insufficient by exactly the amount that his are greater.'

Far from being a helpful pointer towards our own true values, envy is more likely to be an illustration of how easily our attention is captured by what shiny jewels others have and we don't, especially when we feel the social pressure to acquire certain goods that we perceive most people to have. We'll probably feel more envy towards our neighbour's new car than the yachts of the super-rich.

The solution to envy is not to try to emulate the achievements of others. As Russell points out, there will always be people who are doing better than us, but what we have 'does not cease to be enjoyable because someone else has something else'. It is the habit of comparing that we need to break. 'You can get away from envy,' says Russell, 'by enjoying the pleasures that come your way, by doing the work that you have to do, and by avoiding comparisons with those whom you imagine, perhaps quite falsely, to be more fortunate than yourself'.

That last point is important. From the outside, people's lives tend to look more perfect than they are, and you never know what demons and troubles the apparently blessed have to put up with. Rather than envy other people's lives, we should make the most of our own – it is, after all, the only one we have.

See also: Competition, Consumerism, Gratitude, Jealousy, Perfectionism

Reading
Bertrand Russell, *The Conquest of Happiness* (George Allen & Unwin, 1930)

Euthanasia *see* Assisted Dying

Evidence

Whether or not there is more bare-faced lying in the world today, the supply and flow of untruths has surely increased significantly, clogging the arteries of the information super-highway. Picking out the true from the false can be difficult. One of the most useful tools for helping with this is asking the simple question: what's the evidence?

Philosophers have long appreciated the importance of basing our beliefs on facts. For instance, all the orthodox schools of Indian philosophy count *pratyaksha* (perception or observation) as a valid form of knowledge. The *falsafa* school of the Islamic Golden Age also put great emphasis on 'demonstrative proof', or reasoning from evidence.

However, making evidence the most important source of knowledge is historically more unusual. In the Islamic tradition, all thinkers have accepted the role of revelation and there have been fierce debates about what to do if evidence appears to contradict it. Among the Indian orthodox schools, only the materialist Charvaka (or Lokayata) school has given priority to *pratyaksha*, claiming it is the only valid source of knowledge. Most other schools also maintain the validity of *shabda*, the testimony of reliable experts, usually the authors of the ancient sacred Vedas and other seers.

In the West, evidence has been in competition with logic. Since Plato, many philosophers have believed that the surest knowledge comes from the application of reason alone, not from inferences based on sense perception. These rationalists have been opposed by empiricists, who believe that evidence is the basis of all knowledge of the world. The person who did most to help shift the debate in favour of the empiricists was the Renaissance philosopher and statesman Francis Bacon.

Bacon was one of the first to offer an account of the scientific method. The core claim in his *New Organon* was that 'Man, being the servant and interpreter of Nature, can do and understand so much and so much only as he has observed in fact or in thought of the course of nature. Beyond this he neither knows anything nor can do anything.' He had no time for the rationalists, saying, 'It cannot be that axioms established by argumentation should avail for the discovery of new works, since the subtlety of nature is greater many times over than the subtlety of argument.'

The principle might seem clear, but Bacon was acutely aware of how difficult it is for humans to follow the evidence wherever it leads. In this, he anticipated many biases of thought that we usually regard as discoveries of modern psychology. For example, he says, 'The human understanding is of its own nature prone to suppose the existence of more order and regularity in the world than it finds.' He also accurately describes what we now call 'confirmation bias', saying that 'The human understanding when it has once adopted an opinion . . . draws all things else to support and agree with it.'

However, it is naive to believe that if we follow the kind of scientific procedure advocated by Bacon we can avoid all error and nonsense. Take the case of evidence-based medicine. In conventional healthcare, treatments are supposed to be assessed along recognisably Baconian lines. They are tested in comparison with alternatives, placebos or nothing to make sure that any apparent beneficial effects are real. Their efficacy is explained by principles of cause and effect that have been established through careful investigation. In contrast, alternative medicines are rarely tested rigorously, and when they are, most fail. The mechanisms by which they are supposed to work are often also unknown to science, such as homeopathy's 'memory of water'.

So it would seem that the evidence is clearly on the side of conventional against alternative medicine. But the case may be less clear-cut than it seems, not because the evidence for alternative medicine is better than is believed, but because the evidence for the conventional kind is sometimes shakier than we suppose. One reason for this, as Paul Feyerabend argued, is that in practice scientists work with a much less rigorous method than we might think. There is a lot of trial and error, guesswork, not knowing why things work. 'Given any rule, however "fundamental" or "necessary" for science,' he wrote, 'there are always circumstances when it is advisable not only to ignore the rule, but to adopt its opposite.'

Conventional treatments are sometimes simply the ones that seem to work better than any others. In time, it is not unusual to find that many either don't do much good at all or have serious side effects. More worryingly, the evidence we see is highly selective: only positive results tend to be published, while trials suggesting that things don't work are buried.

There are also many conditions for which no conventional treatment has been found to work reliably. Many forms of back pain and digestive problems, for instance, can be particularly hard to treat. In such cases, trying something in the absence of good enough evidence might be worth a punt. But be aware of the risks: if a treatment is powerful enough to change the body, it is always possible that the effects will be bad as well as good. 'Natural' remedies are no exception to this principle. And of course, there are plenty of cases where the evidential gap between conventional and alternative treatments is so vast that it would be foolish to ignore it. Anyone who chooses coffee enemas over chemotherapy to treat cancer is flying in the face of the evidence.

Bacon would have appreciated these difficulties. He would never have endorsed the simplistic adage that 'the evidence speaks for itself'. He took an extremely balanced view that recognised the importance of both observation and thought: 'The men of experiment are like the ant, they only collect and use; the reasoners resemble spiders, who make cobwebs out of their own substance. But the bee takes a middle course: it gathers its material from the flowers of the garden and of the field, but transforms and digests it by a power of its own. Not unlike this is the true business of philosophy; for it neither relies solely or chiefly on the powers of the mind, nor does it take the matter which it gathers from natural history and mechanical experiments and lay it up in the memory whole, as it finds it, but lays it up in the understanding altered and digested.'

Reading Bacon, it is clear that basing your views on evidence isn't a simple matter of opening your eyes and looking. As Kant argued, intellectual maturity requires the courage to use your own mind. Accepting whatever evidence is put in front of you without question is an easy way to avoid exerting your brain. As he wrote, 'I have no need to think, if only I can pay; others will take care of that disagreeable business for me.' We should not be so lazy.

See also: Argument, Intuition, Knowledge, Rationality, Superstition, Truth

Reading
Paul Feyerabend, *Against Method* (Verso, 1975)
Francis Bacon, *Novum Organum Scientiarum* or *The New Organon* (1620)

Evil

Scarcely a day goes by without us being aware of some serious wrongdoing, whether in our neighbourhood or in the world. But every now and again something comes to our attention – torture, genocide, child rape – that seems to demand stronger condemnation than just 'that's bad'. The sense that something evil has happened can be visceral. But does 'evil' really exist and, if so, how should we respond to it?

Theologians and philosophers have debated the nature of evil for millennia. Today there is something of a consensus that evil is an extreme form of 'bad', not a separate category. It is true that some psychopaths and sadists do seem fundamentally different from ordinary people. They either lack the kind of empathy that makes most humans sensitive to the suffering of others, or they positively enjoy feeling someone else's pain. The evil of such people is nowadays considered a form of mental illness and they are usually locked up in what are officially hospitals rather than prisons.

It is more difficult to understand the wicked acts committed by people who are not mentally ill. Philosophers and psychologists who have studied this tend to come to the disturbing conclusion that they are not fundamentally different from everyone else, which has the chilling corollary that anyone is capable of doing evil in the wrong circumstances.

Hannah Arendt's *Eichmann in Jerusalem* is one of the key texts in this debate, despite her own insistence that the book is not 'a theoretical treatise on the nature of evil'. It is rather a carefully observed account of the trial of one man who was condemned to death for crimes against the Jewish people. But what she recorded clearly has wider resonance.

Arendt wrote that 'the trouble with Eichmann was precisely that so many were like him, and that the many were neither perverted nor sadistic, that they were, and still are, terrifyingly normal'. Indeed, when recruiting soldiers for the Einsatzgruppen, the Nazi death squads who were responsible for mass killings across German-occupied Europe, 'a systematic effort was made to weed out all those who derived physical pleasure from what they did'.

So how could a 'normal' person like Eichmann have sent so many innocent people to their deaths? Arendt's answers are deeply disturbing. 'It was sheer thoughtlessness', she wrote, 'that predisposed him to become one of the greatest criminals of that period.' He simply didn't think and so *'never realised what he was doing'*.

This seems extraordinary, unbelievable. How could he not have known what he was doing? It wasn't that he was a kind of zombie, doing his work in a trance. At one level he was aware of all that he did. But he didn't attend to what he was *really* doing, to the real meaning and significance of it.

Could any normal person really do the same? It seems they could. We have many techniques at our disposal to help us to avert our gaze from what should be obvious. Eichmann describes one of these as 'a kind of Pontius Pilate feeling'. Arriving at a conference to decide the 'final solution' to the 'Jewish problem', he had doubts about the proposed violent path. But everyone else seemed so comfortable with the idea that it became normalised. 'At that moment,' said Eichmann,

'I felt free of all guilt.' As Arendt put it, 'Who was he to judge?' So many sex abuse scandals have followed this pattern: too many people accept what goes on as just the way things are.

The most important lesson from history about evil is that we should not think of it as something that only concerns others. We all have the capacity to do evil, and to guard against it we have to carefully examine the consequences of our own actions. We also have to make sure we don't go along with the wicked acts of other people, or allow their acceptance of wrongdoing as some kind of justification for our own. In short, we have to be constantly vigilant for manifestations of what Arendt called 'the fearsome, word-and-thought-defying banality of evil'.

See also: Courage, Duty, Empathy, Human Nature, Self-Deception, War

Reading
Hannah Arendt, *Eichmann in Jerusalem: A Report on the Banality of Evil* (Viking, 1963)
Jonathan Glover, *Humanity: A Moral History of the Twentieth Century* (Yale University Press, 2000)

F

'No one would choose to live without friends, even if he had all the other goods.' Aristotle

Failure

Make a list of your failures. On second thought, don't – unless you are exceptional, it's likely to be a depressing exercise. Even those who have never failed an exam in their life usually have failed relationships, enterprises, interviews, jobs, careers.

We all know the standard advice on dealing with failure: learn from it, bounce back and do better next time. (*See* **Resilience**.) 'What does not kill me makes me stronger,' as Nietzsche said. Very true, as long as you make it so. Nietzsche was not describing a kind of karmic law of the universe: it's not *inevitable* that failure strengthens us. He was advocating resolution, a determination to make the best of any bad situation.

Neither is it inevitable that success will ultimately ensue, as a positive thinking interpretation of Nietzsche's aphorism might have it. Of course, if we fail, we need to pick ourselves up, brush ourselves down and start again. Our efforts might pay off. David Hume reported that his first book, *A Treatise of Human Nature*, for which he had much hope, 'fell dead-born from the press'. Convinced that the problem was with the manner rather than the matter of the work, he later reworked it with greater success. But a lot of the time failure is not the prelude to success. It might just be failure, period – we don't know. So maybe we need no more than Samuel Beckett's realistic, sober encouragement to keep going: 'Ever failed. No matter. Try again. Fail again. Fail better.'

Nietzsche offers a good case against taking his maxim as a crass piece of positive thinking. Plagued by ill health, he wrote and published without any great success in his lifetime. By the time his reputation began to grow, he was already insane. Worse, his posthumous reputation was shaped by his anti-Semitic sister who had married a Nazi and promoted a distorted version of her brother as the philosopher of the Third

Reich. There were many difficulties that didn't make him stronger before one of them killed him.

More useful than Nietzsche's bold aphorism is the example of his life, since it invites us to rethink what success means. He didn't achieve fame or wide recognition in his lifetime and he ended it a broken man. But he did succeed in doing what he wanted to do: living the life of a writer and thinker.

He was not the only philosopher who could have made this claim. Søren Kierkegaard was ridiculed and mocked by Copenhagen society. Five of his six siblings died before they were three. He had spinal problems from a young age, which probably contributed to his early death at the age of 42. His worldly success came too late for him to enjoy. But was his life a failure? Only by the most superficial measure.

Failing in our endeavours is normal and inevitable. The greater failure we should try harder to avoid is the failure to live according to our values. This is something we can work on – whether the result is success or another failure is beyond our control.

See also: Achievement, Frustration, Resilience, Success, Vulnerability

Reading
Friedrich Nietzsche, *The Gay Science* (1882)

Faith

Faith is treasured and despised in equal measure. Many people say their faith is important to them and are more offended by mockery of it than they are by personal criticisms; others dismiss it as the wishful woolly thinking of the feeble-minded who need a crutch to get through life.

But what exactly is faith? The word is often used loosely to cover pretty much any belief that is less than 100 per cent certain. This seems too permissive: it doesn't require faith to take a medicine that might not work, merely a rational judgement about probabilities. Faith is belief not in the absence of *conclusive* evidence (which is usually an impossibly high standard anyway), but in the absence of *sufficient* evidence.

According to Søren Kierkegaard, faith is a bold leap beyond or even against reason. The archetype of faith, Abraham, went along with God's command to sacrifice his only son even though it contravened all morality, all that he wanted and everything he believed about what a good god would demand. In his faith, he trusted God in defiance of reason ('trust' being the meaning of the Latin root of 'faith', *fides*).

For William James, faith also goes beyond reason, but in a paradoxically reasonable way. James believed there are some hypotheses that are live (it is possible to believe in them), open (we don't know for sure whether they are true) and momentous (it matters a great deal whether we believe them or not). The existence of God is one such hypothesis. Reason alone cannot tell us whether it is true – it dumps us short of where we need to be to make our decision. Therefore it is reasonable to rely on faith to take us the final mile.

In their different ways, Kierkegaard and James both make the point that as long as the existence of God is uncertain from a rational point of view, there is some justification in believing in him on the basis of faith. (*See* **Risk** for Pascal's take on this.) How persuasive you find this will depend on how uncertain you think God's existence is.

Many atheists think that while the evidence against God's existence is not conclusive, it is so unlikely that the possibility is neither 'live' nor 'open', in James's terminology. Bertrand Russell was one such non-believer. He said that while he was technically an agnostic, since 'I cannot prove that either the Christian God or the Homeric gods do not exist,' he nonetheless did 'not think that their existence is an alternative that is sufficiently probable to be worth serious consideration'.

Another question is whether faith is the preserve of religions. Sometimes non-believers are accused of basing their conclusions on faith, since they cannot prove that God *doesn't* exist. But faith is required to go beyond reason to believe *in* something without sufficient evidence; it requires no faith *not* to take that leap.

There is such a thing as secular faith, however, which manifests itself any time we believe something in the absence or in defiance of good evidence. Faith in science means holding the unscientific belief that it can solve all our problems and provide us with a guide to life; faith in the future means believing everything will turn out for the best when we have good reason to doubt it; faith in friends and family means trusting them even when the evidence suggests that we shouldn't.

Do we all need some kind of faith to live without despair? Not everyone thinks so. But even if you believe we do, it's worth weighing things up carefully before taking the leap. The title of Kierkegaard's masterpiece on faith was *Fear and Trembling*, which conveys how terrifying it is to entrust yourself to something in the absence of any real grounding or guarantee that there will be something on the other side. If after consideration you decide there is no more rational way forward, go ahead and jump. Good luck – you'll need it.

See also: Commitment, Hope, Optimism, Religion, Trust

Reading

Søren Kierkegaard, *Fear and Trembling* (1843)
Bertrand Russell, *Why I Am Not a Christian and Other Essays* (George Allen & Unwin, 1957)
William James, *The Will to Believe* (1896)

Fame *see* **Reputation**

Family

In a world where increasingly little is sacred, the family continues to be an object of veneration. 'Family-owned' lends a business an air of trustworthiness, while politicians unite in praising 'hard-working families'. But for many of us, whether it's the ones we were raised by or born into, or those we have started or are trying to start, families often become fractured and fractious. Knowing that the sunshine-drenched, perma-happy, cornflake-packet family is a myth doesn't stop us worrying that our own family is too far from the ideal.

The near universal reverence for family is especially hard for those who don't give it a central place in their lives, and who may come to wonder whether something is wrong with them. But these refuseniks can make a good case that they have the backing of the West's greatest thinkers. Even Jesus was far from enthusiastic about the family, in contradiction to the endless rhetoric of Christian family values. 'If you come to me but will not leave your family, you cannot be my follower,' he said. 'You must love me more than your father, mother, wife, children, brothers, and sisters.' The only evidence the Anglican wedding service offers that Jesus even supported marriage is that he attended the wedding feast at Cana.

A remarkably large proportion of the canonical thinkers of the Western philosophical tradition never married, including Plato, Descartes, Locke, Spinoza, Hume, Kant and Schopenhauer. Nietzsche believed that every philosopher should react to the birth of a child by saying, 'A shackle has been forged for me.' His remark is typically hyperbolic, but it makes an important point: to start a family is a serious commitment, potentially incompatible with any calling that demands almost all your attention, not just being a philosopher. (*See* **Relationships**.)

Most of us do want families of our own, however, follow-ing the example of philosophers such as Socrates, Aristotle and Hegel. But this does not always work out the way we'd like. Here we might find help in non-Western philosophies, which tend to be much more positive about family.

Confucianism, for instance, places a great deal of impor-tance on *xiao*, often translated as 'filial piety' but better rendered as 'family reverence'. In its original form, *xiao* entailed strict, traditional roles. The three core family relations – father to son, husband to wife, elder brother to younger brother – form a set with two other key social relations – ruler to ruled and friend to friend. Familial and social harmony are intimately linked, as expressed in the old Chinese proverb, 'When the family is harmonious, everything thrives.'

However, the essence of *xiao* is transferable to times when familial relations are more fluid. The importance of *xiao* is that everyone has to stand in the proper relation to others, fulfilling their duties and obligations. This is something we can do even when the nuclear family has been split.

In fact, non-Western philosophies often understand the notion of family more broadly anyway. One of the contem-porary Chinese words for ethics, *lunli*, means 'the patterns in human kinship and relations'. The immediate family is just one node in a web of human relations. In many cultures where philosophies are transmitted orally, kinship is a central concept that extends to all life, even the environment.

It is often said that we are reinventing the family for the modern age, with friends becoming like kin and more compli-cated arrangements of step-parents and siblings. An alterna-tive interpretation is that the nuclear family was the real rein-vention, and we are returning to an understanding of family that is more linked to wider society and broader networks. Perhaps it is not that we have failed at making family work, but that our model has failed us. To make a success of family life, we have to question our assumptions about what it is.

See also: Community, Home, Marriage, Parenthood, Pets

Reading
Confucius, *The Classic of Filial Piety*

Fate

What will be, will be. *Al-maktoob* ('it is written'). *Que sera, sera.*
All around the world, there are phrases and idioms that
express the idea that what happens is in some ways determined by fate or predestined by God. It's a belief that can
provide some comfort when things don't go the way we
hoped. 'It just wasn't meant to be,' we tell ourselves. It can
help us to set aside our worries about the future and just see
what happens, but it can also be a source of despair or resignation. If everything is fated, why bother trying to do
anything at all? If what will be will be, then how can anything
I do change it?

Before deciding whether fate should make us feel reassured or despondent, we need to decide if it is real. To do
that it helps to distinguish between two different ideas that
many people confuse.

The first is that everything has already been decided by
some deity or supernatural force. If that's true, certain
outcomes will happen whatever we do. If there's a bullet with
my name on it but the sniper due to fire it leaves it behind,
either it will get back to him somehow or someone else will
shoot it instead.

It takes a very particular religious worldview to think that
someone or something is deliberately and consciously making
sure that everything happens according to a cosmic master-
plan and that nothing anyone can do will stop it. Although
this is how some interpret the Islamic idea of *al-maktoob*, few
others buy into that kind of fate.

The second, more popular version of fate is that the universe is like some giant clockwork mechanism, in which inexorable chains of cause and effect blindly do their work, like lines of dominoes falling. We may think that our choices change the unfolding of history, but everything we decide is simply the result of the combined forces of nature and nurture.

This kind of fate, however, isn't really fate at all but *causal determinism*. The key difference is explained by what Eddy Nahmias calls 'bypassing'. Fate means that certain things will happen no matter what you do – it 'bypasses' your thoughts, decisions and actions, none of which change anything. Causal determinism, in contrast, does not imply that things will happen no matter what you do. Yes, there is a sense in which you were bound to do *that* rather than something else, but what happens cannot bypass your mind, your body and your choices.

You might think this difference doesn't matter, since with or without bypassing whatever happens is equally inevitable. But what *kind* of inevitability governs the universe makes all the difference. If you believe in fate, you are going to die on a certain day anyway, so you might as well eat badly and live dangerously. But if causal determinism is true, then what you do makes a difference – go easy on the cookies and don't go scuba diving in shark-infested waters.

Thinking about this can be mind-boggling. Accepting causal determinism might make us feel less free than we thought we were. (*See* **Free Will**.) Still, the clear take-home message is that even in a world of causal determinism our choices make a difference and we have no option other than to choose. That is the only fate we cannot avoid.

See also: Choice, Commitment, Free Will, Luck, Responsibility, Superstition

Reading

Eddy Nahmias, 'Intuitions about Free Will, Determinism, and Bypassing', in Robert Kane (ed.), *The Oxford Handbook of Free Will* (Oxford University Press, 2011)

Fear

The physiologist and psychologist Walter Bradford Cannon was the first to describe the 'fight-or-flight response' that occurs when we perceive threats. The philosophy of fear could be said to be concerned with the same pair of responses, but in quite a different way. The question is: should we fight our fear or flee from what scares us?

Popular wisdom sees fear as something to be conquered. We are urged to be fearless and told that 'we have nothing to fear but fear itself'. But you need only to pay attention to the source of that last slogan to see it cannot be that simple. In his 1933 inaugural address, Franklin D. Roosevelt made it clear that the kind of fear he was talking about was 'nameless, unreasoning, unjustified terror'. He would have agreed with Aristotle, who said that we are right to have fears, and if someone did not fear anything 'he would be a sort of madman or insensible'.

The question, then, is not *whether* to fear but *what* to fear and *how* to deal with it. But what *is* fear? Aristotle says it is an 'expectation of evil' and defined it as 'a kind of pain or disturbance resulting from the imagination of impending danger, either destructive or painful'.

A lot hinges on the words 'expectation' and 'imagination'. If we have false expectations or overactive imaginations, our fears will be misplaced. Some philosophers have tried to convince us that most of our fears are like this. Most notably, the Stoics thought that death, illness and poverty weren't bad, so it was illogical to be afraid of them. Their only concession to anything like common sense was to say that if you are caught up in a shipwreck you are allowed an initial wobble, as long as you quickly recover from it. Unless you share their view that only moral virtue genuinely matters, you are not going to be persuaded.

As long as there are bad things that might happen, fear is inevitable. According to Robert Solomon, fear is universal because the world is a dangerous place: 'To be alive is to be vulnerable. Fear, like anger, is an engagement with the world.' It helps us by alerting us to many kinds of danger, and is an invaluable tool for navigating through life's hazards.

Of course fear can be irrational, but Solomon believes it is not typically so. It is not irrational to fear grizzly bears if you are on an ill-judged solo hike, or the taxman if you've been under-declaring your income. We have the concept of phobia precisely to distinguish unusual, irrational fears from more common, reasonable ones.

That is not to say our assessment of our own fears is always or even usually accurate. We are primed to see more threats than really exist, simply because it is safer to fear too much than too little: 'better safe than sorry' is a good evolutionary strategy. To check if our instincts are leading us astray, we can start by identifying our most common objects of fear – the ones we avoid at all costs or worry about. We can then do a reality check by asking ourselves some of Aristotle's questions. Is the danger serious? Is it impending? If it is both, all we can do is tell ourselves that we'll deal with whatever happens as best we can. Sometimes we can't offer any more reassurance than 'we'll get through this'.

When we examine our own reactions, we might notice that we have a general disposition to fearfulness. Lars Svendsen has made the helpful suggestion that, like other emotions, fear should be seen as a habit of noticing certain frightening features of a situation. When we are fearful, he says, 'we habitually focus on what is potentially dangerous in everything we encounter in life'. If this is true of us, we can make an effort to

F

cultivate different habits of attention and action. (*See* **Habits**.) Aristotle would approve.

A philosopher's approach to fear has its limitations. It is all very well asking us to check if our fears are rational, but irrational fears by their nature tend to be resistant to reason and evidence. Even if we become convinced that a fear is groundless, it won't necessarily leave us. Knowing that flying is safer than driving doesn't stop most people feeling nervous at take off. This is an example of what Peter Goldie calls the 'cognitive impenetrability' of emotion. And the closer the object of fear, the harder it is to use reason to dislodge it. If you decide to challenge your fears, therefore, you'd better make a start away from the situations that evoke it.

See also: Anxiety, Emotions, Habits, Hope, Pessimism, Risk, Superstition, Uncertainty, Vulnerability, Worrying

Reading
Peter Goldie, *The Emotions: A Philosophical Exploration* (Oxford University Press, 2002)
Robert C. Solomon, *True to Our Feelings* (Oxford University Press, 2007)

Fear of Missing Out *see* **Travel**

Feelings *see* **Emotions**

Food and Drink

Food and drink cause a great deal of pleasure but also much guilt. There's a thin line between being a hearty trencherman and a greedy pig, often drawn arbitrarily and inconsistently.

There's also a great deal of moralising about eating: feed your children the 'wrong' food and you are a wicked parent; eat 'dirty' rather than 'clean' food and you defile your soul as well as your body.

It's little wonder that in the West food has the taint of sinfulness when most of its leading philosophers have been so dismissive of it. Although gourmands are sometimes called 'epicures', the ancient Greek philosopher who lent them his name was not one of them. Epicurus advised that 'plain fare gives as much pleasure as a costly diet' and so it was better 'to habituate one's self . . . to a simple and inexpensive diet that supplies all that is needful for health'. It took very little for him to feel like he was feasting. 'Send me a pot of cheese, so that I may be able to indulge myself whenever I wish,' he wrote to a friend.

Plato was particularly scathing about culinary pleasures, which he thought involved nothing more than a blind giving in to appetite. 'Cookery,' he wrote, 'never regards either the nature or reason of that pleasure to which she devotes herself, but goes straight to her end.'

Even the usually sensible Aristotle downgraded eating and drinking to the lowest level of pleasures, because they centred on the 'servile and brutish' senses of touch and taste, which give us 'pleasures as beasts also share in'.

This disdain for our animal appetites has endured. John Stuart Mill thought we should promote happiness and pleasure but insisted on a distinction between higher and lower pleasures, with eating and drinking relegated to the second category. 'Few human creatures would consent to be changed into any of the lower animals, for a promise of the fullest allowance of a beast's pleasures,' he said. (*See* **Pleasure**.)

And yet in recent centuries there are countless examples of philosophers who enjoyed eating well, even though they rarely talked about it in their professional work. David Hume was a keen cook who moved house because although it was 'very chearful, and even elegant' it was 'too small to display my great Talent for Cookery, the Science to which I intend to addict the remaining Years of my Life'. Before Albert Camus got into the car that crashed, cutting short his life in 1960, he had lunch at Au Chapon Fin at Thoissey, then one of France's top restaurants.

As more philosophers have come to embrace our embodied nature, they have increasingly endorsed bodily pleasures, including eating. But that doesn't imply advocating a blind pursuit of pleasure that always leaves us wanting more. Epicurus was right to warn us not to become dependent on fancy foods, but mindful and appreciative enjoyment of food deserves a place in the good life. Even austere Zen Buddhists advocate giving care and attention to the preparation and eating of food. Dogen claimed that with the right attitude it is possible to 'build great temples from ordinary greens'.

And anyway, eating is not just an animal pleasure after all. There can be creativity in food production, sociability in its consumption and intellectual appreciation of what we eat and how it was made. When we sit down to eat, we bring mind and body to the table. No one should feel guilty about enjoying one of life's quotidian delights. Aristotle was wrong to equate human cuisine and animal sustenance. As Jean Anthelme Brillat-Savarin said, 'Animals feed; man eats; only a man of thought knows how to eat.'

See also: Asceticism, The Body, Carpe Diem, Desires, Mindfulness, Pleasure, Self-Control, Vegetarianism

Reading
Julian Baggini, *The Virtues of the Table* (Granta, 2014)

Forgiveness

It's not only life that trips us up. Sometimes it's people we know, even love and trust. Rare is the person who is never wronged or who never does wrong. How are we supposed to respond to this?

In the Christian world, a key part of the answer to this question is forgiveness, which is often said to be Jesus' distinctive contribution to moral philosophy. If so, it is a much more interesting one than the glib suggestion that we should offer unconditional absolution and move on.

In a key passage in Matthew's Gospel, the disciple Peter asks Jesus, 'Lord, how oft shall my brother sin against me, and I forgive him? till seven times?' Jesus answers, 'Until seventy times seven.' On the face of it, this seems to be a call for forgiveness without limit or conditions. But if you look at the rest of the teaching, things become more complicated.

The most important point is that Jesus does not say that forgiveness is unconditional. In Luke's Gospel, he says the brother should be rebuked and 'if he repent, forgive him', but in Matthew's he also makes it clear that the brother has to play his part in the process. You start by trying to work it out between you, and if that fails you bring in other mediators. As a last resort, 'tell it unto the church: but if he neglect to hear the church, let him be unto thee as an heathen man and a publican'.

This kind of forgiveness does not brush aside misbehaviour as though it could and should be forgotten. Jesus often forgives people, but he never diminishes the seriousness of what they've done. When he saves a woman caught committing adultery from stoning, he tells her to 'sin no more'. To forgive is not to pretend there was no wrongdoing: it requires facing up to it.

For this to be constructive, we have to be compassionate towards the wrongdoer. Jesus said to the woman's accusers, 'He that is without sin among you, let him first cast a stone at her.' In order to forgive others we have to admit that none of us is faultless, and that we all need to be forgiven at some stage, too.

Jesus' ideas about forgiveness are useful for non-Christians because they are mainly about how we interact with each other, not with God – we forgive in order to restore relationships. This was implicitly recognised by the Truth and Reconciliation Commission in post-apartheid South Africa, which called for testimonies from perpetrators and victims alike, in an attempt to heal society and allow the country to move on. But although it gave amnesty to people who confessed to wrongdoings, it never asked anyone to forgive. Reconciliation does not always require you to go that far.

If you are struggling to forgive, you need to start by acknowledging the wrongdoing rather than trying to ignore or downplay it. Remember that we all mess up from time to time and deserve the opportunity to put things right. Ask the person in question to acknowledge their error and make up for it in some way. If, after you've tried earnestly, they refuse to do so, the relationship remains broken through no fault of your own. Forgiveness does not work simply by being granted to people – they have to take it willingly.

See also: Anger, Betrayal, Loyalty, Relationships, Trust, Vulnerability

Reading
Matthew's Gospel, Chapter 18
Luke's Gospel, Chapter 17

Freedom
One of the defining characteristics of modernity is the widespread desire for individual liberty. For large periods of human history, people have been content to play their part in the

family, tribe or nation. Today we refuse the roles cast upon us by others and demand self-determination. But our yearning for freedom often remains just that. What is this freedom we seek, and why is it so often elusive?

There is no better place to start thinking about freedom than Isaiah Berlin's seminal essay 'Two Concepts of Liberty'. The first of these is *negative* freedom, which means freedom from interference. You are free in this sense when no one stops you from doing what you want.

In practice, having this freedom might not enable you to do much at all. You have absolute negative freedom alone in the middle of the desert, but you may not live long enough to be able to do anything with it. What you need in such a situation is the *positive* freedom to do whatever it is that you want or have to do.

Berlin says that the desire for positive freedom 'derives from the wish on the part of the individual to be his own master ... I wish to be the instrument of my own, not of other men's acts of will.' This is not just a matter of people leaving us alone. Becoming one's own master also requires resources and self-control.

If you are stuck in the middle of the desert, you'll need to reach out to potential rescuers to get to safety. But other people are just as central in more ordinary situations. To direct your own life you need a good education, a living wage, a decent home, healthcare and so on. In short, individual liberty of the positive kind presupposes membership of a functioning society. The price you pay for this is that it restricts some of your freedom by requiring that you follow laws and pay taxes.

Crucially, positive freedom also demands the self-control and self-awareness to direct our own lives instead of being pushed around by the whims of desire and impulse. We are not free if we are 'a slave to nature' or to our own 'unbridled passions'.

True freedom then is not a matter of being as independent as possible and doing whatever we like. It depends both on living in an enabling society and on having sufficient self-mastery. A good model of this kind of freedom is jazz improvisation. Jazz musicians take the music where they want, without being restrained by a score. But two things are necessary for this magnificent freedom to be expressed. One of these is people: past teachers, other band members, the giants who shaped the tradition. Then there is the mastery that can come only from years of practice and self-discipline.

If we assume that true freedom is all about doing what we want and ignoring others, we'll never find it. We do not get freedom for free: it requires social support and personal effort.

See also: Authenticity, Choice, Consumerism, Free Will, Politics, Self-Control

Reading
Isaiah Berlin, *Two Concepts of Liberty* (Clarendon Press, 1958)

Free Will

There are times in life when it seems like we're not in control of what we do. You resolve to be more patient with an annoying parent but find yourself baiting them within minutes the next time you meet. In an unguarded moment you cheat on your partner, and as soon as you've done it you can't believe you've jeopardised the most important relationship in your life. You hear yourself lying to a trusted friend and feel as though you're hearing someone else's voice. At times like these, we might doubt we have free will.

Most of the time, we assume we are acting freely. Sometimes we can't say or do what we want because of outside pressures, but our capacity to choose, to make up our minds, seems fundamental. It's what makes us humans rather than robots.

But sometimes that difference blurs. When we see people behaving in the same way again and again, we suspect they are unable to do anything different. When we remark on how like their father or mother a person is, we seem to be accepting that a lot of how they think and act was programmed into them at birth.

Doubts about free will are routinely reinforced by scientists. Stephen Hawking once wrote, 'it seems that we are no more than biological machines and that free will is just an illusion'. The bestselling Dutch neurobiologist Dick Swaab tells us, 'Free will is a pleasant illusion'. More than once Einstein said, 'I do not believe in free will.'

Many find this disturbing. It threatens our sense of who and what we fundamentally are. Resolving the issue definitively is difficult, if not impossible. Free will is one of the most contested problems of philosophy. There are, however, some key insights that can help us to get beyond simplistic and absolute denials of it.

A good place to start is with Daniel Dennett, who asked the simple and powerful question: what kinds of free will are worth wanting? He argues that the kind we are constantly told we don't have isn't one of them. This is the capacity not merely to make choices but to be the ultimate originators of our choices. In other words, the buck stops with us: our choices are not determined by any combination of our genes and prior circumstances. 'Libertarianism', as this is known, says that our 'will' – our capacity to choose – is independent of the usual chain of cause and effect that governs the universe. We could always have done other than what we actually did.

At first glance this looks like a common-sense definition of free will. In reality it is a concept that is almost exclusive to modern Western philosophy. No such idea of free will is found in the philosophical traditions of ancient Greece, China, India, the Islamic world, or the philosophies transmitted orally in Africa, Australasia, Central and South America. And if you think about it, it's not clear that libertarian free will even makes sense. A capacity to make choices that are not grounded in biology, experience and circumstances would not be an engine of freedom but a generator of random, meaningless actions. It's the opposite of what we really want, which is for our choices to be consistent with who we are, what we believe and what we value. No one would prefer those things to just emerge independently of their history.

The kind of free will we should want, argues Dennett, is more limited. It is not the capacity to break free from the laws of cause and effect. It is merely the ability to be free from the coercive control of others, to be agents who can 'decide our courses of action, and to decide them wisely, in the light of our expectations and desires'.

Dennett's account is a version of 'compatibilism': the view that we have free will even though we are biological creatures, as much subject to cause and effect as any other part of nature. Does compatibilism give us enough freedom to save free will? If our worry is that we have no agency and don't really make choices, then no scientific account of human consciousness holds this. Even if we talk of the brain as the decision-making organ, rather than the whole human being, it is clear that it does indeed process information and generate actions. We are agents in the sense that we act. Even deniers of free will do not deny we have agency, but merely question its nature.

Critics accuse compatibilists of dressing up a diluted version of free will as the real thing. But maybe it is the deniers who are guilty of wishful thinking. Although the belief that we have no free will can be disturbing, it can also be comforting to think that nothing you do is really your fault, that whatever you do you have to do and no one can hold you to account. Jean-Paul Sartre believed that human beings are prone to slipping into this way of thinking, which is why we are constantly in flight from our freedom and the responsibility that goes with it. 'Anyone who takes refuge behind the excuse of his passions, or by inventing some deterministic doctrine, is a self-deceiver,' he wrote.

Sartre's challenge is perhaps more useful than the metaphysical debate about whether free will is real. Even deniers routinely accept that we cannot help acting *as though* we were free. But our beliefs affect how we act: those who believe they have free will are more likely to take responsibility than those who deny their freedom.

So go back to the examples we started with: seemingly unbreakable habits, impulsive mistakes, a momentary feeling of not being in control. We could look at ourselves in situations like these as if from the outside and conclude that at that moment we couldn't have done other than we did. In a sense we'd be right. But we can also recognise that we did what we did because we are who we are, and take responsibility for that. (*See* **Responsibility**.) We can't undo what is done, but we can accept the consequences and learn from the past so that we are more likely to behave differently in the future.

See also: Authenticity, Choice, Consumerism, Fate, Freedom, Guilt and Shame, Responsibility, Self-Control, Self-Deception

Reading
Daniel C. Dennett, *Elbow Room: The Varieties of Free Will Worth Wanting* (new edition, MIT Press, 2015)
Julian Baggini, *Freedom Regained* (Granta, 2015)

Friendship

In the age of social media friends, followers and likes, it is easy to interpret a low friend count as a sign that there is something wrong with us. Aristotle offers a good counterbalance to this tendency. He was in no doubt that for most of us, friendships are an essential part of the good life. 'No one would choose to live without friends, even if he had all the other goods,' he wrote, because 'a human is a social being and his nature is to live in the company of others.'

He asks: 'Should we, then, make as many friends as possible?' Or is it better 'neither to be without friends nor to have an excessive number of them?' Aristotle was clear that we should limit their number, because close friendships require sharing, and it is 'hard to share personally in the joys and sorrows of many'.

He argues that those 'who have many friends and treat everybody they meet as if they were close to them seem to be friends of nobody, except in the sense that fellow citizens are friends'. Anyone who claims to have dozens of close friends is either lying or deluded, although the ideal number of friends is not fixed and partly depends on the kind of person we are.

Aristotle also distinguishes between three kinds of personal relationships that could be loosely called friendships. One is based on mutual benefit, like the friendliness between shop owners and their regular customers. Another is based on doing fun things together, like going clubbing or to football matches. If that's as far as the relationship goes, neither of these is a real friendship for Aristotle, since if the other person ceases to be useful or entertaining the relationship will come to an end.

It is only the third kind that counts as real friendship. In this one, the friends want the best for each other and feel as they do 'because of what they are, not for any incidental reason'. These kinds of friendships are not common, but we can expect them to be lasting.

While it may be excessive to go through our list of friends assigning people to one group or another, it is important to be clear about what a friendship is mainly about, as this can help us to avoid misunderstandings and disappointment. Aristotle was spot on when he observed that 'most differences arise between friends when they are not friends in the way they think'. So 'if a person were to like us for utility or pleasure, but pretend that it was for our character', we'd be right to be annoyed. However, if the friend did not pretend, and it was entirely our own misunderstanding, then we'd have only ourselves to blame.

It's all about clarity. If a relationship primarily involves playing sports together, for instance, it would be wise not to expect deep emotional support at a time of crisis, although there is room to be pleasantly surprised if that support turns out to be there.

Another important point that Aristotle makes is that we should choose our friends carefully, as it's easy to absorb both good and bad habits from them. Relationships won't leave us unaffected, so we should choose friends who are likely to have a good influence.

Epicurus agreed with Aristotle that we should neither be too eager nor too shy in making friends. 'We must not approve either those who are always ready for friendship, or those who hang back,' he wrote. He gave friendship a more central place in the good life, saying, 'Of all the means which are procured by wisdom to ensure happiness throughout the whole of life, by far the most important is the acquisition of friends.' What he had in mind was a network of friends who offer mutual support and help each other to live the philosophical life, which is what he tried to create in the Garden, the community he founded near Athens.

Epicurus was criticised by some for valuing friends only instrumentally. But that may be unfair. Although he thought friendships were important as a means of gaining a sense of safety and security in life, he made it clear that he also considered them intrinsically valuable. 'All friendship is desirable in itself, though it starts from the need of help,' he said. The worry that there is a tension between the two positions could be the result of erecting too sharp a boundary between self-interest and concern for other people. The true value of friendship may lie precisely in its capacity to bind together our own interests with those of others.

See also: Community, Family, Loyalty, Other People, Relationships, Solitude, Vulnerability

Reading
Mark Vernon, *The Meaning of Friendship* (Palgrave Macmillan, 2006)

Frugality *see* Simplicity

Frustration

Whatever your frustration – a traffic jam, a slow-moving queue, the tortuous inefficiency of a bureaucracy – if you can't simply walk away, the best cure is a dash of Stoicism.

A dash, because full-blown Stoicism requires indifference to everything that is not in our power – health, partners, relatives, success. (*See* **Contentment**.) That is asking a great deal, too much for most. But without going that far we can agree that life would be a lot easier if we accepted that the things that are not in our power may well not work out how we'd like and resolved not to get too stressed about it.

Epictetus believed that fretting about what you can't change is the source of much anguish. He gives the example of a singer who 'feels no anxiety while he is singing by himself, but is anxious when he enters the theatre, even if he has a very fine voice and plays his instrument beautifully'. His problem is that 'he wants not only to sing well, but to gain applause, and that lies beyond his control'.

The secret is not so much to lower our expectations of things outside our control as to get rid of them. Anything might happen, so don't be surprised if your plans are disrupted. Every time you take a trip, you might not get to your destination. So if you find yourself stuck in a traffic jam with no alternative route, and you can't get to your best friend's wedding in time, there's nothing you can do about it. If you don't have mobile phone reception and can't even tell people you won't make it, there's nothing you can do about that either. Your frustration probably won't disappear immediately, but give it a few minutes and perhaps a kick of an inanimate object and it can be surprising how calm descends.

So if the situation is out of your hands, you might as well accept it and relax. This is hard enough to do about transport frustrations, let alone when more significant issues are at stake. But the principle is the same, and worth regularly repeating to ourselves: it is completely pointless, and a waste of energy, to stay frustrated about things we can't do anything about.

See also: Calm, Control, Contentment, Pessimism, Stress, Uncertainty

Reading
Epictetus, *Discourses* and *Handbook*

G

'If our life did not fade and vanish like the dews of Adashino's graves or the drifting smoke from Toribe's burning grounds, but lingered on for ever, how little the world would move us. It is the ephemeral nature of things that makes them wonderful.'
Yoshida Kenko

God *see* **Religion**

Gossip

You probably don't like to think of yourself as a gossip. There is something unpleasant about discussing other people when they're not there, especially when we're judging them negatively. But then again, this kind of chit-chat is *fun* and seems like the most natural thing in the world.

Evolutionary psychology tells us that gossip exists for good reasons. Our prehistoric ancestors depended on group cooperation, so sharing information about which members were trustworthy and which ones were not pulling their weight was crucial. This promotes social bonding and is an essential part of social interaction, which is why even now most of our talk is gossip.

Some philosophers, however, have been uncompromisingly negative about light conversation, including talk about others. Epictetus, for instance, said, 'Be for the most part silent, or speak merely what is necessary, and in few words. Speak but rarely, when the occasion calls for it, but not about anything that happens to come up; do not talk about gladiators, or horse races, or athletes, or food and drink, the topics that arise on every occasion, but above all, do not talk about individuals, either to praise, or to blame, or to compare them.'

The Buddha likewise spoke in favour of silence and against idle chatter, by which he meant 'talk of kings, robbers, ministers, armies, dangers, battles, food, drink, clothing, beds, garlands, perfumes, relatives, vehicles, villages, towns, cities, countries, women, heroes, streets, wells, the dead, trifles' and so on.

Should we really all adopt their high-minded position? If we took this advice literally we would probably end up not speaking much at all – you decide whether that would be a good thing or not.

But maybe it's a matter of avoiding the wrong *kind* of gossip, rather than gossip altogether. For this we could make use of another Buddhist discourse, which suggests three criteria for assessing whether our speech is right or wrong: is it truthful? Is it beneficial? Is it pleasing to others? Enjoyable, honest conversation that doesn't harm anyone would get three ticks.

Emrys Westacott's more recent discussion of gossip fleshes out the first two of these tests. On the question of truth, he argues that it is more than a matter of not deliberately spreading malicious rumours about others – even transmitting potentially damaging information without checking its truth is unethical.

On the issue of being beneficial, he suggests that an important question is whether sharing the information is likely to lead to more harm or more good. He gives the example of warning someone that a potential babysitter has a serious drug problem (having first taken care to check that it is true). Among the harms that should be considered is the hurt that people might feel as a result of some fact becoming known about them.

J.L. Austin's concept of 'speech acts' is also relevant to this test. He argues that some utterances do not just transmit information, they can *do* things. Mocking speech can ostracise the mocked; sexist speech in the workplace can disempower women. Gossip can cause real harm by diminishing people's status or making others less likely to trust them. The casual nature of gossip can make us forget that words have power and accusations have consequences.

The Buddhist discourse acknowledges that applying the test isn't a straightforward box-ticking exercise. Some speech does not fulfil all three criteria of being true, beneficial and pleasing, and yet it is acceptable. For instance, in cases of something being truthful and beneficial but not pleasing to others, the Buddha would still say it. Sometimes people need to hear things they don't like, but that only justifies telling it to their faces, not behind their backs.

Banishing gossip altogether is of dubious merit, unless you are planning to live as a hermit. Gossip can have a positive contribution to make to social interaction. But it is worth running the typical content of our conversation through the filters described to make sure that any gossip we engage in is of the benign kind.

See also: Loyalty, Lying, Office Politics, Reputation, Silence

Reading
Emrys Westacott, *The Virtues of Our Vices: A Modest Defense of Gossip, Rudeness, and Other Bad Habits* (Princeton University Press, 2011)

Gratitude

The old advice to count your blessings has been given contemporary scientific endorsement by positive psychologists, who have turned it into a happiness hack: write a gratitude diary every day, listing the things you're grateful for, and you'll be happier, healthier and no doubt more attractive too.

Believing that gratitude will make you happier might be a good enough reason for you to cultivate it. But you might want to stop and ask: to what or whom are we supposed to be grateful, and for what?

The most straightforward kind of gratitude is *to* a particular person. Few of us need prompting to feel grateful to someone who does them a good turn. Gratitude *that*, or *for*, is more complicated. Unlike the first kind, which is interpersonal, this involves appreciating that something good has happened to you, or even that something good exists. We might simply be grateful for the beauty of the autumn leaves, or that it didn't rain on our camping trip.

It is sometimes argued that this isn't *really* gratitude unless you believe in a God to offer your thanks to. It may be better seen as a form of appreciation. But this defines gratitude too narrowly and literally – everyone knows what it means to feel thankful for something good, even if there is no one to thank.

A more serious objection is that there is little about being alive to feel grateful for. As David Benatar argues, 'Each one of us was harmed by being brought into existence. That harm is not negligible, because the quality of even the best lives is very bad – and considerably worse than most people recognise it to be.' Benatar says that we deny this to ourselves because to admit it would be intolerable. In this view, gratitude is just another way of pretending that life is better than it is. 'We live off bread crusts which have been baptised cakes,' as Fernando Pessoa put it.

Benatar's pessimistic assessment has resonances with the Buddhist view that suffering is ever-present in life. This is not the claim that we suffer every minute we're alive, but that everything is impermanent and nothing in this world can produce lasting satisfaction. (*See* **Suffering**.) However, far from this being a reason to stop us appreciating the world around us, there is a connection between awareness of our own transience and appreciation of the evanescent beauty of nature.

The Japanese literary and artistic tradition, which hinges on the Buddhist concept of impermanence, captures this poignantly. The monk Yoshida Kenko wrote, 'If our life did not fade and vanish like the dews of Adashino's graves or the drifting smoke from Toribe's burning grounds, but lingered on for ever, how little the world would move us. It is the ephemeral nature of things that makes them wonderful.'

Everything fades with alarming speed, like the spring cherry blossom, which in Japan has come to symbolise both beauty and sorrow. But instead of stopping us appreciating life, transience can allow us to fully savour it. For example, the next time you have a cup of coffee, imagine that you're taking your last sip and you'll appreciate it much more.

It sounds simple. 'How is it possible for men not to rejoice each day over the pleasure of being alive?' asks Kenko. The answer, he continues, is that people get sidetracked by misguided pursuits. 'Foolish men, forgetting this pleasure, laboriously seek others; forgetting the wealth they possess, they risk their lives in their greed for new wealth. But their desires are never satisfied.' This is especially relevant in our culture of constant striving.

Kenko is critical of those who are unable to make the most of their life: 'While they live they do not rejoice in life, but, when faced with death, they fear it – what could be more illogical?' Every day brings opportunities to 'rejoice in life' by appreciating simple daily pleasures, not only those provided by nature, but also things like sharing food with a friend, or listening to a favourite radio programme.

Of course, being grateful for what we have doesn't mean denying life's imperfections. Let's face it, life will always be imperfect. Gratitude is not about pretending everything is great but being able to find delight in this flawed, bittersweet world.

See also: Carpe Diem, Contentment, Control, Melancholy, Mindfulness, Perfectionism, Simplicity, Vulnerability

Reading
Yoshida Kenko, *Essays in Idleness* (1330–1332)

Guilt and Shame

Guilt is a heavy burden to carry, and life provides endless opportunities for us to add to its weight. Who believes they are a good enough spouse, parent, son or daughter? How many of us get through a single day without eating, drinking, saying or doing something we feel we shouldn't have? Guilt eats at us. Should we simply cast it off?

To answer this, we need to be clearer about what guilt and the related emotion of shame are. This is not easy, as the terms are often given precise technical definitions that don't neatly correspond to their everyday usage. In psychology, for instance, it is customary to distinguish between guilt and shame, the former being directed towards some particular action or behaviour one has done and the latter being a global assessment of one's self.

This distinction may be useful, but it is by no means universal. According to Robert Solomon, both guilt and shame involve self-reproach and moral responsibility, characterised by seeing 'the self as seriously blameworthy'. Compared to basic emotions like fear, they require greater mental sophistication. Your cat might look guilty for stealing your dinner, but is unlikely to be experiencing fully-formed self-condemnation.

Solomon writes that these emotions involve three dimensions of evaluation. First there is 'the felt evaluation of the self by oneself'. Second, there is 'an evaluation of the self imposed by other people'. Third, there is an evaluation of 'the nature of the situation' itself.

For Solomon, the main difference between guilt and shame is the focus, which in shame is on what other people think and in guilt is on our own inner moral compass. Which we feel more of and for what reasons is also in part culturally determined. Anthropologists distinguish between 'shame cultures', which are predominant in Asia, and 'guilt cultures', which are more associated with Christian societies.

To the extent that they lead to reparatory action and self-improvement, guilt and shame can be helpful. They can drive us to make amends and improve ourselves so we don't make the same mistakes again. According to Aristotle (who defines shame as 'a kind of fear of disrepute'), the important point is that we can train ourselves to improve our moral character, since 'if to act nobly is in our power, not to do so, and hence act shamefully, is also in our power'.

Another kind of guilt is a collective one. The failings of the groups we belong to reflect on us, because those groups have shaped who we are and we are part of them. This is more appreciated in shame cultures, where people often feel remorse for things they had no personal role in. Even in guilt cultures it is common for people to say that homelessness, for example, is a failure of society for which we all share some of the blame. Such shame is useful when it spurs us to take up our responsibility as citizens to improve society for the better.

Then there are more nebulous forms of guilt. Many people feel habitually guilty despite the fact that they have done nothing wrong. Such feelings can haunt us for a lifetime. If they are left to fester, they can form a generalised sense of unworthiness and blameworthiness that we carry around with us. Recognising that these feelings are unfounded can be a great release.

We often connect this sense of global guilt with the Judaeo-Christian doctrine of original sin. Sometimes we call it 'Catholic guilt', although it is not confined to that denomination. But perhaps there is also a deeper 'existential guilt' within us. Paul Tillich describes how the awareness of human possibilities brings with it a sense of responsibility for who we are and what we could be. But being finite, we could never fulfil those potentialities, and this is the source of our guilt. To be human is to fall short.

Life without guilt and shame would be a life without conscience or moral self-awareness. They cease to serve us when they lead us to obsess about ourselves and our social standing, or when they are felt without due cause. But so long as harmful self-loathing can be averted, they perform the invaluable function of alerting us to what we've done wrong, giving us the opportunity to make amends.

See also: Dilemmas, Embarrassment, Emotions, Regret, Reputation

Reading
Paul Tillich, *The Courage to Be* (Nisbet, 1952)

H

'I do not want my house to be walled in on all sides and my windows to be stuffed. I want the cultures of all lands to be blown about my house as freely as possible. But I refuse to be blown off my feet by any.'
Mahatma Gandhi

Habits

It's a rare person who doesn't have at least one bad habit: sitting at the computer with a hunched back, always being late, unhealthy snacking. Over a lifetime we can acquire quite a collection of these. We know we'd be better off without them, but once a habit has taken hold it can be difficult to uproot.

Less noticed are the habits that define our moral character. Whether people are kind or heartless, generous or mean, brave or cowardly is also largely a matter of habit. This was a key claim of both Aristotle and Confucius, who believed that we can become better people by training ourselves to do the right thing regardless of how we feel. If we want to become more courageous we push ourselves to do courageous actions, if we want to have more self-control we practise saying no to temptation. 'Wear the clothes of Yao, repeat the words of Yao, and do the actions of Yao, and you will just be a Yao,' wrote the Confucian Mencius. The principle holds for learning skills as well as for developing a good character. 'We become builders by building, and lyre players by playing the lyre,' said Aristotle.

This ability to train ourselves by habituation is unique to humans. Aristotle pointed out that natural processes can't be altered by practice: 'For example, a stone that naturally falls downwards could not be made by habituation to rise upwards, not even if one tried to habituate it by throwing it up ten thousand times.'

If we persist with habituation, over time we will become more inclined to act correctly. The ideal is that doing the right thing becomes so habitual that it is almost automatic. Mencius said, 'The great man does not think beforehand of his words that they may be sincere, nor of his actions that they may be resolute – he simply speaks and does what is right.'

All this applies equally to small daily actions. When we become aware of a habit that doesn't serve us, we can set about replacing it with a better one. It isn't easy, but with application and patience it will work. Eventually we can expect determined effort to give way to established dispositions, so we end up sitting correctly without thinking about it, forgetting that the biscuits are even there and smiling knowingly when others are late, remembering how we once were.

See also: Change, Character, Choice, Free Will, Perseverance, Routine, Self-Control, Virtue

Reading
Aristotle, *Nicomachean Ethics*

Happiness

It is almost universally agreed that happiness is good and that, other things being equal, it is much better to be happy than not. There is now a big industry selling tools and techniques to achieve happiness, often with a seal of approval from experimental psychology. So why does it so often seem that only other people are happy, while we muddle through in various degrees of contentment and discontent? Should we be meditating more, doing yoga or seeing a therapist? Is our niggling dissatisfaction our own fault? Or maybe we should question whether happiness is really attainable. Maybe it's not everything it's cracked up to be. After all, what is happiness, anyway?

The simplest version of happiness is that it is nothing more than feeling good. This notion lies behind the philosophy that promotes it as the highest human good: utilitarianism. The early utilitarians, Jeremy Bentham and John Stuart Mill, agreed that the morality of actions must be judged by how much they increase or diminish human happiness.

Plato would have considered this elevation of happiness to the highest good misguided. He believed that every pleasure was cancelled out by an equal and opposite pain. Our natural condition is equilibrium, being neither happy nor sad. If we become temporarily miserable, or happy, we will in time return to a steady state. For Plato, much of what we call pleasure is actually no more than the relief we feel after recovering from pain. For similar reasons, Schopenhauer wrote, 'All satisfaction, or what is commonly called happiness, is always really and essentially only negative, and never positive.' Plato and Schopenhauer may overstate this, but they point to the truth that happiness does not last. (*See* **Suffering**.)

The most scathing criticisms of the view that happiness is the greatest good came from Nietzsche. In an aphorism that takes a swipe at Mill and Bentham, he declared, 'Mankind does not strive for happiness; only the Englishman does'. For Nietzsche, the idealisation of happiness puts the desire for easy comfort above the aspiration for greatness, which is why he described 'England's small-mindedness' as 'the great danger now on earth'. Happiness is for simple creatures, like the cat curled up in the basket or the child splashing in the paddling pool; serious adults should have higher ambitions.

In the late twentieth century, Robert Nozick devised another way of articulating why it is problematic to make happiness the ultimate goal. Decades before virtual reality became a technological reality, he imagined a machine that would guarantee you a life of happiness, as long as you never left it. Would you choose life inside such a device over taking your chances in the real world? Nozick thought, correctly, that most of us would prefer the organic rough and smooth over simulated serenity. This suggests that we don't just want any old happiness; we want the sort that comes as a result of living the best life we can.

The idea that happiness is the highest human good therefore turns out to be philosophically contentious. Happiness as good mood – 'positive affect', in contemporary psychological parlance – is just too shallow an objective. This is something that even most non-philosophers sense.

A better goal than happiness is captured by the Greek word *eudaimonia*. It is often misleadingly translated as 'happiness', but 'flourishing' is more accurate. Aristotle thought this was the highest human good. To flourish is to live the best kind of life an organism can live. A blooming rose, a cat freely roaming its territory or an eagle hunting its prey are all flourishing. For us, flourishing means using all our faculties, especially the distinctively human ones. Aristotle gave pride of place to reason – which is rather convenient for a philosopher. We might also include creativity, altruism and craftsmanship.

When we live a flourishing life, we are generally happier. But we are not *always* or *necessarily* happy. The tortured genius may be flourishing, and most of us have our ups and downs.

It's good to be happy, but so long as we are not debilitatingly miserable what really matters is to be living the best life we can, becoming the best people we can be. Worrying about how happy we should be doesn't help us to flourish – or even to be happier.

See also: Contentment, Desires, Gratitude, Leisure, Love of Life, Meaning, Pleasure, Success

Reading
Aristotle, *The Nicomachean Ethics*
Robert Nozick, *Anarchy, State, and Utopia* (Basic Books, 1974)

Health and Illness

Descartes has plenty of detractors, but few would disagree with his claim that health is 'the chief blessing and the foundation of all other blessings in this life'. Health is the one thing we are all sure to want, even if the unhealthy ways we live sometimes suggest otherwise. But it is not straightforward to know what health is, what is normal or abnormal and at what point inevitable flaws and niggles turn into illness.

The World Health Organization defines health as 'a state of complete physical, mental and social well-being and not merely the absence of disease or infirmity'. In this view, health becomes indistinguishable from wider well-being. This expansive definition has a downside: if this is what health is, it seems out of reach for most of us. It creates the unhelpful expectation that a state of complete well-being is a norm that we can and should achieve.

Another problematic issue is the extent to which we are responsible for our health. Of course it is good for each of us to take responsibility for doing what we can to be as healthy as possible. However, this is sometimes overemphasised, with the consequence that if we suffer from ill health we might feel as if we have somehow brought it upon ourselves.

Susan Sontag argues that an older notion of disease as punishment for our sins has evolved into one in which repressed emotions are thought to end up expressing themselves through illnesses such as cancer. If this were the case we would be responsible for our illness. Sontag writes powerfully against this blaming of the ill, pointing out that painful feelings and past traumas afflict people who do not have cancer just as much as those who do.

We might add that there are plenty of people who eat well, keep their minds and bodies active and think positively but still get dementia, heart disease or arthritis. We look after ourselves to improve our odds of winning in the health lottery, but we can't guarantee a winning ticket.

We make the mistake of thinking about health as a mechanic thinks about a car, seeing the body as a machine that will work perfectly as long as it is well-maintained. But what if health is not about the state of our organs but about what we can do? This is the thrust of Hans-Georg Gadamer's phenomenological perspective. He argues that health 'is a condition of being involved, of being in the world, of being together with one's fellow human beings, of active and rewarding engagement in everyday tasks'.

If health is primarily about engaging with the world, then the presence of pathology is not necessarily an insurmountable obstacle to having it. Many of the things disabled people cannot do are the result of design decisions rather than biology. When society enables people to get on with their lives despite their disabilities, they are able to enjoy good health, in Gadamer's sense of the word.

Along similar lines, Havi Carel writes that health and illness are not opposites but rather 'a continuum or a blend'. Her questioning of the health-illness dichotomy shows that the relationship between the two states is often much more complicated than we allow. She suggests that 'in the same way that episodes of illness can occur within health, an experience of health within illness is a possible, if often overlooked, phenomenon'. Since health is not something we straightforwardly have or don't have, flourishing is possible even when physiological functioning is impaired.

See also: The Body, Consent, Mental Health, Pain

Reading
Hans-Georg Gadamer, *The Enigma of Health: The Art of Healing in a Scientific Age* (Polity, 1993)
Havi Carel, *Illness* (3rd edition, Routledge, 2018)

Home

In *The Wizard of Oz*, Dorothy learns that there's 'no place like home' the hard way. For many of us the problem is slightly different: there's no place that *is* home, or at least nowhere that really feels like it. This can feel like a real gap in our lives, perhaps even like a personal failing.

For most humans throughout history, home has been the land where they were born, lived and died. When your own self is so intimately tied to a place, home is not just where you belong but something of which you are a part. Stephen Muecke says of aboriginal Australian philosophy that death is widely conceived as 'a return of energy to the place of emanation with which it reidentifies'. The physical environment is as important as the people who live in it and is granted equal respect. That is why the Whanganui River, New Zealand's third longest, was declared a legal person in March 2017, in respect of Maori beliefs.

In developed countries, many of us lack this sense of deep connection with a place. Although we still seem to crave it, the restlessness that comes from not finding it can be a source of creative energy. Throughout his life, David Hume oscillated between enjoying the intellectual stimulation of the city and tiring of its sociability. Sometimes he was convinced he was more at home in the quiet countryside of the Scottish Borders or rural France. He never found that one place he could call home. But he made the most of where he was at any given time. His unsettledness also propelled him to travel and see more of the world than he might have done otherwise. That can be ample compensation for the lack of a place that exerts such a pull one never wants to leave it.

The idea that there is a corner of the world where we could feel at home for ever can be a fantasy. The young and still wealthy Ludwig Wittgenstein had a house built on a small lake in Norway. This was the only home he had that was truly and solely his, but over the course of the next 39 years, he spent less than two years there.

Home can also be where your roots are. As the old adage goes, you can take the person out of a place, but you can't take the place out of the person. Acknowledging the role such a home plays in making us who we are is vital to fully understanding ourselves. That's why it is not necessarily petty chauvinism that makes us feel a special connection to where we come from.

The ideal is to be at home in a place but open to others. Mahatma Gandhi put this beautifully when he wrote, 'I do not want my house to be walled in on all sides and my windows to be stuffed. I want the cultures of all lands to be blown about my house as freely as possible. But I refuse to be blown off my feet by any. I refuse to live in other people's houses as an interloper, a beggar or a slave.'

Others go further. They are cosmopolitans, citizens of the world. In theory, cosmopolitanism enables us to feel at home anywhere. In practice it can mean we feel truly at home nowhere. For those who aspire to global citizenship this might be a price worth paying. But according to Kwame Anthony Appiah, cosmopolitanism can be reconciled with local attachments. He takes as an example his Ghanaian nationalist father, whose final message to his children was, 'Remember you are citizens of the world.' As Appiah says, 'he never saw a conflict between local partialities and a universal morality – between being part of the place you were and part of a broader human community.'

The thought of home is warm, cosy and reassuring. The sense of lacking one can stir painful yearnings, but sometimes it is better to let that ache be and embrace our feelings of rootlessness or restlessness. It's more important to be comfortable with *who* we are than *where* we are.

See also: Authenticity, Community, Family, Patriotism, Travel

Reading
Kwame Anthony Appiah, *Cosmopolitanism* (Norton, 2007)

Hope

It's hard to imagine how life would be tolerable without hope. Hope can keep people going, but when it is dashed we can be left even more shattered than we would have been without it.

That's why although giving hope is a kindness, giving false hope is cruel.

But it is not just false hope that is problematic. Seneca argued that both hope and fear 'belong to the mind that is in suspense, that is worried by its expectation of what is to come'. It is because we desire particular outcomes, which are uncertain, that both fear and hope arise. In fear, we dwell on the outcome we don't want; in hope, on the one we do. Hope and fear are therefore intimately connected. 'Just as the prisoner and the guard are bound to each other by the same chain, so these two that are so different nonetheless go along together: where hope goes, fear follows.'

Seneca agreed with his fellow Stoic Hecaton that we should avoid hope, since 'You will cease to fear if you cease to hope.' If you hope that something will happen, you also fear that it won't. Seneca believed that the best way to banish hope and fear was to stop desiring altogether. Without going so far, we might agree with him that 'Limiting one's desires is beneficial also as a remedy for fear.'

Schopenhauer also mistrusted hope, and agreed that the solution to the ills of humanity is to curb our desires. (*See* **Desires**, **Suffering**.) For him, hope is a 'folly of the heart' because it distorts our thinking and prevents us from grasping the truth. Also, hope is bound to disappoint, whether or not our hopes are met, since what we hope for more often than not does not match our expectations. Schopenhauer can be seen as agreeing with Plato's verdict that hope is 'gullible' in both respects.

So hope often comes accompanied by fear, its evil twin, as well as by wishful thinking and disappointment. But it is natural and comforting, and if we completely got rid of it we would risk losing heart and motivation. A better strategy is therefore to change how we understand it.

Hope is normally based on a desire for a certain outcome and a belief. This need not be the belief that things are or will turn out for the best, which is more characteristic of what we could call optimism. (*See* **Optimism**.) All hope requires is a belief that what we're wishing for is *possible*.

This line of thought led Sartre to conclude that we 'should act without hope' – we should commit ourselves to action, but on the understanding that 'one need not hope in order to undertake one's work'. These slogans are misleading because Sartre meant something quite specific by *acting without hope*. He meant that we should act with a complete suspension of judgement about whether our action will bring about the desired results. We can be motivated and committed without relying on a belief that our preferred outcome will happen, or even that it is likely to happen – all we need to believe is that it's possible.

For Sartre, this meant giving up hope. It might be more accurate to say it requires giving up *excessive* hope, the kind that sees a good outcome as probable. But we can still have hope if that means wishing for what is good and believing it's possible. Hope without expectation enables us to pursue what we value, while avoiding fear and disappointment.

See also: Afterlife, Faith, Optimism, Perseverance, Pessimism, Uncertainty

Reading
Jean-Paul Sartre, *Existentialism Is a Humanism* (1946)

Human Nature

When people disappoint us, it is tempting to shrug our shoulders and put it down to human nature. 'Out of the crooked timber of humanity, no straight thing was ever made,' as Kant wrote. If human beings are essentially weak and selfish, we shouldn't be surprised that when it comes to the crunch they often let others down. But when we see how people help each other in crises and witness examples of extraordinary self-sacrifice, human nature can seem much kinder. So what are we fundamentally – good people corrupted by society or bad ones kept in check by it?

The debate is as old as philosophy itself. The ancient Chinese philosopher Gaozi got there millennia before Kant when he pessimistically suggested that 'Man's nature is like the ch'i-willow and righteousness is like a cup or bowl.' The Confucian Xunzi agreed, saying that 'people's nature is bad' and that 'without ritual and the standards of righteousness, they will be unruly, chaotic, and not well ordered'. Mencius, on the other hand, argued that 'benevolence is the distinguishing characteristic of man'. We all have the seeds of goodness within us; they just need to be cultivated.

The question of who is right seems a profoundly important one. In practice, however, both sides agree that we have to work to cultivate our better natures. For Mencius, natural human goodness withers with neglect, whereas for Xunzi, natural human badness can be overcome with effort. The upshot is the same: nurture goodness or watch the weeds of wickedness spread.

Still, we need to be realistic if our attempts at cultivation are to bear fruit. If we try too hard to work against the grain of human nature, we will do it violence rather than improve it. For instance, the Stoics believed it was possible to train ourselves to be indifferent to all but our own virtue and consider our deaths and those of our loved ones with equanimity. Hume, who tried in his youth to follow Stoic advice, concluded that their theories were 'too magnificent for human nature'. They asked us to 'render happiness entirely independent of every thing external' but 'that degree of perfection is impossible to be attained'.

The realistic view of human nature adopted by Hume is that we are neither wholly good nor bad. Perfection is beyond us, but that does not mean we cannot strive to be better than we are. This kind of realism teaches tolerance of human failings in ourselves and in others, but not indulgence of them. 'Human nature' is never an excuse for bad behaviour, but it does explain why we will always fall short of our highest aspirations.

See also: Character, Nature, Perfectionism, Tolerance

Reading
Julian Baggini, *How the World Thinks* (Granta, 2018), Chapter 21
David Hume, *An Enquiry Concerning the Principles of Morals* (1751), Chapter 7

Humility *see* Pride

I

'These hours of solitude and meditation are the only ones in the day when I am completely myself and my own master.'

Jean-Jacques Rousseau

Identity

Who am I? It's one of the most fundamental questions we can ask. Even when we think we've answered it, we return to it again and again. Crises of identity can occur for a variety of reasons. Your children leave home and suddenly your status as a parent no longer seems primary, and you're not sure what should take its place. You may not label yourself a 'successful professional', but when your career comes crashing down, you're jolted into recognising that without that identity you feel bereft.

Giving things labels and putting them into neat categories makes the world seem more manageable. If you're sick, it often helps just to get a diagnosis, so you can give a name to your pain. We are also quick to think of people as having clear, primary identities: 'arty Alex', 'cerebral Steph', Sporty Spice or Bob the Builder. We could call this the 'essentialising impulse': the desire to attribute to everything some kind of unchanging, defining essence. It's easy to do the same to ourselves, even though we know that, as Walt Whitman wrote, we all 'contain multitudes'.

'What is man but a heap of contradictions!' wrote David Hume. His choice of the word 'heap' is telling, since on another occasion he described the self as a 'bundle of perceptions'. The self contains no immutable, simple essence – it is rather an ever-changing sequence of thoughts and sensations. This flux means that your identity not only changes over time, it is never simple and unitary at any point.

Our identities are 'inescapably plural', as Amartya Sen puts it. 'The same person can be without contradiction, an American citizen, of Caribbean origin, with African ancestry, a Christian, a liberal, a woman, a historian, a novelist, a feminist, a heterosexual, a believer in gay and lesbian rights, a theatre lover, an environmental activist, a tennis fan, a jazz musician . . .'

Ordinarily, however, we are spellbound by what Sen calls the myth of 'solitarist' identity: the idea that one such identity is primary and rules over all the others. Sometimes we are keenly aware of which identity that is, particularly when its assertion is in response to a perceived threat. For example, most heterosexuals do not see their sexuality as their primary identity, but if you face discrimination or persecution for being gay, your sexuality may take on a greater significance. Religious identity tends to be less important when we live among people of the same faith, but is stronger if we find ourselves in a minority.

When life is going smoothly, we may not be conscious of any primary identity at all. Nonetheless, we often assume one, which is why the shock job dismissal, the divorce or the injury that robs someone of their beloved sport threatens an identity we previously took for granted.

Sen's interest in identity was primarily political. He was concerned about how solitarist identities breed conflict, between natives and immigrants, Hutus and Tutsis, Protestants and Catholics. However, solitarist, essentialising identities can be toxic for individual as well as societal well-being. We can feel trapped by the expectations that come with identities given to us by family or society, or when our beliefs cease to align with the religious, moral or political identity those around us assume we must have.

Whether the problem is political or personal, the way forward is the same: don't reduce yourself or others to a single identity and accept the multiplicity and fluidity of all your identities. What makes us unique is not the possession of a singular essence but the idiosyncratic package we become. We should also accept that any tensions there may be between them are part and parcel of what it is to be a complex human being. The question 'Who am I?' is not one that can be answered with a sentence. Its answer is found in the messy totality of all that we think, feel and do.

See also: Authenticity, Change, Community, Integrity, Self-Knowledge

Reading
Julian Baggini, *The Ego Trick* (Granta, 2011)
Amartya Sen, *Identity and Violence* (Penguin, 2006)

Idleness *see* Leisure

Illness *see* Health and Illness

Impostor Syndrome

Do you ever have the uncomfortable feeling that you are not able, talented or qualified enough to do whatever it is you find yourself doing? This sense of inadequacy is often accompanied by the terror that sooner or later other people will realise this too and you will be exposed as a fraud, an impostor.

It should be reassuring to know that impostor syndrome is not categorised as a mental disorder and that it is extremely common. One study showed that almost all medical students at one college had at least mild versions of it, with more than half of them feeling it severely. Men and women seem equally vulnerable to these pangs of inadequacy.

Reminding ourselves that we are good enough and that others are not as able and confident as we imagine is not always sufficient. Sometimes we need to listen to our doubts more carefully.

One such set of cases is where there is simply no way of being sure that you *are* good enough. Philosophers know this feeling well. As Simon Glendinning once said, 'It's always a tricky moment for any philosopher to acknowledge that what you are doing, what you think might be worth doing, might be just a spinning in the wind or just a kind of doing nothing at all, or doing something very badly.' Glendinning believed that professional philosophy has developed ways of demonstrating to itself that it is rigorous and bona fide, but that such self-validation is a mistake. It is, he says, 'unhelpful' for philosophers 'to think of themselves as having freed themselves from something it is impossible to free yourself from'.

Another kind of case is where you can see that you are not as good as some others in your field. The young Simone de Beauvoir realised this after endless student debates with Jean-Paul Sartre, who was three years her senior. 'Day after day, and all day long I set myself up against Sartre, and in our discussions I was simply not in his class,' she wrote in her autobiography.

Beauvoir did not try to persuade herself that she was as good as Sartre, but didn't let herself be discouraged either. She concluded: 'My curiosity was greater than my pride; I preferred learning to showing off.' Her future suddenly seemed more difficult, but also more open. 'Nothing had been done: but everything was possible.' It worked, and she ended up at least Sartre's equal.

Both Glendinning and Beauvoir remind us that impostor syndrome is not always simply a misguided sense of inadequacy that needs to be fought. Sometimes it alerts us to the fact that we have a long way to go to achieve our potential, or that there are no guarantees that what we're doing is good or will be successful. These warning signs should be heeded. A person who never feels impostor syndrome is too confident of the value of what they do, their ability to do it, or both. If we are aware of the possibility that we might fall short, we will be more prepared and determined to push ourselves to do our best.

See also: Authority, Competition, Envy, Insecurity, Perfectionism, Self-Confidence

Reading
Simone de Beauvoir, *Memoirs of a Dutiful Daughter* (1958)

Indecision

How tiresome it is to waste our time and energy seesawing from one option to another and back again, feeling that we should be able to make up our minds and that there's something wrong with us if we can't. There isn't. Making good decisions is difficult. When matters are clear, things decide themselves. A period of wavering is a natural part of the process of moving from uncertainty to action, so there's nothing wrong with short-term indecision. It becomes a problem only when it is chronic and unresolved.

Aristotle called the process of decision-making 'deliberation'. In his view, we deliberate only 'where the consequences are unclear, and where things are not definite'. This point speaks to two common pitfalls that frequently delay or even paralyse decision-making. One is to want to reach the perfect solution, when it is much more common for each option to carry a different set of gains and losses; the other is to demand certainty that things will work out, when in fact every choice is to some extent a leap in the dark. If we wait for the perfect solution, which will definitely turn out well, we may be waiting a long time – better to lower the bar and accept that every option involves downsides and uncertainties.

Being able to deliberate well is an important skill for Aristotle, part of what he calls 'practical wisdom'. But in his terminology, deliberation refers specifically to finding means to ends. So before we even get to deliberate, we must become clear about what ends we seek and what is most valuable in life. (*See* **Values**.) Once we've done that, we can get down to the central task of connecting these values with the situation at hand: we 'establish an end and then go on to think about how and by what means it is to be achieved. If it appears that there are several means available, [we] consider by which it will be achieved in the easiest and most noble way.'

Taking the case of a career change, once we have established our priorities it's a matter of thinking through how each available option fares in relation to them. This is not always easy, as values often clash with each other. (*See* **Ambivalence**.) 'Gut feelings' may help or hinder in this respect, so they will have to be scrutinised to ascertain whether they are telling you something worth listening to or just clouding your judgement. (*See* **Intuition**.)

Bertrand Russell advises not to agonise over decisions or regret them after the event: 'When a difficult or worrying decision has to be reached, as soon as all the data are available, give the matter your best thought and make your decision; having made the decision, do not revise it unless some new fact comes to your knowledge. Nothing is so exhausting as indecision, and nothing is so futile.'

So next time you're undecided, give a thought to the philosophers' advice: do reflect on your values, systematically think through your options and select a reasonable solution that has a chance of working out; do *not* demand perfection or cast-iron guarantees, or revisit the decision unless something new comes to light.

See also: Ambivalence, Choice, Control, Dilemmas, Intuition, Perfectionism, Regret, Uncertainty, Values, Virtue, Wisdom

Reading
Aristotle, *Nicomachean Ethics* and *Eudemian Ethics*

Infidelity *see* **Betrayal**

Inner Life

Jean-Jacques Rousseau may have been a genius, but he was also conceited, arrogant and paranoid. Almost all his friends eventually gave up on him and he ended up living as a recluse in the French countryside, convinced that he was the victim of a cruel and unjust world. This self-inflicted exile, however, taught him valuable lessons about 'the pleasure of conversing with my soul'.

Rousseau said this was 'the only pleasure that men cannot take away from me'. It would be more accurate to say that it was the only pleasure he left himself with. Nonetheless, his self-pitying description points to one of the most important reasons for developing a rich inner life: it is one of the few things that can't be taken from us.

So how do you develop such an inner life? First of all by finding resources in yourself that you may have overlooked or neglected. 'Losing all hope for this life and finding no food left on earth for my soul,' wrote Rousseau, 'I gradually learnt to feed it on its own substance and seek all its nourishment within myself.' Sources of inner stimulation include actively using your imagination and allowing your mind to wander – doing this allows our brains to come up with things we could literally only daydream of.

Second, feed the mind with books, films, art, music and mindful observation of the world, not for the sake of mere stimulation but to nourish reflection and inner dialogue. Habitually looking at the world with curiosity and reflecting on it is not only rewarding in itself but also helps us to gain clarity and insight.

Once you have developed the capacity to be stimulated by your own thoughts, experiences and reflections, you will never be bored and life will never be without interest.

The inner life is thus a source of remarkable self-sufficiency. You learn that your happiness need not depend as much on others as you might have believed, and you might find yourself thinking, as Rousseau did, that 'These hours of solitude and meditation are the only ones in the day when I am completely myself and my own master.'

See also: Leisure, Mindfulness, Self-Care, Self-Knowledge, Simplicity, Slowing Down, Solitude

Reading
Jean-Jacques Rousseau, *Reveries of the Solitary Walker* (1782)

Insecurity

If you're feeling insecure, the obvious remedy is to put protective measures in place to shield yourself from the perceived threats. If you feel financially insecure, live within your means and try to save; if your job is insecure, look for another one; if you're emotionally insecure, see a therapist. On this view, insecurity is a practical problem that we may or may not be able to do anything about.

But insecurity cannot always be so easily fixed, and not just because of practical obstacles. Even when we limit ourselves to consideration of these everyday insecurities, philosophers of many schools, including Buddhism, Daoism and Stoicism, have insisted that nothing close to full protection is an achievable aim. Life is fundamentally impermanent and subject to unpredictable change. Even if you are as secure as can be, you may be struck down by personal disaster, financial ruin, illness – or literally by lightning.

Material, physical and emotional security are never enough to make us feel completely protected. According to Paul Tillich, our strivings for safety are fundamentally driven by death anxiety. Unable to fully accept our mortality, we seek to make ourselves as secure as possible, ignoring the fact that our fortresses are really sandcastles facing the coming tide. Our misguided focus on creating security leads us to make prisons for ourselves in which we hide from reality. We would do better to emerge from these cells and accept that 'no absolute and no final security is possible'.

R.D. Laing identified another form of insecurity that was not easily fixed by seeking greater protection. In his view, we are *ontologically* secure when we have a firm sense of identity and reality; our experiences fit together as those of a single, coherent life; and we are able to relate to others as well as be separate from them. In ontological *in*security, on the other hand, our sense of identity becomes blurred and we oscillate between 'complete isolation or complete merging of identity'. Our subjective experience becomes 'swamped, impinged upon, or congealed by the other'. In this condition of uncertainty and confusion we are constantly threatened by the 'ordinary circumstances of everyday life'. Although Laing was mainly addressing the problem of psychosis, the general point applies to all of us: in order to feel secure in the world, we need to feel secure about who we are.

Together, these diverse philosophical perspectives on insecurity add up to a useful set of principles for dealing with it. The upshot is to accept that the world cannot be relied upon to deliver security and that the only kind of security we can develop is to be comfortable with who we are and what we believe. Inner security enables us to stay anchored in the choppy waters of life.

See also: Anxiety, Contentment, Fear, Resilience, Self-Confidence, Vulnerability

Reading
R.D. Laing, *Self and Others* (Tavistock, 1961)
Paul Tillich, *The Courage to Be* (Yale University Press, 1952)

Integrity

There's not much higher praise than calling someone a person of integrity. But becoming such a paragon of virtue isn't easy. Sometimes we find our integrity under threat. Maybe we have the offer of a great job but with a company whose values we don't agree with. Or we might have the opportunity to take a trip of a lifetime on the kind of long-haul flight we habitually criticise as environmentally ruinous.

But integrity is hard to maintain for a deeper reason: it's not entirely clear what it even is. The word comes from the Latin *integer*, meaning 'whole' or 'intact'. To have integrity means maintaining your values in their wholeness and being true to what is most important to you. A person who lacks integrity will do what is expedient in any given case, undermining the coherence of their moral selves.

This seems simple enough in theory, even if it isn't easy to do in practice. But it would be simple only if it was always evident what our values demanded of us. Few of us, however, sign up to such a clear-cut moral code.

The complications of integrity are evident in the Confucian tradition. Like Aristotle, Confucius believes that the cultivation of character is the basis of good action. The *junzi*, or exemplary person, is someone of the highest integrity, who remains true to the good in all circumstances. But because situations differ, such an individual will tailor their behaviour accordingly. Confucius says, 'The *junzi* is true, but not rigidly trustworthy.' At times it can be necessary even to betray trust, if keeping a promise requires you to do something worse, such as endangering an innocent life.

The Confucian principle behind this is *quan*, or discretionary action. The origins of this word have the meaning of 'weight', suggesting that *quan* requires the careful weighing up of different courses of action. This contrasts with the simple following of rules, which would require only routine implementation. Such rigidity is frequently criticised by Confucius: 'As long as one does not transgress the bounds when it comes to important Virtues, it is permissible to cross the line here and there when it comes to minor Virtues.'

The virtue of the *junzi* contrasts with two false forms of integrity. One is to remain blindly true to fixed principles. This can lead to what Bernard Williams calls 'moral self-indulgence', in which we make ourselves feel good by not doing something we consider wrong, even if taking a more holistic view would lead us to make an exception. For example, a journalist might refuse to write for a newspaper because of its political views, even though its readers would be the very people who would most benefit from her perspective. Or an environmentalist might refuse to take a long-haul flight to see a dying relative, causing severe hurt to one person while making an insignificant contribution to the fight against climate change.

The second bogus form of integrity is the idea that it means being 'true to yourself', come what may. For one thing, we are not all good, so being true to yourself in this sense sometimes actually means going along with something that you really ought to challenge. For another, the whole idea rests on an assumption that we all have some kind of unchanging essence of self that we can remain true to. (*See* **Identity**.) It is more honest and realistic to accept that the self is always a work in progress. Sticking steadfastly to who you are today means not making the effort to become a better you tomorrow.

Both of these false forms of integrity mislead us into thinking that integrity is about being fixed and unbending. Real integrity is more difficult than that. It means holding fast to what is right and being willing to adapt your behaviour accordingly. Integrity is not something we simply possess but a skill that requires constant practice.

See also: Ambivalence, Authenticity, Character, Dilemmas, Duty, Identity, Responsibility, Trust

Reading
Bernard Williams, 'Utilitarianism and Moral Self-Indulgence' in *Moral Luck* (Cambridge University Press, 1981) pp. 40–53
Confucius, *Analects*

Intuition

Should you trust your intuitions? We often have strong gut feelings that we can't rationally justify, but that we don't want to ignore. At the same time, we tend to be as suspicious of others' intuitions as we are certain of our own. Would you be happy for a police officer to stand up in court and say 'I just *know* she's guilty, m'lord', and for the judge to accept that? 'I just know it' seems good enough for ourselves but woefully inadequate for others.

It is tempting to think of intuition as a mysterious ability to detect the truth directly, and in one sense of the word it is indeed like this. Most philosophers agree that there are certain fundamental truths or principles that cannot be proven. Take basic maths, for example: when you understand what 'one', 'two' 'plus' and 'equals' mean, you can just *see* that 'one plus one equals two' must be true.

This is why, although Aristotle described science as a kind of 'demonstrative reason', it cannot demonstrate the basic principles it rests on: a building cannot be its own foundation. Hence 'it is intuitive reason that grasps the first principles', not demonstrative reason. Descartes similarly thought that logical argument had its limits and some things could be seen to be true only by what he called 'the natural light'.

Just how much of our knowledge rests on intuition is contentious. Both Aristotle and Descartes limited the role of intuition to the basic foundations of knowledge. Some philosophical traditions, however, believe that with the right training it is possible to sharpen intuitive powers to the point of grasping the ultimate nature of things. Several Indian schools of philosophy acknowledge the authority of *rishis* (seers), people who have practised *anvikshiki* (literally 'looking at') and so can attain direct realisation of reality. This is why alongside logic and argument, much Indian philosophy involves practices like yoga and meditation.

More modestly, the eighteenth to twentieth-century moral intuitionists argued that moral principles were among the things that could not be demonstrated to be true and had simply to be grasped. That it is wrong to cause unnecessary harm, for example, is self-evident.

None of these defences of intuition justify the sense we often have that a particular judgement is correct in the absence of any supporting evidence. The fact that some knowledge can only be intuited does not mean we are licensed to rely on intuition in cases where it is both possible and desirable to use evidence and argument instead.

There is, however, another form of intuition that has a legitimate role in making everyday judgements. This is what Aristotle called practical wisdom, the ability to make good judgements that are based on experience. (*See* **Wisdom**.) We can't always fully explain or justify why we've made such a judgement, but nor is it a mere hunch. For example, it is practical wisdom that could alert a doctor to a suspicious set of test results that don't look obviously wrong to a junior colleague. Hence, Aristotle argued, 'we ought to attend to the undemonstrated sayings and opinions of experienced and older people or of people of practical wisdom not less than to demonstrations; because their experienced eye enables them to see correctly.'

That such intuition is real is not in doubt. The hard question is: when do we actually have it? When we find ourselves tempted to rely on gut feelings, we can ask ourselves two useful questions. First, do I have good reason to believe that my intuitions *in this kind of situation* are generally reliable? Intuition is not a global skill: your hunches about racehorses might be spot on but those about potential romantic partners could be terrible. Second, do I need to trust my intuitions or are there more dependable ways of getting to the truth? There's no point in ignoring good evidence and arguments if they are available.

We ought to be careful when using intuition – it is always tempting to believe that our own inklings are more trustworthy than they really are. The role of intuition is to do what reason cannot, not do reason's job for it.

See also: Argument, Evidence, Knowledge, Rationality, Superstition, Unconscious, Virtue, Wisdom

Reading
Aristotle, *Nicomachean Ethics*, Book Six

Irrationality *see* **Rationality**

J

'Jealousy is the price that has to be paid for there to be a certain sort of love from a certain sort of person, and one might not wish to be without that certain sort of love from that certain sort of person.' Peter Goldie

Jealousy

'The Jealous Kind', 'Suspicious Minds', 'Who Is He (And What Is He to You)?', 'Jealous Guy'. There are so many songs about jealousy. When something is a perennial theme in popular music, you know it's an emotion that almost everyone feels. And if you listen to those songs, you'll find it is portrayed as bitter, destructive, irrational, uncontrollable. How can we tame such a beast?

We often use the word 'jealousy' interchangeably with 'envy', but unlike envy, jealousy typically arises in the context of a relationship, when we believe we are threatened by a 'rival'. (*See* **Envy**.) Jealousy need not be personal or sexual, but it tends to be.

One of the things that makes jealousy so difficult and complex is that it tends to loosen our grip on reality. It is, at the very least, a 'magnifier of trifles' as Friedrich Schiller put it. In his interesting analysis, Peter Goldie points out that both the relationship and the threat could be completely imagined. Correcting our distorted vision is difficult because jealousy can pull us in opposite directions, making us susceptible 'both to doubt and to credulity'. On the one hand we are overly suspicious, taking insignificant things as confirmation of nefarious goings-on; on the other, we are 'also susceptible to being unduly assuaged by reassurances from the lover or rival'. In these circumstances, it can be difficult to know whether we're being paranoid or naive.

Apart from the fact that it messes with our critical faculties, there are other reasons why jealousy is problematic. In particular, it tends to instigate self-defeating behaviour and it can be underscored by the unsavoury habit of treating our loved ones as possessions.

Given all this, we'd be justified in asking, what is the point of jealousy? Surely we'd be better off without it? According to Goldie, 'jealousy is the price that has to be paid for there to be a certain sort of love from a certain sort of person, and one might not wish to be without that certain sort of love from that certain sort of person.' In his view, jealousy can sometimes 'involve mutually held legitimate expectations which do not involve treating the lover in an ethically unjustifiable way'. For instance, jealousy might be legitimate if the justified expectation of keeping promises were not met.

For Goldie, the challenge with jealousy is to manage it. He acknowledges that it is a 'character trait which should not be left unchecked' because it 'does tend to get out of control'. We should always be wary of jealousy: it's not known as 'the green-eyed monster' for nothing.

See also: Betrayal, Emotions, Envy, Relationships, Trust

Reading
Peter Goldie, *The Emotions: A Philosophical Exploration* (Oxford University Press, 2002)

Joy *see* **Happiness**

Justice

It can be really hard to be on the receiving end of an injustice, large or small. But it's something we all have to deal with, whether it's being unfairly slandered by gossip, not getting your fair share of an inheritance, or missing out on an opportunity because someone else has cheated.

The sense of justice is not something created by philosophers. It seems to be innate. Primatologists such as Frans de Waal have found that monkeys refuse rewards if they see others getting more than them. When children complain that 'it's not fair!' before anyone has explained to them what fairness means, we tell them that they need to learn that life is not fair. To some extent that's true, but it's hardly the end of the story. Isaiah Berlin once characterised philosophers as adults who persist in asking childish questions. 'What is justice?' is one of these.

One of the first answers to this question was given short shrift by Plato. In the *Republic*, Polemarchus suggests to Socrates that justice is giving people their due. Socrates tears this to shreds. The answer is not wrong, merely hopelessly vague. No one in an acrimonious divorce denies that each party should get their due – they just have incompatible views of what that means. The whole problem of justice is determining precisely who is due what and why.

Plato's positive account of justice, however, is incomplete and unsatisfactory. A just state is one in proper order, which for him means that philosophers rule and each person sticks to their allotted role: ruler, soldier or worker. The main legacy of the *Republic* was to lay down the gauntlet for future philosophers to come up with a better definition of justice.

One of the most influential has been the liberal view of John Rawls, who devised a powerful thought experiment to reveal our deepest intuitions about justice. Imagine that you have to decide who gets what in society from behind a 'veil of ignorance', not knowing what position you will personally be in when the distribution takes place. So you don't know whether you'd be born to a middle-class family in a rich nation or a poor farmer in a developing one. Rawls thought that in such a situation, most people would choose a fairly egalitarian distribution of goods.

The thought experiment transfers to more personal contexts: if you are sincere about working out what a fair divorce settlement is, don't think about what you would get but instead imagine what would be fair for anyone in that situation. And if you do think of yourself, imagine you are in the position of the other party.

Rawls's veil of ignorance is a tool to get us to think more impartially, which seems to be the key to justice. If the concept still appears to lack a precise definition, perhaps that is not as much of a problem as philosophers have thought. Amartya Sen has argued that we have been too transfixed by the search for an idea of perfect justice – most of the time, we get on fine without one. To put it crudely, like monkeys and children, we all know obvious injustice when we see it.

In less clear cases, Sen argues, the problem is that there are always competing versions of justice. He asks us to imagine we are giving a flute to one of three children. Do you give it to the one who has no toys, the only one who can play it or the precocious child who made it? There is no algorithm for answering this – each option fits one dimension of justice but goes against others. Justice can mean fair outcomes, fair opportunities or fair processes, and sometimes these point us in different directions.

When we feel that we are victims of injustice, we should be reassured that our hurt and even rage is one of the most natural feelings in the world. However, we should try to take a more objective viewpoint to check whether our sense of injustice is being distorted by self-serving bias. If it isn't, it is helpful to remember Sen's point that the lack of perfect justice is not just the result of living in an imperfect world, but is often due to the impossibility of meeting all the different demands of justice.

If, after all this, we conclude that there is a real, avoidable and serious injustice, the question that remains is pragmatic: is this a fight that can be won, or one that is worth the battle even if it isn't? Save your energy for the cases where the answer is yes. To combat a serious injustice that can be remedied is noble; to rage against minor ones that can't is an exhausting waste of time and effort.

See also: Competition, Office Politics, Politics, Right and Wrong

Reading

John Rawls, *A Theory of Justice* (Harvard University Press, 1971)

Amartya Sen, *The Idea of Justice* (Allen Lane, 2009)

K

'Let us not pretend to doubt
in philosophy what we do
not doubt in our hearts.'
Charles Sanders Peirce

Kindness *see* **Empathy**

Knowledge

In our sceptical age, it sometimes seems that the only thing you need to know is that nobody knows anything. Scientists, bankers, doctors, dieticians and economists have all been shown to have been wrong on a number of important occasions. The fictional spies' adage 'trust no one, suspect everyone' has become a mantra for our times.

Many people believe that philosophy encourages this scepticism. One of the few things people know about Socrates is that he claimed to be the wisest person in Athens precisely because he knew he knew nothing, while others were under the illusion that they knew something. However, one of the things people falsely believe they know is what this actually means. Plato, whose dialogues feature the fictionalised Socrates, set a very high bar for true knowledge. We can be said to know only if we have absolute certainty of what is eternally and unchangingly true, beyond any question of being wrong. Little wonder that nothing we think we know passes this test. For Plato, even science is a form of opinion, since it concerns itself only with the world of observation and perception.

So when Socrates said he knew nothing, he was using 'know' in a very particular and restrictive way, which changes the rules of the ordinary knowledge game. For example, when a scientist says we know the speed of light, she is not necessarily claiming that this is an eternal and unchanging truth about ultimate reality. Rather it is a tested and verified fact about the observable universe, and that is good enough to count as knowledge.

Not all philosophers have been as idealistic as Plato about knowledge. The American pragmatists had no time for radical scepticism. 'Let us not pretend to doubt in philosophy what we do not doubt in our hearts,' said one of its leading lights, Charles Sanders Peirce. The pragmatists followed British empiricists such as John Locke and David Hume, who grounded knowledge in our experience of the world rather than in pure logic. The spirit of both these schools is captured in the answer Wittgenstein suggested you should give to a sceptic who says 'I don't know if there is a hand here': *look closer.*

Socrates nearly admits that he is using 'knowledge' in an artificially narrow way. Even to say that the one thing he knows is that he knows nothing is an acknowledgement that there is a legitimate use of 'know' that falls short of timeless absoluteness.

Despite their disagreements, Western philosophers have tended to think of knowledge as the possession of truths that can be articulated in words. Such 'propositional knowledge' includes statements like 'one plus one equals two', 'Paris is the capital of France', 'TripAdvisor restaurant reviews are not to be trusted', or anything else that can be expressed as a sentence. This 'knowing that' contrasts with 'knowing how', which is a skill that can't always be put into words.

This kind of knowledge has a more central role in Asian philosophy. In the *Zhuangzi*, for example, a butcher called Ding knows how to cut meat so well that it appears to just fall from the bone. When he acts, 'sensible knowledge stops'. In the Western tradition, most philosophers would hesitate to say that Ding has knowledge, but it seems perfectly natural to say that he knows more about butchering than any theoretician.

An example of know-how that straddles the traditions is the kind of moral knowledge that both Confucius and Aristotle believed good people had. For them, knowing the right thing to do morally was a matter of skill rather than of possessing a correct theory. (*See* **Wisdom**.)

Some scepticism about knowledge is justified. Whenever anyone claims to know something with absolute certainty, your inner Socrates should be roused to question their excessive confidence. But as long as our claims to knowledge are less emphatic and subject to revision, there is no reason to dismiss them. And we should also grant know-how due respect – the doers of this world know things that mere thinkers cannot.

See also: Argument, Authority, Evidence, Intuition, Rationality, Truth, Uncertainty, Wisdom

Reading

Robert B. Talisse and Scott F. Aikin (eds), *The Pragmatism Reader* (Princeton University Press, 2011)

Zhuangzi, in Philip J. Ivanhoe and Bryan W. Van Norden (eds), *Readings in Classical Chinese Philosophy* (2nd edition, Hackett, 2005)

Ludwig Wittgenstein, *On Certainty,* translated by Denis Paul and G.E.M. Anscombe (Blackwell, 1969)

L

"The mind requires some relaxation and cannot always support its bent to care and industry. It seems, then, that nature has pointed out a mixed kind of life as most suitable to the human race.'
David Hume

Leisure

In our hyperconnected society, many of us feel as though we're 'always on'. Words and phrases we use, like 'switch off' and 'downtime', make it sound like we are machines to unplug. These metaphors suggest that what we really need from our time off work and chores is to do nothing, sit back and relax. Is that what we should be seeking from our leisure time?

The title of Bertrand Russell's famous essay 'In Praise of Idleness' might suggest so. But for Russell idleness means time away from paid labour, not inactivity. This makes room for leisure, which is activity that 'we do for its own sake, not as a means to something else', in Robert and Edward Skidelsky's later formulation. They add that all 'recreations involving active, skilled participation . . . are leisure in our sense', which means that work can also be leisure when our main motivation to do it is not money. It also means that some things we call leisure are not really, either because they are means to an end (working out at the gym, for example) or because they are too passive (slumping on the sofa with a takeaway, half watching whatever is on television).

Russell also thought that leisure was active rather than passive. While the constructive leisure he had in mind was not 'pure frivolity', he denied that he was thinking 'mainly of the sort of things that would be considered "highbrow"'. He quaintly suggested 'peasant dances' as an example of an ordinary person's leisure, and elsewhere he wrote approvingly about watching games, going to the theatre, playing golf and reading.

The value of active leisure is also integral to the concept of 'flow', developed by the psychologist Mihalyi Csikszentmihalyi. This is a state in which we are so absorbed in the task at hand that all other concerns seem to drop away. For this to happen, the challenge needs to match our skills. If the goal is pitched too low we get bored; if too high we get anxious. The ideal is to be stretched but not overwhelmed. Unlike happiness, which we cannot control, with flow it is in our power to direct our attention so as to create more opportunities for it.

Flow often occurs when we're engaged body and mind in a craft. It is not surprising that there has been a resurgence of interest in crafts in recent years, as they bring many benefits. Take knitting, which can train the ability to shift your attention from stresses and worries to a constructive activity, help you to practise patience, satisfy a creative yearning and generate a sense of mastery through learning new skills and seeing the results of your work.

According to Aristotle, leisure was a vital part of the flourishing life. For him, however, leisure *was* of a highbrow kind. Counterintuitively, it referred mainly to intellectual activity that is valuable for its own sake, in particular study and 'contemplation'. Other important activities, like politics and war, are only a means to an end, which is why they are not as valuable.

An understanding of leisure that looks down on relaxation or 'mere entertainment' seems excessively demanding. But if you look at what philosophers do rather than what they say, you can see that many of them also value downtime. Wittgenstein liked to watch Hollywood westerns and A.J. Ayer enjoyed dancing and watching Tottenham Hotspur play football. The take-home message from Aristotle, Russell and the Skidelskys is not that switching off is bad, but that leisure should not be *only* or *mostly* of this kind.

David Hume made a good case for including periods of pure relaxation in our leisure time. He attributed a breakdown in his youth to overwork and so learned early about the need for a balanced life, in which there is time to recharge and remind ourselves that there is more to life than what primarily occupies us. 'The mind requires some relaxation,' he wrote, 'and cannot always support its bent to care and industry. It seems, then, that nature has pointed out a mixed kind of life as most suitable to the human race.'

Some form of rest and relaxation is also important to create a space of openness and receptivity to the world, which otherwise disappears under the weight of too much activity. As the poet W.H. Davies put it in 'Leisure', 'What is this life if, full of care, We have no time to stand and stare.'

Davies is hinting at what might be called the spiritual potential of leisure. Kierkegaard wrote more explicitly about this, arguing that although work is commonly recommended to keep idleness at bay, it is only when one is bored that idleness is a problem. Otherwise, it is 'so far from being the root of evil that it is rather the true good'. This is because 'restless activity' keeps us distracted from the kind of serious contemplation and introspection required to stop life being lived on autopilot: 'There is an indefatigable activity that shuts a person out of the world of spirit.' The portrait he paints of such people is easily recognisable today: 'There are people who have an extraordinary talent for transforming everything into a business operation, whose whole life is a business operation, who fall in love and are married, hear a joke, and admire a work of art with the same businesslike zeal with which they work at the office.'

The call to leisure and idleness is a call to challenge the assumption that productivity is always the sovereign value. Most of us could probably do with bringing more leisure into our lives. 'To be able to fill leisure intelligently is the last product of civilisation,' as Russell put it. To know how to do that, we need to ask ourselves what we need more of in our lives purely for its own sake. Find that, and you've found your leisure.

See also: Achievement, Balance, Boredom, Busyness, Calm, Inner Life, Slowing Down, Work

Reading
Bertrand Russell, *In Praise of Idleness and Other Essays* (George
Allen & Unwin, 1935)

Loneliness *see* Solitude

Loss

It's amazing how the most trivial loss can be annoying, even
when it's just a small amount of money, or a biscuit you were
saving for later. We are, psychologists say, 'loss averse': once
we have something, no longer having it bothers us much
more than not having it in the first place. It's always worth
asking yourself how you would feel if you'd never had the
thing that you're now so cross is gone. If the answer is 'fine',
your greatest loss is the time and energy of getting vexed
about it.

Our built-in lack of perspective on loss frequently distorts
our sense of priorities. Kierkegaard put it elegantly when he
wrote, 'The greatest hazard of all, losing one's self, can occur
very quietly in the world, as if it were nothing at all. No other
loss can occur so quietly; any other loss – an arm, a leg, five
dollars, a wife, etc. – is sure to be noticed.'

'Loss of self' is a complex notion for Kierkegaard, but his
general point can be grasped without delving deeply into it:
distracted by life, we can forget who we really are and lose
touch with our deepest values and integrity. Everyday losses,
especially major financial ones, can be very inconvenient, but
as long as they leave us and our loved ones intact, they remain
relatively trivial.

We might also benefit from reminding ourselves that loss
is not an aberration but part and parcel of life. As Seneca put
it, 'Our minds need frequent prompting to love things on the

understanding that we are sure to lose them, or rather that we are already losing them.'

This is a central theme in Japanese thought. Kakuzo Okakura sees this insight ritualised in the art of flower arranging. He notes the 'wanton waste' of Western bouquets and recoils at the number of flowers that are cut only to be 'thrown away on the morrow', lamenting 'this utter carelessness of life'. The Japanese master arranger, in contrast, will use few stems, sometimes only one, and when it fades, 'tenderly consigns it to the river or carefully buries it in the ground'. Such a reverent attitude to nature's resources makes us more appreciative of things while they last and more prepared for when they are gone.

Some losses are, of course, profoundly important. (*See* **Bereavement, Health and Illness**.) But if we really stopped to think, when we're upset about something we've lost, nine times out of ten we'd realise that either we are perfectly fine without it or that our loss was inevitably the price we would have to pay for being able to enjoy it in the first place. Every bloom becomes a wilted flower, every loss is proof that we once gained.

See also: Bereavement, Change, Death, Health and Illness

Reading
Søren Kierkegaard, *The Sickness unto Death* (1849)
Kakuzo Okakura, *The Book of Tea* (1906)

Love

Love is almost universally counted among the most important things in life. Love, wrote the poet Philip Larkin, is 'what will survive of us'. According to Aristophanes' imaginative myth about the origins of romantic love, as told in Plato's *Symposium*, what we call man and woman were originally parts of the same first humans. Zeus tore them in two in order to diminish their power, and humans have sought to find their 'other half' ever since. Aristophanes says that 'when one of them meets with his other actual half, whether he be a lover of youth or a lover of another sort, the pair are lost in an amazement of love and friendship and intimacy, and would not be out of the other's sight, as I may say, even for a moment.'

This captures the sense in which a couple become a single unit, 'one flesh' as the Christian marriage service puts it. It's an enduring image, still evident whenever we talk of our 'other half' or 'soulmate'. An insight into this comes from David Hume, who argues that we are not entirely separate atoms of being but 'bundles of perceptions', the sum total of our sensations and experiences. When we share many of those with another person, it is as though the very boundaries of ourselves open up and the other becomes part of us.

This is why it can be so painful to separate from someone with whom you have intimately shared your life, and why we use the language of being 'torn apart' or 'ripped open' to describe how vulnerable and hurt we feel. There is no escaping this. We have to grieve for the shared self that has ceased to exist, even if it had become so problematic that it was no longer viable. At those times it can be hard to remember that the same fluidity and openness that allowed us to be so bound up with another in the first place will in time allow us to re-form ourselves without them.

We often assume that we are powerless before a feeling like love, which we take to be fundamentally irrational. 'The heart has its reasons, of which reason knows nothing,' wrote Pascal. But head and heart are more connected than the common distinction between them suggests. The Japanese language enshrines the intimacy of the relationship: the word *kokoro* means 'heart-mind', referring to our feeling-thinking minds.

One of the least poetic descriptions of love in history helps to illuminate this. Spinoza thought that we could 'clearly

L

understand the nature of Love', which he concluded 'is nothing else but pleasure accompanied by the idea of an external cause'. This is why 'he who loves necessarily endeavours to have, and to keep present to him, the object of his love.'

You can't imagine those lines appearing on many valentine cards, but Spinoza's dry definition really does boil it down brilliantly. Love is extremely diverse: familial love is not like romantic love, we don't love chocolate or books the way we love people, and our love for humanity lacks the focus of love for a particular human. But in each case there is some object of that love, which evokes in us some kind of positive feeling, if not pleasure. We may not always want to keep the objects of our love physically close – studies suggest parents are happier when their children leave home, for instance – but we certainly want to know that they are in good shape.

The key word in Spinoza's definition is 'idea'. A feeling of pleasure cannot be love if you have no idea what the external cause of it is. In love, the positive feeling is linked with an idea of what causes it. This is why head and heart cannot be separated – how we feel and what we think are intimately related.

So even if the initial stirrings of love are outside our control, it can be worth thinking about why we feel the way we do. Sometimes love traps us in a destructive relationship, for instance. Seeing more clearly how the object of our love causes us more grief than joy can change how we feel about them.

Love isn't just about romance. There is a more impartial kind of love, which transcends the appreciation of individual lovable characteristics. The Stoics had a version of this universal love, based on the fact that we all belong to the community of rational beings. Students were advised to progressively expand their sense of fellow feeling from themselves and their families to neighbours, the community, and ultimately to all humanity.

Universal love has found its strongest expression in religions. In Christianity, we are all equally worthy of God's love, and are encouraged to love our neighbour out of general benevolence rather than specific affection, or even approval. Jesus said, 'love your enemies and pray for those who persecute you'.

Buddhism strongly encourages relating to all beings with kindness and benevolence. According to the *Metta Sutta*, 'as a mother protects with her life her child, her only child, so with a boundless heart should one cherish all living beings, radiating kindness over the entire world.'

This kind of love is less a spontaneous feeling and more an attitude that we can choose to develop. Several Buddhist meditations are devoted to this. For instance, we might imagine radiating kindness in all directions, as if blowing a conch shell from the top of a mountain. Developing kindness towards all beings is a practice worth adopting. It could transform our experience of life, whatever the ups and downs of romantic love.

See also: Commitment, Dating, Empathy, Family, Friendship, Monogamy, Other People, Parenthood, Relationships, Self-Love, Sex

Reading
Baruch Spinoza, *Ethics* (1677), Book 3
Simon May, *Love: A History* (Yale University Press, 2011)
Plato, *The Symposium*

Love of Life

One common sentiment in funeral eulogies is that the deceased 'loved life'. Sometimes this is a euphemism for debauchery, but it usually captures something more innocent and important. As long as a person has love, or 'zest', for life, there is a reason to get up in the morning, no matter how tough the day ahead will be.

Those who have this lovely quality show a deep appreciation of the experience of being alive, which can manifest itself in a range of attitudes, from curiosity about the world to simple delight in the familiar things we encounter every day.

Interestingly, this enjoyment might persist even when things are not so good. Russell points out that some people manage to maintain their zest for life through all sorts of unpleasant experiences: 'They say to themselves in an earthquake, for example, "So that is what an earthquake is like", and it gives them pleasure to have their knowledge of the world increased by this new item.'

Russell is not so naive as to believe that love of life can persist no matter how extreme the situation. His claim that it tends to be diminished by ill health is, however, debatable. People usually imagine that becoming ill or disabled would ruin everything, but often their love of life is undimmed. Sometimes it even increases, since the experience makes them appreciate what they have more.

In Russell's view, cultivating sources of zest is a route into happiness, as the more things we are interested in, the more opportunities for happiness we will have. This may be true, but it is not the main reason to nurture it. Zest seems more important than happiness, as it can coexist with sadness at life's inevitable misfortunes.

You might wonder, isn't it just a matter of luck whether you are born with such a disposition? There is some truth in this: some are more naturally zestful than others. But whatever our baseline, the way we live can help the quality to flourish or wither. The key is to identify the things that reliably make us glad to be alive. Through this exercise, we may come to realise that we don't make enough room for them, even though we could easily do so. This is a case when absence makes the heart grow cooler rather than fonder. Make the sources of zest present and it will thrive.

See also: Carpe Diem, Gratitude, Happiness, Midlife Crisis, Retirement, Suicide

Reading
Bertrand Russell, *The Conquest of Happiness* (George Allen & Unwin, 1930)

Loyalty

The country singer Tammy Wynette stood by her man. Maybe she was right to do so. We appreciate the loyalty of friends, colleagues and family in difficult times. But we also know that many people have remained too loyal for too long, to people who didn't deserve it. As with so many virtues, loyalty is a 'Goldilocks' quality: you need not too much, not too little, but just the right amount.

That's the easy part. It is more difficult to work out what that perfect balance is. It helps to distinguish between two kinds of loyalty. One we might call 'personal loyalty', which concerns you and the people you are loyal to. For example, if a friend has let you down one too many times and you are considering breaking off the friendship, that's just between you and them. The other we could call 'civic loyalty', when wider society is involved. If a friend is engaged in criminal activity, as well as your relationship to them you also have to consider your loyalty to your community, social group or country.

With personal loyalty, the moral stakes are typically lower. We have no duty of loyalty other than to stand by our commitments and responsibilities. Beyond that it is a question of how much a relationship deserves working on when it seems to be breaking down. In such cases, a good principle is to ask yourself whether loyalty would be deserved if the boot was on the other foot. You might also use the strategy, advocated by Confucius and Aristotle, of thinking about how you tend to err. If you know you have been excessively loyal in the past, you might want to challenge yourself to be less so now; if you've tended to give up on people too easily, that might be a signal to work harder this time.

With civic loyalty, cultural expectations play a large part. For example, for most of Chinese history, loyalty to family was sacrosanct. For many centuries it was a crime to give evidence against your parents, even if they had done wrong. Protecting family bonds was considered more important than upholding civic justice.

Although almost everyone places some value on loyalty, the trend in Western ethics has been towards embracing universal principles that allow no room for special favours. The Enlightenment values of equal rights and the equal importance of interests mean that it would be unjust to treat someone differently because of some personal tie. This is why politicians now get into trouble if they employ family members as aides, and businesses are criticised if they give children of staff preferential treatment on work experience programmes. Loyalty has slowly been restricted to the private realm. As citizens, we are expected to be impartial.

However, this expectation only goes so far. Personal bonds are an important part of a good life, and if we ignore them we deny what Bernard Williams calls the 'separateness of persons'. (*See* **Altruism**.) That is to say, if we treat everyone exactly the same, we neglect what makes each person different, and part of that difference is how they relate to each other.

Personal and civic loyalty both matter, and so they are always in some kind of tension. When the demands of justice test our allegiances, we need to consider two things. The first is the seriousness of the situation: you can rightly expect not to be grassed up by a friend for a minor misdemeanour, but you can't expect them to cover up systematic fraud or any kind of abuse. The second is balance of evidence: friends deserve the benefit of the doubt, but only if there is real doubt to give them the benefit of.

It is also important to remember that loyalty isn't all about whether you back someone or not. True friendship might require helping someone to admit their wrongdoings and either pay the price or make amends. The same applies to loyalty to organisations, communities and country. Loyalty does not require blind faith in friends, family, country or allies. It means believing that when they are wrong, they deserve the chance to make things right, and our help to do so.

See also: Character, Community, Duty, Family, Forgiveness, Parenthood, Patriotism, Trust

Reading
Bernard Williams, 'Persons, Character and Morality' in *Moral Luck* (Cambridge University Press, 1981)

Luck

In March 2014, Tan Bee Jeok, a flight attendant for Malaysia Airlines, switched her shifts. Cabin crew do this all the time, but on this occasion it meant that she avoided working on flight MH370, the plane that subsequently disappeared somewhere over the South China Sea, never to be recovered. Four months later, a change of shift by her husband and colleague Sanjid Singh put him on flight MH17, which was shot down by Russian-backed separatists over eastern Ukraine, killing everyone on board.

Each incident alone is a remarkable example of luck, good and bad respectively. However, for both to happen in the same family is an extraordinary coincidence, one that many feel is too extraordinary to be a coincidence.

Such extremes of fortune are rare. But we have all experienced both kinds of luck, and it's the bad variety that can be hard to take. We try as best we can and still don't get the career break or find the life partner we crave. We happen to be in the wrong place at the wrong time and catch a nasty disease, or have a life-changing accident. We think we've found the home we wanted, only for the neighbour from hell to move in next door.

However, many people struggle with the idea that events happen purely by accident. They find it comforting to think that everything happens for a reason and that luck is made, perhaps by ourselves.

Human beings have devised many ways of explaining away those offensively capricious occurrences. On the Indian subcontinent, most philosophical systems have for millennia embraced the idea of *karma*, which originally meant little more than the principle that actions have consequences. In the early Brahmanical tradition it referred mainly to the need to get rituals right in order for them to have the desired effects. Over time, it evolved into the idea that actions have consequences for the agent: good actions are repaid with good effects, bad actions with bad effects. In Buddhism, this expanded to include good and bad thoughts as well as deeds. Outside of India, many believe a less formal version of this, captured in the saying 'what goes around comes around'.

When a believer in *karma* describes someone as 'lucky', they mean that they are 'karmically gifted' and that their good fortune is the consequence of actions in a past life rather than their efforts in this one. This retains the idea that luck in the here and now is outside our control, while at the same time asserting that good or bad fortune is something we have earned.

One way of dealing with the fact that 'shit happens' is to argue that flourishing does not require good fortune. An early example of this in the Western tradition is Plato, who argued in two separate dialogues that 'no evil can happen to a good man' and that 'he who has wisdom has no need of luck'. His idea was that a person of perfect virtue placed no value on the kinds of things that fortune affected, such as bodily health or material wealth, and sought only wisdom, something the slings and arrows of fortune cannot scratch.

In the sixth century, a similar point of view found an advocate in Boethius. Living at the time the Roman Empire was crumbling, he spent much of his life involved in scholarly work. However, after venturing into politics, he fell into disfavour, was thrown into prison and was eventually executed. It was in prison that he wrote his masterpiece, *The Consolation of Philosophy*, a dialogue with a female personification of philosophy.

Boethius represents himself as grief-stricken, complaining that it is not fair for him to be deserted by the goddess Fortune, having lived justly all his life. He is particularly tormented by the memory of his past prosperity. Lady Philosophy reminds him that Fortune is fickle by her very nature. Boethius, she says, is paying the penalty for his mistaken expectations: 'dull-witted mortal, if Fortune begin to stay still, she is no longer Fortune.'

Lady Philosophy imagines Fortune defending herself and saying, 'I turn my wheel that spins its circle fairly; I delight to make the lowest turn to the top, the highest to the bottom. Come you to the top if you will, but on this condition, that you think it no unfairness to sink when the rule of my game demands it.'

So the first point is that there are things – wealth, honours, power, fame – that are ultimately the gift of Fortune. The wise know that these may be taken away at any time, so consider them a loan rather than something they rightfully own. But the even more important point Philosophy makes is that Boethius has not been deprived of anything valuable, as what is truly of value cannot be taken away: 'If . . . you are master of yourself, you will be in possession of that which you will never wish to lose, and which Fortune will never be able to take from you.'

This has strong echoes of the Stoic view that virtue is the only good and vice the only evil. All the other apparently good things that so many of us lust after are in Stoic jargon called 'preferred indifferents'. They include not only fame and riches, but also things like relationships, health and even life itself. These preferred indifferents are thought to be of limited value: it's fine to enjoy them if they happen to come our way, but we shouldn't compromise other values to get them or be unduly upset if we lose them.

This is an ennobling idea, but it is too rarefied for most. As Aristotle wrote, 'those who maintain that, provided he is good, a man is happy on the rack or surrounded by great disasters, are talking nonsense.'

In most discussions of luck, the focus is on what Thomas Nagel calls 'circumstantial luck', which refers to whether we find ourselves in good or bad life situations – living through a time of peace or war, or having the opportunity to have a good education. However, Nagel also draws attention to 'constitutive luck', which concerns the kind of person we are, with our particular inclinations and temperament, which is a combination of nature and nurture.

When you consider how much in life depends on circumstantial and constitutive luck, the disturbing possibility arises that even morality becomes a matter of luck. Whether you are able to act morally will depend on such things as your temperament, whether your upbringing nurtured your pro-social capacities and the situations you find yourself in. Someone who became a concentration camp guard in the Third Reich might fundamentally be no better or worse than someone who grew up in a peaceful society and was never tested. Many of us have driven while too tired or agitated, but it is those who end up causing an accident as a result that are judged to have behaved badly.

A realistic view of the role of luck should make us more willing to accept that chance plays a huge role in our lives. This should, in turn, make us more compassionate to ourselves and others, as we realise that the difference between a person who does something wrong and one who doesn't could just be luck.

If we are to take comfort from luck, it is perhaps by considering the outrageous improbability that our world even exists and that we were born into it. It is pure luck that we are here to listen to the birds, feel the warmth of the sun, sip wine. Set against that, most, if not all, of our misfortunes are a price worth paying.

See also: Calm, Control, Fate, Regret, Risk, Superstition, What If

Reading
Boethius, *The Consolation of Philosophy* (c. 523)
Thomas Nagel, 'Moral Luck' in *Mortal Questions* (Cambridge University Press, 2012)

Lying

'Sorry I missed the party – I wasn't feeling well.' 'That shirt suits you.' 'I'm so excited for you!' Few people will consider such lies to be anything other than sensible attempts to grease the wheels of social intercourse. But there are many other times when the decision to tell the truth or not carries a lot more moral weight. Do you say, 'You're going to be fine' to someone who is not likely to be? Do you keep a one-off infidelity secret? Do you report a colleague for inappropriate behaviour?

One of the few things we can be certain about is that anyone who says they have never lied is a liar – beyond that, it is all rather complicated. Immanuel Kant tried to strip away the complexities by asserting that 'To be truthful in all declarations is . . . a sacred command of reason prescribing unconditionally, one not to be restricted by any conveniences.' Honesty is an absolute duty, lying is never justified. Benjamin Constant, one of his contemporaries, saw the problem with that. He accused Kant of insisting that 'it would be a crime to lie to a murderer who asked us whether a friend of ours whom he is pursuing has taken refuge in our house'. Kant's reply has been picked apart by scholars ever since. Let's just say that he didn't unambiguously deny the accusation.

Assuming that most of us are not absolutist about lying, the question becomes: when are we permitted, or even obliged, to do it? The simple utilitarian answer is that lying is justified when it has better consequences than telling the truth. One of the founders of utilitarianism, John Stuart Mill, seemed to have Kant and Constant in mind when he gave an example of such a justified lie: 'when the withholding of some fact (as of information from a malefactor, or of bad news from a person dangerously ill) would save an individual (especially an individual other than oneself) from great and unmerited evil, and when the withholding can only be effected by denial.'

The problem with the utilitarian approach, as Mill recognised, is that it is of vital social importance that we trust people to be generally honest. If we know that people will lie whenever it seems to them that the consequences of doing so are good, the whole institution of truth-telling is undermined. 'Any, even unintentional, deviation from truth,' said Mill, 'does that much towards weakening the trustworthiness of human assertion, which is not only the principal support of all present social well-being, but the insufficiency of which does more than any one thing that can be named to keep back civilisation, virtue, everything on which human happiness on the largest scale depends.'

Confucius and Aristotle would have cheered Mill for this. They both believed that the key to being good is the cultivation of good character, and that includes being honest and trustworthy. 'They who know the truth are not equal to those who love it, and they who love it are not equal to those who delight in it,' said Confucius. The only way to become such a person is to practise honesty so that it becomes a habit, though not such a blind one that exceptions cannot be made. But if we become too utilitarian in our approach to lying, we cultivate a calculating approach to human interaction, which corrodes character.

But what principle can we appeal to when testing whether a lie is justified? Perhaps that of the ethics of care, which developed from the work of the psychologist Carol Gilligan. Gilligan argued that male-dominated Western moral philosophy has become characterised by rules and principles that conform to stereotypes of male rationality. It has neglected the virtues of care that are more associated with women, especially mothers, and so are assumed to be less important. The ethics of care claims that relationships, in particular those of caring and being cared for, are central to morality.

The ethics of care does not promote hard and fast rules, but it does suggest an important question to ask whenever contemplating a lie: what would be the most caring thing to do in this situation? To answer this requires careful and caring thought, as well as absolute honesty. Often we tell ourselves that we are helping someone by hiding the truth from them when we are really just making life easier for ourselves. We also have to be careful not to second-guess what is in another person's best interests. Genuine care means respecting their actual desires and values.

Care ethics also reminds us that one of the most corrosive effects of lying is the damage it can do to relationships. Being lied to can be extremely hurtful, even when the matter is not very serious. Lying not only breaks bonds of trust, it is often deeply patronising, as if implying that the person lying can handle the truth but the person lied to cannot.

A life without lies would be not only impossible but cruel; a life without the presumption of truth, however, would be even more intolerable. There are good reasons why moral theorists of all stripes promote the cultivation of honesty as a prime virtue and urge us to restrict lying to when the lie is either trivial and harmless or absolutely necessary.

See also: Habits, Infidelity, Loyalty, Right and Wrong, Trust, Truth

Reading

Carol Gilligan, *In a Different Voice: Psychological Theory and Women's Development* (Harvard University Press, 1982)
Alasdair MacIntyre, *Truthfulness, Lies, and Moral Philosophers: What Can We Learn from Mill and Kant?*, 'The Tanner Lectures on Human Values' (1994), available online at tannerlectures. utah.edu

M

'If one has a proper education, one never runs out of things to do.' Aubrey de Grey

Meaning

Viktor Frankl called the desire to find meaning in life a 'primary motivational force'. But in our darker moments it can feel like life has lost its meaning, and that all the activities we normally throw ourselves into with gusto have become drab and pointless. When meaning is absent, where can we find it? The search is especially difficult because the very words we use are unclear and confusing. What does it even *mean* for life to have meaning?

Many assume that meaning has an objective reality – maybe given by some God or divine creator – and provides a structure for the whole of humanity to live by. Most religions see themselves as offering such a universal true view. However, according to Frankl – and the vast majority of philosophers today – there is no such abstract meaning of life. But if that is the case, all roads seem to lead to nihilism. Doesn't it follow that nothing in life has value? And does that mean we're doomed to absurdity and despair?

Fortunately, the belief that life has no intrinsic meaning does not imply that nothing is truly of value. As Frankl puts it, meaning has to be discovered *within* the world. Each of us can have a full and meaningful life, in which we find many things valuable – work, relationships with loved ones, a passion for wild orchids, or just everyday enjoyment. This kind of meaning is personal and idiosyncratic: what gives meaning to your life may not be what gives meaning to mine.

Despite this variety, Frankl thought that the ways to find meaning in life fall under three general categories. The first is 'creating a work or a deed'. This does not necessarily mean producing a masterpiece or a best-selling novel, just creating or accomplishing something we value. The second is 'experiencing something or encountering someone'. This could be nature, art or music, or loving a person. The third is 'the attitude we take toward unavoidable suffering'. Frankl knew about this through his experience of being in Auschwitz. When all else fails, he tells us, we can find meaning by turning difficulties into opportunities to grow as a person.

When meaning is lost, we can look for it in these three areas. Think about what you most appreciate doing, or the people and places that nourish you, and you'll more than likely find sources of meaning. And even when nothing seems to be on the horizon, there is always the possibility of finding meaning by confronting suffering to build inner strength.

See also: Authenticity, Cosmic Insignificance, Purpose, Self-Actualisation

Reading
Viktor Frankl, *Man's Search for Meaning* (Beacon Press, 1946)

Melancholy

These days, it is unusual to hear people say they're feeling melancholy. It's more common to say we're 'low', or 'down', and we are often quick to reach for the word 'depressed'. We forget that words matter, and that how we describe our experience will affect how we feel. If we say we're depressed, we're by definition semi-diagnosing ourselves with a pathological condition, when we might just be feeling a bit sad or upset about something.

The varieties of feeling blue are more numerous than our default vocabulary allows. Kierkegaard drew a distinction between unhappiness and spiritual despair, for instance. He wrote, 'I am in the deepest sense an unhappy individual who, from my earliest years, has been nailed fast to one or another suffering that drove me to the brink of insanity.' The strange thing, he noted, was that this had 'no relation to my spirit, which on the contrary . . . has acquired a resilience that is rare'.

What is interesting about this is that Kierkegaard teased apart phenomena that are often lumped together, and that it might be useful to disaggregate. In his case, he thought it was possible to be psychologically unhappy and spiritually resilient at the same time. Taking this approach further, we could try to disentangle other concepts, such as unhappiness, sadness, melancholy and depression.

Just as we can be sad or unhappy without being depressed, maybe melancholy and depression needn't be yoked together. The word 'melancholy' comes from the ancient theory of humours, in which it referred to a psychological state of fear and sadness caused by an excess of black bile. But meanings change, and melancholy has been used in different ways at different times, sometimes merging with, sometimes diverging from depression – a word that has also undergone mutation. As Susan Sontag quipped, 'Depression is melancholy minus its charms.'

Melancholy and depression overlap, of course,. But the fundamental idea is that not all melancholy states are pathological. We could reclaim melancholy as a non-debilitating response to the world – a kind of existential unease, a sadness about the human condition and the inevitable suffering that life brings. Perhaps surprisingly, affirming this sentiment need not produce a disengagement with the world or interfere with our motivation, enjoyment and zest for life.

This is particularly the case when melancholy is associated with art, music and nature. Sad, moving music can be a joy to listen to. Most notably, in Japanese aesthetics the concept of *mono no aware* captures the heightened appreciation that comes from the awareness, inevitably tinged with sorrow, of the transience of everything. Understood in this way, as a bittersweet mood that evokes reflection and contemplation, melancholy can enrich rather than impoverish our experience.

See also: Gratitude, Perfectionism, Pain, Suffering

Reading
Søren Kierkegaard, *Papers and Journals: A Selection,* edited by
Alastair Hannay (Penguin, 1996)

Memory

It is a quaint accident of history that most of us carry around
with us something called a 'phone'. Telephone calls are
nowadays one of their least-used features. Perhaps a more
accurate name would be 'memory capture device'. Go to any
event or tourist sight and you will see people taking photos or
videos, sometimes with such intent that they spend more time
looking at the tiny screen than at what is actually around
them.

The acquisition of memories has overtaken the acquisition of things as the biggest growth market in capitalist
economies. A look at the prices of many festivals, detox retreats
and activity-based holidays such as sledging with huskies
shows how lucrative a sector this is.

There are very good reasons why we value memories so
much. They are a large part of what makes us, perhaps the
biggest part. John Locke argued that what makes you the
same person over time is not that you have the same body or
the same soul, but that you have the 'same consciousness'. This
is what allows a person to 'consider itself as itself, the same
thinking thing, in different times and places'. Memory is
essential for this. It is only because you can remember yourself
in different times and places in the past that you can think of
yourself as having the same consciousness over time, and
hence being the same person. If you have total amnesia, you
literally forget who you were.

Using technology to help us to remember can therefore
serve a valuable purpose. Andy Clark and David Chalmers

M

have argued that human beings have always used things outside their bodies to extend the functioning of their minds. Paper diaries, for instance, are ways of storing memories and plans outside the brain, and digital photos and videos can also be seen as ways of increasing our brains' storage capacity. It is not just computers but people who store things in 'the cloud'.

Many philosophers, however, have argued that although memory is necessary for personal identity, it is not sufficient. As Alasdair MacIntyre puts it, there also needs to be a 'narrative unity of human life': your memories and experiences have to fit together in a way that provides some coherent sense of an unfolding life story.

One important aspect of this view of identity is that we are, to some extent, the authors of our own narrative. It is up to us to make sense of our experiences and live our lives in such a way that when we look back on them, it is not just one thing after another.

The narrative view has its critics, but for most of us there is a ring of truth about it. That ring is an alarm bell for those who find themselves too busy simply acquiring memories. Filling up the memory bank creates a very simple personal narrative: 'I'm a person who has done lots of things.' Maybe that's enough. But often the richest and most meaningful lives involve projects and a sense of development.

Think of how the most powerful experiences tend to be located in an unfolding story. A concert by a great band may be fantastic, but it will mean more to someone who has followed the group and is deeply engaged with their work. Your Instagram post from a Michelin-starred restaurant may look impressive, but you won't fully appreciate the meal unless you are a discerning cook and diner.

Those endless snaps and selfies also create another problem. To get the most out of any moment, we have to be truly present in it. Paradoxically, if we try too hard to capture

219

an experience for posterity, we diminish its intensity and make it less memorable.

Also, the sheer volume of material we store outside our brains often makes memory retrieval almost impossible. We have so many photos that we never look at them. Meanwhile, we are in danger of so under-using our organic memory circuits that they atrophy from neglect.

Experiences may have replaced goods as the object of our spending in the late capitalist economy, but we still risk replicating the old consumerist mistake of thinking that more always means better. To create a satisfying narrative of our own lives, we need to curate our memories more carefully and locate them in a story of ourselves that makes them enduringly meaningful, not just fleetingly 'awesome'.

See also: Achievement, Carpe Diem, Consumerism, Identity, Pleasure

Reading
Julian Baggini, *The Ego Trick* (Granta, 2011)

Mental Health

Awareness of mental health has been increasing rapidly recently. You will probably have heard that one in four people will experience a mental health problem every year. But greater awareness is not the same as deeper understanding, and there are reasons to think that the idea of mental health is not as clear as the bold statistical claims would suggest.

The current common-sense view is that mental disorders are as real, objective and categorisable as physical ones. But this has been questioned. According to Thomas Szasz, the concept of mental illness differs fundamentally from that of physical illness. Physical illness involves a 'deviation from the clearly defined norms of the structural and functional integrity of the body'. We know what it means for a heart to work properly and so also know that something is wrong when it doesn't. The idea of mental illness, on the other hand, is measured against 'ethical, legal and social' standards, and is therefore inevitably based on value judgements. This line of thinking led Szasz to conclude that mental illness is a myth.

Others, like the psychiatrist and philosopher Bill Fulford, have argued that *both* physical and mental illness are value-laden. Fulford illustrates this with reference to the work of R.M. Hare, according to whom value terms have a descriptive and an evaluative component. For instance, a good strawberry (evaluation) is one that satisfies certain criteria, like being sweet and maggot-free (description).

The crucial point is that when evaluations are largely shared – like in the case of the strawberry – they come to appear descriptive. Whether you like strawberries or not, it seems clear what a good one should be like. If there is a lot of disagreement, however, our judgements remain more obviously value-laden, as in the case of 'a good painting'.

According to Fulford, the same applies to health and illness. The reason why physical health seems relatively objective and straightforward is that there is more agreement about what satisfactory functioning looks like. But this masks the fact that value judgements are still being made. Hence some deaf people, for example, argue that deafness is not a disability but merely a way of being differently abled.

In the case of mental health, there are more diverse views about standards of normality and what should be considered problematic, so it remains more obviously value-laden. This is why, Fulford says, there is an anti-psychiatry movement but not an anti-cardiology one.

According to current practice, psychiatric diagnoses are based on objective descriptions of symptoms. However, insofar as they contain implicit judgements about standards of normality, they are evaluative and not merely descriptive. The World Health Organization, for instance, says that mental disorders are generally 'characterised by some combination of *abnormal* thoughts, emotions, behaviour and relationships with others' (our italics).

But our ideas of what is normal change, and with them so do our positive and negative judgements. It wasn't until 1973 that the American Psychiatric Association removed homosexuality from its list of mental disorders. There is currently a lot of talk of 'neurodiversity', with Asperger's syndrome and the hearing of voices being seen not as pathologies but as ways of being different.

Despite the dissimilarities between the problems of body and mind, we can talk about physical and mental health using the same word because they share what Wittgenstein called a 'family resemblance'. But while it can be useful to draw attention to the common features, we should not allow these to obscure the differences.

This matters because how we think about these issues will affect how we relate to our own and other people's mental health, in a helpful or unhelpful way. Of course, if you're experiencing some kind of mental health issue you should recognise it as a problem and seek help. But we should avoid making too many assumptions about what is normal. Let's remember that it's possible to flourish in ways that depart from common standards. Wittgenstein seems to have been a troubled soul in many ways, but while perhaps not a textbook example of mental health, he had a deeply meaningful life, which he described as 'wonderful' on his deathbed.

The World Health Organization defines mental health as 'a state of well-being in which every individual realises his or her own potential, can cope with the normal stresses of life, can work productively and fruitfully, and is able to make a contribution to her or his community'. This is fine as an ideal to aspire to, but if this is full mental health then hardly anyone is completely healthy. Avoiding unrealistic standards is good for your mental well-being.

See also: Anxiety, Health and Illness, Melancholy, Stress

Reading
Thomas Szasz, *The Myth of Mental Illness* (Harper, 1961)

Midlife Crisis

The signs are diverse: some leave their apparently happy families, some get their first tattoo, some head to India for a spiritual retreat, others splash out on a Harley Davidson. The cause is called a 'midlife crisis', and it can take various forms. We may wake up to find that the things we had previously valued and maybe vigorously pursued suddenly seem worthless, like when people dedicate themselves to a career only to realise years later that it had not given their life meaning. Or projects that were once valuable come to an end and we're left asking, 'Now what?'

The term 'midlife crisis' misidentifies the problem, since not everyone in midlife has a crisis, not every such crisis comes in midlife and it is not always as strong as a crisis. It is, however, common to go through a phase in which we become unsettled and start questioning our values and lifestyle.

Kieran Setiya, the author of *Midlife*, has mined philosophy for help in getting through such a period. He draws a useful distinction between things and activities that have *existential* value and those that have merely *ameliorative* value. The latter are maintenance tasks that just have to be done, like taking the cat to the vet, paying the bills, or mowing the lawn. When we have settled down in a routine, which is typical of middle age, life sometimes seems to become just one long list of these. It's not that they have no value at all. But what is missing, writes Setiya, are activities that are valuable in themselves:

they have what he calls 'existential value'. Part of the solution to a midlife crisis can be to identify what these are for you and make more time for them.

Another point to consider is that things that are meaningful at one stage of life can become irrelevant in another, and vice versa. Plato, for instance, believed that people should not start studying philosophy until they had acquired some experience and maturity. In Hinduism there are traditionally four ideal stages of life: studying, raising a family, gradually withdrawing from the world and renunciation.

Life can be a bit like the old Eric Morecambe joke about playing all the right notes but not necessarily in the right order. There might be nothing wrong with our life in itself, but maybe we haven't moved on from an earlier stage, or have settled into a later one too soon. We are all different, and we should not be too prescriptive about what is appropriate for what phase of life. But another route to avoiding a midlife crisis (or any other life-stage crisis, for that matter) is to keep evolving our goals and interests so that they are appropriate for wherever we are in our lives.

See also: Achievement, Ageing, Boredom, Carpe Diem, Inner Life, Leisure, Meaning, Retirement, Routine

Reading
Kieran Setiya, *Midlife: A Philosophical Guide* (Princeton University Press, 2017)

Mindfulness

Mindfulness is the not-so-latest-by-now big thing, touted as the means to health, wealth, calm, happiness, peak performance, success and pretty much every other worldly goal you can think of. That's ironic, considering that it began as a spiritual practice to aid detachment from temporal concerns.

This ersatz meditation has been called 'McMindfulness' to draw attention to how it has been co-opted by corporate and economic interests.

That's not to say mindfulness should only be of interest to card-carrying Buddhists who embrace its metaphysical goal of ending the cycle of rebirth. Nor does it mean that there is no value in adopting secular mindfulness techniques for practical goals, and it is certainly good to cultivate more mindful attention in daily life. However, if you limit mindfulness to these uses you might miss one of its most important aspects.

Let's start with the Buddha, where it all began. The word 'mindfulness' is the common translation of the Pali word *sati*, which in the early Buddhist texts refers primarily to holding one's attention on a meditative practice, be it observing one's experience, developing an attitude of benevolence or reflecting on death.

In the normal course of events we are not so mindful, which means that we automatically react to things around us, running after what appears good and trying to get away from what appears bad, without the mental space to reflect on whether our impressions are correct or what we're doing is advisable.

Through the practice of mindfulness – in other words, by paying close attention to our experience – we can begin to create a gap between our never-ending urges and our behaviour. In the early Buddhist texts mindfulness is likened, among other things, to a cowherd keeping an eye on his cows from the distance and to a gatekeeper monitoring who enters a town.

The Stoics had similar analogies about attention. Epictetus, for instance, said that the philosopher 'keeps watch over himself as over an enemy in ambush', and that 'we should be satisfied if, by never relaxing our attention, we shall escape at least a few errors.' As in Buddhism, becoming more aware of the desires and aversions that normally shape and even rule our conduct makes us better able to avoid being enslaved by them and to choose a wiser course of action instead.

For both schools of thought, becoming more mindful means being able to catch our impressions of good and bad as soon as they occur, which gives us the chance to question the values implicit in our desires. Then we can spot when we are being moved to action by greed, envy, insecurity or any other impulse that on reflection we would not endorse. If we develop mindfulness we create the space for a reasoned response instead of being unthinkingly shunted into habitual behaviour patterns. Whether or not we choose to take up formal meditation, mindfulness is what we need if we want to be more reflective and autonomous.

See also: Busyness, Calm, Desires, Inner Life, Self-Control, Silence, Slowing Down

Reading
Antonia Macaro, *More than Happiness* (Icon, 2018)

Mistakes

We all make mistakes. But the standard hackneyed advice about how to deal with them is not very helpful. Some of it is true but trite. Most obviously, of course, you should try to learn from your mistakes. But did anyone ever err and then think, 'nothing worth remembering here'? Some other saws are misguided. It is foolish to insist that we can learn only from our own mistakes. Sensible folk learn as much as they can from observing others go awry, which is one reason why it's still worth reading philosophers whom history has judged to have been wrong.

When mistakes can't be undone (*See* **Regret**), any lessons learned from them can seem like too little, too late. It can also be harder than folk wisdom suggests to work out what the lesson is. Many mistakes seem clear enough: we had a wrong view or made a wrong judgement, for instance, and in hindsight we see what the correct one was. But our biggest mistakes tend to be rooted in something more than an isolated belief.

Also, when we go badly wrong, it is often not so much *what* we think as *how* we think that is misguided. Consider for example Gilbert Ryle's now classic idea of the 'category mistake'. He tells the story of some tourists who ask to be shown Oxford University and are taken to the colleges, the Bodleian Library, the Sheldonian Theatre, the Ashmolean Museum and so on. The bemused tourists then ask, 'But where is the university?' They haven't realised that the university is not a single building or campus but an institution spread over several sites. They have been thinking of 'the university' as one kind of thing, whereas it is entirely another.

Ryle defined category mistakes in a technical, narrow way, but the concept illustrates the broader kind of error of mistaking one kind of thing for quite another. A lot of our failures to see the true nature of a problem are like this. For instance, we think we're working for the wrong company but we're actually in the wrong job; or we think we're doing the wrong job when we're simply working for the wrong company. Or we think the problem is not working hard enough when it's really a lack of talent, or vice versa.

Mistakes about other people often also involve wrong categorisations. We might not understand why someone is religious, for example, because we think they are wedded to beliefs we find wacky when really it's a matter of belonging to a community and living a certain way of life: we've confused commitment to a community with commitment to a belief. Or we might think someone is being off with us when they are simply reserved with everyone, confusing the way someone reacts to us specifically with how they react to people in general.

Once we become alert to how easy it is to make such mistakes, we can get better at spotting them before they lead us to make practical errors. One clue is bafflement: if we can't even make sense of what's going on, we're probably thinking about it in the wrong way. Another clue is persistence: if a problem remains despite repeated attempts to solve it, perhaps we haven't understood what the real issue is. Often our biggest mistake is to take it for granted that we know what the problem is when we should be questioning how we understand it.

See also: Dilemmas, Forgiveness, Guilt and Shame, Luck, Regret, Resilience

Reading
Gilbert Ryle, *The Concept of Mind* (University of Chicago Press, 1949)

Moderation *see* Balance

Money *see* Wealth

Monogamy

The desirability of monogamy is the great unsettled question of the sexual revolution. In the heyday of free love, people were clear that to restrict yourself to sex with just one person was not groovy. As time passed, monogamy rehabilitated itself in an altered form. Lifelong monogamy has been widely rejected, but serial monogamy has become the new social norm. Recently, however, free love has made something of a comeback in the form of polyamory: the idea that consenting adults should not be confined to one sexual partner at a time. So is monogamy for squares?

Carrie Ichikawa Jenkins would not go that far, but she does believe that society is overwhelmingly and unjustifiably 'mononormative', meaning that it assumes a person can be seriously in love with only one other person at a time. She does not promote polyamory as superior to monogamy but simply argues that it is a reasonable lifestyle, one that she and her husband Jonathan Jenkins Ichikawa have embraced.

To make this case, Ichikawa and Jenkins have to rebut objections to polyamory. One is that it is bad for sexual health. They retort that 'considered and ethical non-monogamy is likely to be a substantially better option health-wise than the frustrated drunken flings, clandestine affairs or otherwise ill-considered hook-ups that are the fate of many of those who attempt monogamy despite not being well suited to it and eventually fail in the attempt.'

Another is that 'Non-monogamy is inevitably psychologically damaging. Sexual jealousy is unmanageable, always and for everyone, so all non-monogamous relationships eventually suffer and break down.' Their response to this is that it is too much of a generalisation. They also point out that jealousy is a big factor in a lot of monogamous relationships.

Ichikawa and Jenkins say that many people object to polyamory on the basis that it is not natural, but in many countries a majority now believe that it is monogamy that is unnatural. Opinion is divided. According to a major UK survey, 41 per cent believe that humans are naturally monogamous and 39 per cent think we are not. But what is or is not natural is beside the moral point. Contraception, Viagra and sex toys are not natural, but people don't see that as a reason not to use them. Sex is at root an animal instinct, but so is the desire to punch someone in the face. It is not high-minded to believe that we should not allow our behaviour to be shaped by raw feeling alone.

Many certainly find monogamy difficult. One reason for this is that, as Bertrand Russell put it, 'sooner or later sexual familiarity dulls the edge of passion'. The monotony of monogamy gets to almost everyone in the end. But many worthwhile things are difficult. Many people choose monogamy knowing that there is a trade-off in terms of sexual excitement. It's simply that they value the tender intimacy of a long-term partner over the more intense thrill of sex with someone they have less of a bond with.

To ask which of monogamy or polyamory is the right or best choice for all human beings seems misguided. It is much more individual than that. It's a question of honestly assessing our own situation, including our assumptions. In some cases this might mean challenging a mononormative default position; in others it means checking whether it is wishful thinking, and the desire to have our cake and eat it, that makes us believe we can adopt the complications of poly-amory without paying too high a price. Whatever conclusion we come to, the key moral priority in any intimate relationship is that we are honest, trusting and trustworthy with our partners, no matter how many we have.

See also: Human Nature, Jealousy, Love, Relationships, Sex

Reading
Carrie Jenkins, *What Love Is: And What It Could Be* (Basic Books, 2017)
Bertrand Russell, *Marriage and Morals* (George Allen & Unwin, 1929)

Moods

Reading Heidegger is enough to put many people in a foul mood. Simon Blackburn called him a 'dismal windbag', while Rudolf Carnap accused him of writing 'nonsensical pseudo-propositions'. His work is certainly difficult, but whatever you think of it there are elements worth extricating, including his original analysis of moods.

For Heidegger, a mood is not a subjective mental state in the way we normally think of emotions like anger or joy. Moods emerge from our engagement with the world, and since this is constant, 'we are never free of moods'. Hence a mood 'comes neither from "outside" nor from "inside", but arises out of Being-in-the world.' Moods provide the background of our experience and so even the 'pallid lack of mood which dominates the "grey everyday" through and through' is still a mood.

These moods act as filters on our perception of the world, changing how it 'discloses itself to us' differently at different times. If we are bored, say, we might notice certain features and filter out others. The German term for 'mood' is related to the tuning of musical instruments, conveying this sense of tuning into the world in particular ways.

A mood discloses some things but occludes others. When we're happy, the world reveals itself to us in an upbeat light, and at that time we are disconnected from what is apparent in a gloomier vision; if the world is revealing itself to us in its gloomy features, the opposite is true. There are different modes of experiencing the world, and the mood we're currently in is just one.

Although we tend to think of moods as being outside of our control, Heidegger argued that we are not passive before them. He writes that we 'can, should, and must' master them. Since we are always in some mood or other, he suggests that 'when we master a mood, we do so by way of a counter-mood'. We can dislodge one mood only by tuning into another one. So when you notice that you are in an unhelpful mood, you can try to see the world through another filter and attend to what your current mood is blanking out. When you do that, the world reveals itself differently and your mood changes with it.

See also: Emotions, Melancholy, Self-Control

Reading
Martin Heidegger, *Being and Time* (1927)

Mortality

'Why was I born if it wasn't forever?' cries the eponymous protagonist in Eugène Ionesco's *Exit the King*. He is far from alone in finding it difficult to come to terms with mortality. Is there any good answer to his desperate question?

Some philosophers have argued that there is nothing to worry about, because we are not mortal after all. For example, Socrates was cheerful when facing his own execution because, according to Plato, he believed that at death the soul is released 'from the chains of the body' and 'departs to the invisible world, to the divine and immortal and rational'. (*See* **Afterlife**.)

The majority of Indian philosophies also teach that death is not the end for the true self. What we think of as individual selves are in reality part of *Brahman*, the universal self. It is to this that we return once we have escaped the cycle of death and rebirth.

While most philosophers have been less sanguine about our post-mortem prospects, today a number of them believe that immortality, or something close to it, is within our grasp. These 'transhumanists' believe that with the aid of technology we can overcome our fleshy limitations and either extend our lives indefinitely or upload ourselves into virtual realities, where we will live invulnerable to the perils of the physical world.

Transhumanists reject the idea that we should come to terms with our mortality. On the contrary, they think that mortality is dreadful and we should fight it tooth and nail. 'Searching for a cure for ageing is not just a nice thing that we should perhaps one day get around to,' says Nick Bostrom, one of their leading lights. 'It is an urgent, screaming moral imperative.'

If you don't agree with Plato that immortality is our natural state, or with Bostrom that it is an unnatural one we are likely to achieve soon, you could persuade yourself that immortality is an undesirable goal anyway. Bernard Williams argued this in an essay about the Karel Čapek play *The Makropulos Case*, later adapted into an opera by Janáček. The protagonist is a woman who has found an elixir of life and is now aged 342. 'Her unending life has come to a state of boredom, indifference and coldness,' says Williams. She comes to see immortality not as a blessing but a curse, and chooses to stop taking the elixir and die.

Williams does not conclude that mortality should lose all its sting. The desire to live is strong and 'so long as it remains so, I shall not want to die.' But it is also true 'that an eternal life would be unliveable'. Mortality is not ideal, but it is better than the alternative.

Not everyone is convinced. 'It's pathetic, isn't it?' says Aubrey de Grey, a gerontologist who is trying to find a 'cure' for ageing. 'If one has a proper education, one never runs out of things to do. I've got at least a 1,000-year backlog already of things I haven't done and by the time I'm through it I'll have at least another 1,000.'

Whether you side with Williams or de Grey, for the foreseeable future there is little choice but to try to come to terms with mortality as best you can. One way to do this is to remind yourself that the gift of life and the price of mortality cannot be separated: life just *is* ever-changing and impermanent, a cycle of growth and decay.

East Asian philosophies tend to emphasise this. A typical passage in the Daoist text the *Zhuangzi*, for example, says, 'Life is a loan with which the borrower does but add more dust and dirt to the sum total of existence. Life and death are as day and night; and while you and I stand gazing at the evidences of mortality around us, if the same mortality overtakes me, why should I loathe it?'

It's easy to nod at the wisdom of such sentiments. Even so, like Ionesco's king, most of us will be less than completely reassured by the comforting words usually offered to the mortal. 'You are inscribed forever in the annals of the Universe,' one tells him, promising a different kind of immortality. 'Who's going to look up the archives?' replies the king. His queen counsels that 'life is exile', a brief break from the natural state of non-existence. The king is unmoved: 'But I like being in exile.'

Ionesco himself did not believe that the philosophy in his play could help people to come to terms with mortality. 'Humanity has never been satisfied with reality such as it is,' he said. 'I wrote this play to learn how to die, but I haven't succeeded.' We can accept our mortality to a certain degree, but that does not require us to be cheerful about it.

See also: Afterlife, Ageing, Bereavement, Carpe Diem, Cosmic Insignificance, Death, Love of Life, Virtual Life

Reading
Bernard Williams, 'The Makropulos Case' in *Problems of the Self* (Cambridge University Press, 1973), pp. 82–100

Motivation

You want to learn to speak Hungarian, run a marathon or redecorate the kitchen, but somehow you never quite get round to it. Perhaps the problem is weakness of will. (*See* **Self-Control**.) Or maybe it's more honest to admit that you're just not motivated enough.

Motivation is a curious thing. Plato argued that if you believe that something is good, you will automatically be motivated to do it. Hence he was forced to conclude that it is impossible to know what's good and not do it.

Plato had too simplistic an idea about how the human mind works. Nowadays we'd be more likely to accept that our desires and beliefs are often contradictory and engage in ongoing internal battles for supremacy. To understand what is going on when motivation is lacking, we need to examine how these tussles are playing out.

The first question to ask is: do I really want to do the thing I say I want to do? Could it be that we say 'I want to' when we really mean 'I *think* I ought to', because that's what everyone says, even though we don't agree? Perhaps the reason I'm not motivated to train for a career is that I'm not convinced it would make my life better, even if it improved my job prospects.

If you remain convinced that the desire is real, the next question is: do I have other competing desires that are incompatible? I may genuinely want to learn Hungarian, but also want to sit down and relax in the little spare time I have. When a motivation meets an equal (or stronger) but opposing one, the most likely consequence is inaction.

A third question is: am I motivated by the goal itself or by something for which it is a means to an end? We find some things intrinsically motivating, meaning we want to do them for their own sake. But much of what we're motivated to do is not like that. I don't want to drink less, I want to be healthier, and cutting down on alcohol is just a means to that end. If we want to act in such cases, we need to keep reminding ourselves what our ultimate motivation is.

One last question is: am I really motivated to do what it takes to achieve what I want? Kant claimed that 'to will the end is to will the means': if you really want something, you have to be committed to doing what it takes to get it. If you love the idea of crossing the marathon finishing line but can't be bothered to train, it is questionable whether your motivation is genuine.

When we ask these questions, we often find that we are not as motivated as we thought we were. If we still decide that, on balance, we do want to act, we have to find ways of turning that desire into action. One way to do this is to harness whatever *truly* motivates us to supercharge that for which motivation is weak. Ultimately, the motivation that works has to be rooted in the end you desire, not the means to it.

See also: Ambivalence, Commitment, Desires, Dilemmas, Indecision, Perseverance, Self-Control, Self-Knowledge, Values

Reading
Antonia Macaro, *Reason, Virtue and Psychotherapy* (Wiley-Blackwell, 2006)

N

<blockquote>'When all is said and done,
we cannot rise above nature.'
Soga Ryojin</blockquote>

Narcissism *see* Self-Love

Nature

When Spinoza argued in seventeenth-century Amsterdam that God and nature were one and the same thing, he was branded an atheist. In today's secularised world, nature is the closest thing many have to a deity – we even use the name of a goddess, Gaia, to refer to the world we fear we are destroying. Communing with this goddess is also presented as a path to a kind of salvation. Studies tell us that being out in nature is good for our physical and mental health, and many find it deeply moving to feel a connection with forests, animals, mountains and rivers. The words 'biophilia' and 'ecophilia' have been coined to name our love for such places.

And yet the very way we think about 'nature' in the developed world suggests that we are more profoundly alienated from it than we feared. The 'nature' we typically seek is found not in towns and cities but in places where buildings are absent and people invisible. 'Natural' and 'human' have become almost opposites: the less humans have intervened, the more natural we believe a place, food or health product is. Of course there is a distinction between the human and the non-human, but this is not to be confused with the division between the natural and the non-natural.

The Norwegian Arne Næss argued that it was a mistake to 'try to trace a border between the self and "its" geographical surroundings'. An essential feature of ecological thinking is 'the insistence that things cannot be separated from what surrounds them without smaller or greater arbitrariness'. For Næss, every part of nature – human and non-human – has value and importance. He talks about the 'ecosphere' to refer to 'rivers (watersheds), landscapes, cultures, ecosystems, "the living earth"'.

The interconnectedness of all nature is prominent in many non-Western philosophies. David Mowaljarlai, a Ngarinyin from Western Australia, uses the term 'pattern thinking' to describe a common aboriginal way of relating everything in the natural world to everything else. This is why Deborah Bird Rose says that aboriginal understandings 'incorporate a non-human-being-centred view of the world, which also tends to be an ecological one. "Man" is just one living being among plants, animals, even the inanimate environment – all are kin.'

If we think of nature in this way, we lose the romantic sense of it as somehow other but we gain more of a sense of its omnipresence. The British landscape, for example, is almost all a result of human intervention, but that does not make its lush greenery any less natural. We can become more attuned to the workings of nature all around us: the changing weather, pot plants and even electricity, the incredible force of nature that powers our homes.

That is why the Japanese love of nature is compatible with their technophilia. People are often sceptical about Japan's supposed reverence for nature when modern cities like Tokyo seem so alienated from it. But as the twentieth-century Japanese philosopher Soga Ryojin puts it, 'When all is said and done, we cannot rise above nature.' In Japanese thought, such an elevation is inconceivable, as is the elevation of nature above the human. Everything is at the same level – cities and machines are as much a part of nature as anything else. The true opposite of 'natural' is not 'artificial', but 'supernatural'.

The separation of nature and the human is probably a hangover from a religious worldview in which God and our immortal souls belong to a higher plane than the material world. Overcoming this is important for how we think about the current environmental crisis. Despite the efforts of many well-intentioned theologians to update the Christian message, our culture has been shaped by a creation myth in which God gave humankind dominion over nature. The legacy of this is that the environment has been seen as a resource like any other.

Næss's 'deep ecology' counters that the environment has its own intrinsic value, independent of human interests. He defined deep ecology's first principle as 'the flourishing of human and non-human life has inherent value. The value of non-human life forms is independent of the usefulness of the non-human world for human purposes.'

To say that nature has its own value, however, is not to say that it is entirely good. No culture that is close to nature takes such a rose-tinted view. In Japan, a land of typhoons, earthquakes and tsunamis, there can be no illusion that 'natural' means 'good'. Nature is neither good nor bad but indifferent. It brings life and death, pain and pleasure, health and illness, without any concern for how they are distributed.

To see nature as either better than us or something we have dominion over is to make the mistake of seeing it as something *other* to us. It is rather something to which human beings inextricably belong – as the Maori of New Zealand say, 'I am the river and the river is me'. We should not be asking what we can do for the environment, but what we can do as parts of the environment to make sure we flourish together. If we don't, it will be us who perish. Gaia will survive.

See also: Cosmic Insignificance, Human Nature

Reading
Arne Næss, *Ecology of Wisdom* (Penguin Classics, 2016)

Needs

We use the word 'need' often and loosely in daily life: we 'need' more money, a new coat, a holiday or a drink. Sometimes we are vaguely aware of a distinction between what we *need* and what we *want*, but we don't normally question whether our needs are genuine, or what would happen if they weren't fulfilled.

What *do* we need? The question is more complex than it looks. It's easy enough to say what we need in relation to a particular goal: in order to become a doctor I need to get a medical degree, in order to buy a house I need to acquire a sufficient amount of money. But what do we all need as human beings regardless of our specific goals? Beyond food, drink and oxygen to stay alive, it all becomes much more complicated. Are there universal basic needs that have to be fulfilled if we are to lead a good life?

Many lists of basic needs have been proposed, and although they vary, they typically include physiological needs, safety, social affiliation, respect and autonomy. One such list has recently been put together by the economist Robert Skidelsky and his son Edward, a philosopher. They use the term 'basic goods' to refer to things they consider the '*sine qua non* of a decent human existence' – if we come to lack one of them, our quality of life will be impaired.

The Skidelskys include all the usual elements in some form, with the idiosyncratic addition of leisure and harmony with nature. They acknowledge that the inclusion of the latter is controversial, but they believe it is essential to have some sense of connection with animals, plants and landscapes, especially when so many of us live in cities and can easily become alienated from our rural surroundings.

As for leisure, it seems counterintuitive to see this as a need when it is understood as rest and relaxation. But the Skidelskys' definition is close to that of the Greek philosophers, who understood leisure as any activity undertaken for its own sake. (*See* **Leisure**.)

The Skidelskys acknowledge that there can be much individual and cultural variation. As Emrys Westacott reminds us, what people consider necessary 'varies according to time, place, and social class. These concepts are relative. A normal lifestyle for an Athenian citizen in Diogenes's day required far fewer accoutrements than are needed by a twenty-first-century New Yorker.'

Even basic needs are not set in stone: some people might choose to reject one or more of the above-mentioned goods altogether. Some philosophies challenge our common-sense perception of what is necessary for a good human life. An extreme example of this is asceticism. Some of the ascetics active at the time of the Buddha, for instance, were strict to the point of not allowing themselves even the basics needed for survival. (*See* **Asceticism**.)

Separating our needs from our wants turns out to be a tricky business. Most of the time, when we feel we need something, it's more a case of really, really wanting it. It's easy enough to see that we don't need a fur coat or gold-plated door handles. Conversely, some things really *are* essential to functioning, such as a wheelchair for a person with paraplegia. But what about a car? It may not be a need in a city, but what if you live in an isolated rural environment? Or what about a smartphone? There are farmers in developing countries who now rely on one to get their goods to market at the right time and for a fair price.

Maybe it would be best to get away from the binary choice between needs and wants. It's more of a spectrum: at one end there is a tiny number of absolute needs (food, water, shelter, oxygen); at the other are completely optional wants. In between there are all sorts of gradations – from things that really matter for a flourishing life to items that might be nice to have but are not indispensable.

If we think in these terms, it is not a matter of deciding what is a need and what is a want but of challenging our tendency to assume we have more needs than we do. The Skidelskys write that while needs are finite and objective, 'wants, being purely psychic, are infinitely expandable, as to both quantity and quality.' We end up feeling that we must have what our neighbours have, or what advertisers want us to want. More is never enough. The best way to counter that dissatisfaction is to question how much we really need in the first place.

See also: Asceticism, Consumerism, Contentment, Desires, Leisure, Simplicity, Wealth

Reading
Robert Skidelsky and Edward Skidelsky, *How Much is Enough?* (Penguin, 2012)
Emrys Westacott, *The Wisdom of Frugality* (Princeton University Press, 2016)

Neighbours *see* Other People

Noise
Trucks thundering by, neighbours' loud music and arguments, washing machines, drilling, air conditioning units, mysterious hums – with so many and diverse sources of noise, quiet is hard to find in our crowded towns and appliance-filled homes. We are so used to noise that we might even find the rare moments of silence spooky and switch on the radio or television even if we're not listening. It's easy enough to break the silence, but what can we do when we're plagued by noise we can't switch off?

Seneca addressed the problem of noise in one of his letters. Lodging above a bathhouse, he was exposed to 'every sort of awful noise that grates on the ears': the grunts of the men doing their training, ballgames, someone singing in the bath chamber, the screeches of the tweezer man ('he is never silent unless he is plucking someone's armpits and making him cry instead'), 'the cries of the drink man, the sausage man, the bakery man, and all the different sellers of cooked food', and so on.

As a good Stoic, Seneca explains that it's not the noise itself that is the problem, as real tranquillity has to come from inside ourselves. 'How does it help to have silence in the neighbourhood, when one's emotions are in tumult?' So, he writes, 'I force my mind to pay attention to itself and not to be distracted by anything external. It does not matter what is making a noise outside, so long as there is no turmoil inside.'

If we wanted to take his advice, we'd have to work on our reaction to noise. Instead of wallowing in the thought that this is awful and should not be happening, and blaming the neighbours, we could be mindful of these feelings of irritation and choose to focus on something more important. We might try to remember that 'noise' is any sound we find problematic, so if we don't allow it to irritate us it simply becomes another background sound.

Even Seneca acknowledges this is easier said than done. He unexpectedly concludes that it's 'easier sometimes to be away from the racket' and so he will be leaving his lodgings.

There's no reason not to go for the common-sense solution if it's available. But sometimes it isn't. Seneca is quite right that peacefulness begins within, so the skill of managing our reactions to daily irritants is well worth developing, even if you'd have to be a saint to find the tremors of the neighbour's sub-woofer no more irritating than the chirp of the song thrush.

See also: Calm, Frustration, Other People, Tolerance

Reading
Seneca, 'Letter 56'

O

'Act that you treat humanity,
whether in your own person or
in the person of any other,
always at the same time as an
end, never merely as a means.'
Immanuel Kant

Objectification

You might think 'objectification' is a recent, feminist concept. The classic statement of its core principle, however, comes from the eighteenth-century pen of Immanuel Kant: 'act that you treat humanity, whether in your own person or in the person of any other, always at the same time as an end, never merely as a means.' When we break this rule, we treat people as mere tools for our purposes, turning them into objects rather than subjects.

Transactional relationships, such as ordering a coffee from a waiter, are of course fine as long as we don't deny people their agency and fundamental humanity. The injunction is about not treating people *merely* as a means.

The implications of this are particularly thorny in the sphere of sexual relationships. In his lecture 'Duties towards the Body in Respect of Sexual Impulse', Kant says that pure sexual desire makes the other person just an object of one's own appetite, ignoring their humanity, needs and wants. 'As soon as that appetite has been satisfied, the person is cast aside as one casts away a lemon which has been sucked dry.'

This made him oppose any arrangement that reduces sex to a transaction. He was against prostitution because 'Human beings are . . . not entitled to offer themselves, for profit, as things for the use of others in the satisfaction of their sexual propensities'. If we do this, we sacrifice our humanity. His objection is not just to the exchange of money. 'Concubinage', in which no profit is involved, is also inadmissible, as one person is still treated as a thing and 'the rights of the two parties are not equal'.

According to Kant, the sexual impulse can be properly satisfied only in marriage. This is because in the context of a committed relationship sexual desire goes hand in hand with affection, and 'one devotes not only sex but the whole person' to the other in a reciprocal arrangement. Kant's view on this seems both idealistic and overly restrictive, since wedlock is not the only context in which sex can be a genuine relationship between equals. But the basic principle survives being updated for a more liberal age.

That is why many contemporary feminist thinkers have agreed with the essence of Kant's argument, while rejecting his traditional family values. Andrea Dworkin, for example, sounds very Kantian when she writes, 'Objectification occurs when a human being, through social means, is made less than human, turned into a thing or commodity, bought and sold.' Most feminists, however, view the phenomenon of objectification as much more pervasive in patriarchal societies than Kant realised.

Some argue that we are entitled to make ourselves objects for others as long as we do so voluntarily. Kant disagreed, claiming that 'a man is not at his own disposal.' In the sexual domain, he argued, 'to allow one's person for profit to be used by another for the satisfaction of sexual desire, to make of oneself an object of demand, is to dispose over oneself as over a thing and to make of oneself a thing on which another satisfies his appetite, just as he satisfies his hunger upon a steak.'

In the contemporary feminist debate, whether women can ever genuinely consent to being objectified is a key question. Borrowing Marx's concept of 'false consciousness', it is argued that a woman may believe she is expressing her will by dressing to impress, but this is only because she has internalised patriarchal values that she would not endorse if she were more politically aware. It's an influential argument, but many balk at the implication that some women do not know what is in their own best interests.

This links with the question of whether it is possible to see ourselves as objects without realising it. Simone de Beauvoir argued that self-objectification can occur when we come to view ourselves too much through the other's gaze. 'Society even requires woman to make herself an erotic object,' she writes in *The Second Sex*. This is most obvious in the pressures women face to look a certain way, which can lead them to treat themselves as objects designed to please men. 'The goal of the fashion to which she is in thrall is not to reveal her as an autonomous individual but . . . to offer her as a prey to male desires: fashion does not serve to fulfil her projects but on the contrary to thwart them.'

Of course, both men and women can be excessively concerned with their looks, and the rise of male grooming and body hair removal suggests that this particular gender gap is closing. But it is still women who have felt the greater pressure to conform to certain ideal standards. Without us realising, self-beautification may enslave while appearing to empower.

Some more recent philosophers have defended the desire to look attractive. Janet Radcliffe Richards makes the point that in conditions of equality it would not be wrong for either men or women 'to want, and try to please, the other'. This becomes a problem only when it is not a genuine choice, equally open to both sexes, but a social demand unequally placed on women.

Martha Nussbaum goes further, arguing that objectification is not necessarily negative. The main question is whether equality, respect and consent are preserved or whether someone's humanity is being denied.

The issue of objectification is not as simple as Kant's principle suggests. Perhaps it is possible to treat and view ourselves and others as though we were objects in some specific and limited ways. However, Kant and feminist philosophers are surely right to warn us about the dangers of turning people into mere instruments of our desires, or ourselves into instruments of the desires of others.

See also: Authenticity, Consent, Consumerism, Free Will, Other People, Self-Deception, Sex

Reading
Simone de Beauvoir, *The Second Sex* (1949)

Office Politics

Ask anyone who works in an office what they least like about it, and the chances are they'll answer 'the politics'. Even organisations that have a strong social purpose often foment cliques and cabals, bitching and bullying.

When anything is ubiquitous, it's usually a sign that it is practically unavoidable. Confucius can help us to accept the inevitability of office politics and deal with it better.

A key idea in Confucius is *li*, usually translated as 'ritual' or 'ritual propriety'. This may give the impression that *li* is of no interest to the modern world – when was the last time you performed a ritual of any kind, let alone at work? But *li* always concerned more than just formal rituals. In its wider sense it covers social propriety of every kind, including what we'd call etiquette. When, in meetings, you shake hands, dress appropriately and allow others to speak, you are following *li*.

Confucius understood that for *li* to work, everyone has to understand how they stand in relation to everyone else. In Confucius' time, this required sensitivity to hierarchy, which was the main way in which society was structured.

Times have changed. Hierarchies have become flatter, social conventions more informal and notions of what is appropriate more flexible. Still, the fundamental importance of *li* remains. A group can be harmonious only when people understand how they relate to one another and behave appropriately. A lot of office politics is the result of the breakdown of *li*. In those conditions, all we can do is follow Confucius's advice and fulfil the obligations of our role as best we can. If you think this means keeping quiet and being compliant, think again. Confucius believed in challenging conventions when they are wrong, but understood that to do this effectively you have to understand the power relations involved and act accordingly.

Confucius also accepted that sometimes the politics is so toxic that a good person is powerless to do anything about it. 'When bad governance prevails,' he said, the good person 'can roll his principles up, and keep them in his breast.' If you have done your best and the office is still poisonous, Confucius is realistic enough to accept that all you can do is keep your head down or get out.

See also: Authority, Career, Competition, Gossip, Loyalty, Work

Reading
Confucius, *Analects*

Optimism

In popular culture, optimism is usually portrayed as the good guy, pessimism the villain. As Bing Crosby told us, we have to accentuate the positive and eliminate the negative. In intellectual circles, the opposite is true: a serious thinker is seen as sober and gloomy, smiles are a sign of shallowness.

Optimism is easy to mock if it means believing that we live in the best of all possible worlds. That is the view that Voltaire attributed to his satirical creation Pangloss, the professor of 'metaphysico-theologico-cosmolo-nigology'. Pangloss's commitment to this view is in defiance of all evidence, including an earthquake in Lisbon in which 'thirty thousand inhabitants of all ages and sexes were crushed under the ruins'. Pangloss consoles survivors by telling them 'all that is is for the best'. No one is convinced.

As Steven Pinker points out, the Panglossian view is actually deeply pessimistic, since it suggests that things can't get any better. A true optimist would not think that a world in which nearly half the population lives on less than $2.50 a day and more than 750 million people lack adequate access to clean drinking water is as good as we can get. The less extreme view that things will *inevitably* get better – what Roger Scruton calls the 'moving spirit fallacy' – is not much more credible.

You might think that even if it is irrational to overestimate how good things are or will be, so what? Hasn't positive psychology proved that we'll be happier and healthier if we are optimistic, even though there is also good evidence that the moderately pessimistic see things more accurately? If the choice is between accuracy and happiness, why choose the truth?

One answer is that we value the truth, and would not choose to be a cheerful ignoramus. We might also doubt that being blind to the truth would be good for us in the long term. This brings to mind another kind of optimist that Roger Scruton has criticised as downright dangerous: the idealist who offers the false hope of a utopian future in which we live in a perfect, rationally-ordered society and all injustice is ended. This excessive belief in the power of human reason to design an ideal society, argues Scruton, is responsible for the totalitarian nightmares of history.

Thankfully, many people who believe in a better future are not guilty of fallacious thinking. They see improvement as a possibility we must work to attain rather than an inevitability. John Dewey called this view 'meliorism', a term that we should often use in place of optimism. Meliorism is 'the idea that at least there is a sufficient basis of goodness in life and its conditions so that by thought and earnest

251

effort we may constantly make things better.' Dewey accuses optimism of encouraging 'the fatalistic contentment with things as they are', arguing that 'what is needed is the frank recognition of evils, not for the sake of accepting them as final, but for the sake of arousing energy to remedy them.'

Even many people who might appear to advocate the kind of blind optimism Dewey criticises are actually meliorists. Martin Luther King famously said, 'The arc of the moral universe is long, but it bends toward justice.' But his life bore witness to the fact that he did not trust history to do its work without the aid of men and women. The rhetoric of excessive optimism is often just a gloss put on a more realistic meliorism in order to galvanise and encourage. There is nothing naive or foolish about believing that human beings have the capacity to take purposive, collective action and make things better, as long as you accept that success is neither inevitable nor without cost. (*See* **Hope**.)

The best kind of optimism might even be rooted in a rather dim assessment of the human condition. The Holocaust survivor Victor Frankl advocates what he calls 'a tragic optimism', which is 'to say yes to life' despite the 'tragic triad' of pain, guilt and death that inevitably comes with it. This possibility of saying yes is rooted in 'the human capacity to creatively turn life's negative aspects into something positive or constructive'.

The most admirable optimist is actually a meliorist who sees the world as it is. In the best of times that means making the most of a full glass; in the worst of times it means retaining the capacity to see what is good in a near empty one.

See also: Carpe Diem, Control, Gratitude, Happiness, Hope, Love of Life, Perfectionism, Pessimism

Reading

Viktor Frankl, *Man's Search for Meaning* (Beacon Press, 1946)
Roger Scruton, *The Uses of Pessimism* (Oxford University Press, 2010)
Voltaire, *Candide* (1759)

Other People

One of the most famous pronouncements ever is Sartre's 'Hell is other people', which at first glance is pretty damning about the role of people in our life. While it is true that others can create more heartache than just about anything else, we also know from personal experience, as well as from countless studies and surveys, that relationships can give life meaning. It seems that other people are the source of both the best and worst things in life.

To resolve this seeming paradox, we could start by looking more carefully at Sartre's famous aphorism. It comes from his play *No Exit*, in which three deceased characters find themselves in hell. But instead of torture and eternal flames, their damnation is to be locked in a room together, making each other miserable forever.

Sartre explained that he did not mean that our relationships with others are always bad. He was talking about a very specific way in which we can make life hell for one another. He argued that our self-image is based mainly on other people's views of us, which tend to put us in very definite boxes: 'he's stubborn', or 'she's good with people'. This leads us to see ourselves as fixed, unchanging entities, rather than beings who are free to make choices and change. We become trapped by the perceptions of others, which we internalise and thereby make prisons for ourselves. At the end of Sartre's play, the door opens but the characters choose not to leave. We can be braver, however, and refuse to be defined by how others see us.

For different reasons, the Stoics also appear to be down on people. Both Seneca and Marcus Aurelius thought it was a good idea to start each day by mentally preparing ourselves to find people unpleasant and uncooperative. For instance, Marcus advises, 'When you wake up in the morning, tell yourself: The people I deal with today will be meddling, ungrateful, arrogant, dishonest, jealous and surly.'

However, a more careful look would reveal that the Stoics could actually be quite forgiving. If we remind ourselves that we all behave badly more often than we'd like and that wisdom is hard to gain, Seneca advises, we will find it in us to be understanding of other people's flaws and misbehaviours. Taking a dim view of others can be the road not to misanthropy but to sympathy and fellow feeling. If we're all in the same boat, all benighted to a greater or lesser degree, we had better make allowances for people's failings.

On a more positive note, Aristotle wrote at length about *philia*, which he believed was one ingredient of the good life. This Greek term is the root of the English suffix '-phile', meaning a lover of something, as in 'Francophile' or 'technophile'. It is usually translated as 'friendship', but in fact covers the full spectrum of positive human relationships – from the ones we have with close family and friends to those with neighbours and colleagues, fellow gym-goers and local shopkeepers. These are all people with whom we get on well, in one way or another. Aristotle says that there is some kind of *philia* in every community.

The basic ingredient of *philia* is mutual goodwill, and we know from the Stoics that we can choose to embrace this without having to force ourselves into an idealised view of humanity. We can simply treat other people with the same compassion and sympathy with which we would like them to treat our far-from-perfect selves. As Marcus wrote, 'To feel affection for people even when they make mistakes is uniquely human.'

See also: Altruism, Community, Empathy, Friendship, Love, Objectification, Relationships

Reading
Jean-Paul Sartre, *No Exit* (1944)

P

"'Unendurable pain brings
its own end with it. Chronic
pain is always endurable.'
Marcus Aurelius

Pain

If you want life, you have to put up with pain, physical and emotional. That's difficult enough when it is sporadic, harder when it is ongoing, prolonged suffering. (*See* **Suffering**.) No philosophy can take this away, but some might just help us to deal with it better.

Epicurus offered some surprisingly practical and common-sense advice: lighten the moments of pain with memories of good times. It seems that he even managed to do this on his deathbed, writing to his friend Idomeneus, 'On this truly happy day of my life, as I am at the point of death, I write this to you. The disease in my bladder and stomach are pursuing their course, lacking nothing of their natural severity: but against all this is the joy in my heart at the recollection of my conversations with you.'

This might sound glib, but Viktor Frankl reports using a similar method to help himself to cope with being in Auschwitz. 'My mind clung to my wife's image, imagining it with an uncanny acuteness,' he recalled. 'I heard her answering me, saw her smile, her frank and encouraging look. Real or not, her look was then more luminous than the sun which was beginning to rise.'

Another of Epicurus' tips is to remember that 'pain, if extreme, is present a very short time, and even that degree of pain which barely outweighs pleasure in the flesh does not last for many days together.' Similarly, Marcus Aurelius believed that 'Unendurable pain brings its own end with it. Chronic pain is always endurable.' His 'always' seems optimistic, but more often than not mild pain is tolerable and extreme pain short-lived, which is reassuring to remember when suffering from either kind.

For the Buddha, there is one kind of pain and suffering that is inevitable and another that we bring upon ourselves. He illustrates this with a famous simile. 'Suppose they were to strike a man with a dart, and then strike him immediately afterward with a second dart, so that the man would feel a feeling caused by two darts. So too, when the uninstructed worldling experiences a painful feeling, he feels two feelings – a bodily one and a mental one.'

What are these two darts? One is the ache or pain we felt in the first place; the other is the mental web we spin around it: it's terrible, it's never going to go away, it's not fair, we can't cope with it, we don't deserve it. But we don't have to do this – with training, the Buddha tells us, we'll be able to accept our pain without adding to it.

The Buddha's example was of physical pain, but the same could apply to painful mental experiences, which we often make worse by judging ourselves, or telling ourselves we shouldn't be feeling what we're feeling. In either case, removing the second dart means changing our reactions to the pain that life throws at us; in particular, responding to it by simply noticing it and mindfully allowing it to pass, knowing that, like everything else, it is impermanent.

All of this advice sounds simple, but you will have to find out by trial and error which, if any, brings you solace at times of pain. However, there does seem to be a sound general principle behind all three ideas: we can't avoid pain and suffering, but our responses can either turn up or turn down its intensity.

See also: Health and Illness, Mindfulness, Suffering

Reading
Epicurus, *The Art of Happiness* (Penguin Classics, 2013)

Parenthood

Before taking advice from a philosopher about parenthood, there are a few things you should know. One is that a dispro-portionate number of them, including Nietzsche, Kierkegaard,

Sartre, Beauvoir, Kant, Hobbes, Locke, Plato, Hume, Mill, Schopenhauer, Spinoza, Adorno, Popper and Wittgenstein, never had children at all. The writer Carl Cederström went through a list of the twenty greatest philosophers of all time and found that thirteen of them were childless and two of the remaining seven as good as, for all the contact they had with their offspring.

Another thing you should know is that many of those who did have children were far from model parents. One of Bertrand Russell's sons, Conrad, went ten years of his youth without even speaking to his father, while his daughter Katherine wrote of 'his straight back and the invisible wall of concentration that cut him off from us'.

The worst was Jean-Jacques Rousseau, who had five children by his common-law wife and insisted that she give them all up to an orphanage. The reasons he gave for this varied: he didn't have enough money to bring them up, it would bring dishonour on her, and the education they'd get at the orphanage would be better than the one they could give them. None were convincing.

Of course, some great philosophers *have* had children, including two of the greatest of all, Confucius and Aristotle, both of whom wrote about the importance of good family relations. The Confucian principle of *xiao* ('family reverence') underscores the need for domestic order. Family harmony requires hierarchies, with parents and children fulfilling different roles. (*See* **Family**.) That's why parents who truly love their children can't be too indulgent with them.

The most obvious reason why philosophers tend to be childless is that having children around the house is not conducive to intellectual work, not least because of sleep deprivation. The writer Cyril Connolly's remark that 'There is no more sombre enemy of good art than the pram in the hall' has been applied to philosophy too. There are many excellent parent-philosophers who prove that this is not a necessary truth. However, single-minded devotion to any kind of vocation is hard to balance with the demands of parenthood, even if it is not strictly incompatible. Simone de Beauvoir seemed to recognise this when she said, 'By remaining childless I was fulfilling my proper function.'

In today's have-it-all society, this obvious fact has been forgotten or wished away. We don't take seriously the idea that some life projects may require so much of our energy and devotion that they make other valuable things impossible. If you are not prepared to divide your focus, think twice before starting a family.

One reason why this is not said enough is that somehow the idea has spread that the childless are selfish and parenthood makes people less egocentric. This is nonsense. Aristotle says that 'one's offspring is a sort of other self', which is why 'parents . . . love their children as themselves'. Parenthood does not make us less selfish but gives us an expanded self, a kind of double-ego that is often put even more firmly at the centre of our universe than our solo version. Parents routinely do whatever is in their children's best interests, whether or not it is at the expense of others. Competing for places at good schools, for instance, is hardly an example of pro-social altruism.

One argument that having children is a selfish rather than a selfless act is that fulfilling your desire to have a 'mini-you' does your child no favours at all. David Benatar has argued that it is *Better Never to Have Been*, the cheery title of his book. Benatar provides statistics to prove that a huge number of human lives are full of pain and suffering. To give just a taste, in the first 88 years of the twentieth century, between 170 and 360 million people were shot, beaten, tortured, knifed, burned, starved or killed in various other gruesome ways by governments; there were 109.7 million conflict-related deaths in the twentieth century; and there are around 800,000 suicides every year.

Benatar claims that 'human lives fall short on the good things but abound in the bad'. He also has a simple argument for why non-existence is by far the safer bet. Life is a mixture of pleasure (good) and pain (bad). Non-existence is the absence of pain, which is good, and the absence of pleasure too, which is not in itself bad. If you do the maths, it's clear which option comes up in greater credit.

Benatar's message for would-be parents is clear: 'Not having children might make our own lives less good, but starting lives that are not good, merely for our own gratification, is unduly selfish.'

Most people do not find Benatar's challenging case entirely convincing. Nonetheless, the considerations he raises are a useful corrective to the general pro-parenting rhetoric found in most societies. There are very good reasons not to be a parent, and it seems somewhat bizarre that the onus tends to be on the childless to justify their choices rather than on those who bring yet more people into an overcrowded world.

At the very least, parents ought to concede that the desire to have children is not rational. 'If the act of procreation were neither the outcome of a desire nor accompanied by feelings of pleasure, but a matter to be decided on the basis of purely rational considerations,' asked Schopenhauer, 'is it likely the human race would still exist?'

See also: Education, Family, Home, Pets, Selfishness

Reading
David Benatar, *Better Never to Have Been: The Harm of Coming into Existence* (Clarendon Press, 2006)
Jean Kazez, *The Philosophical Parent* (Oxford University Press, 2017)

Patriotism

Almost everyone at least sometimes cheers their national sports team or feels some pride in being the citizen of a particular country. But we are also aware that flag-waving is

frowned upon by many as the innocent-looking twin of
nationalist xenophobia.

Patriotism is almost universally viewed as both natural
and good. It seems impossible to imagine a successful polit-
ician anywhere in the world declaring that they were not
patriotic. Yet philosophy's ethos is more in line with the view
of the ancient Greek Cynic Diogenes, who when asked where
he was from replied, 'I am a citizen of the world.'

Martha Nussbaum is one such cosmopolitan, a term that
literally means 'citizen of the universe'. She argues that the
'emphasis on patriotic pride' is 'morally dangerous', and that
'Our primary allegiance is to the community of human
beings in the entire world.' Although there is no problem in
having a particular affection for our country, our first loyalty
should be to universal values and all humanity rather than to
any specific group.

Defenders of patriotism argue that it is not the same as
blind nationalism. Alasdair MacIntyre, for example, says that
patriotism 'is not to be confused with a mindless loyalty to
one's own particular nation which has no regard at all for the
characteristics of that particular nation.' In the same way that
a loving parent sometimes has to set their child straight, a true
patriot does not back their country when it is wrong but
works to right that wrong. Richard Rorty believes that
without patriotism we would actually be less likely to engage
in this kind of internal criticism: 'You can feel shame over
your country's behaviour only to the extent to which you feel
it is your country.'

It's clear enough why parents take a special interest in
their own children, but why should a patriot take a greater
interest in their country than in humanity as a whole?
According to MacIntyre, we are the individuals we are only
because of the communities and cultures we have grown up
in. Nations are part of what forges our identity. To deny that
there is an intimate link between where we come from and

who we are is as absurd as denying our parents' roles in shaping us. So even if you do not feel a visceral affection for your country, you should at least begrudgingly accept its part in making you, just as you might have to acknowledge that you take after your parents in ways that you're not happy with.

Rorty argues that the right kind of patriotism is necessary for a united, harmonious society. He approves of the project of creating a national identity based on a 'community of communities', or what John Rawls calls 'a social union of social unions'. National belonging is what enables diverse citizens to see that they are all in it together. The alternative is a multiculturalism based on 'the politics of difference'. Without patriotism, society is fragmented and disunited. Rorty argues that 'there is no incompatibility between respect for cultural differences and American patriotism.'

Patriotism can be more inclusive and open if we remember that the countries we feel part of are constantly changing and evolving. Italians are justly proud of their cuisine, but they would do well to remember that without basil from the Asian spice routes and tomatoes from the New World, some of their most famous dishes would never have been created. Patriots should be glad that none of their ancestors have set their national identity in stone and should not try to do so themselves.

It's easy to see why philosophers and other intellectuals are suspicious of patriotism. As Hume wrote, 'The heights of popularity and patriotism are still the beaten road to power and tyranny.' The line between a legitimate love of one's country and unquestioning parochial xenophobia is thin, but it is clear enough, and with care we can avoid crossing it. We do not need to choose between being cosmopolitans and patriots. We can have dual citizenship, of the world and of specific nations.

See also: Community, Family, Home, Identity, Loyalty, Politics, Pride

Reading
'The Unpatriotic Academy', Richard Rorty, *New York Times*, 13 February 1994
'Patriotism and Cosmopolitanism', Martha C. Nussbaum, *Boston Review*, 1 October 1994
'Is Patriotism a Virtue?', Alasdair MacIntyre (The Lindley Lecture, University of Kansas, 1984) in Igor Primoratz (ed.), *Patriotism* (Humanity Books, 2002)

Perfectionism

We live in an age that promises us the perfect everything: skin, sex, home, holiday, phone, furniture. If perfection eludes us – as it always will – it's easy to assume we must be doing something wrong.

Of course, we're not so naive as to believe that perfection is really possible. But it can easily become the measure against which we judge ourselves. To counter this, we could look to Japanese aesthetics, which actively celebrates imperfection. The sensibility behind this is most evident in Zen Buddhism, which has appreciation of impermanence at its heart. This attitude is manifested in a principle called *wabi-sabi*, which praises qualities such as simplicity and imperfection.

An example of this is found in the poet Ton'a's remark that 'It is only after the top and bottom edges of the silk have frayed, or when the mother-of-pearl has peeled off the roller, that a scroll is truly impressive' – an observation that the Buddhist monk Kenko judged to be 'astonishingly fine'. Some took this further: it is said that when a famous tea master was given an exquisite Chinese painting he proceeded to replace the gold brocade in the scroll with a subdued damask and the ivory roll with a branch from a quince tree.

According to Dogen, the founder of the Soto school, humans tend to cherish the perfect and unblemished while looking down on what seems flawed. But this is a distorted perspective. Dogen encourages us to see things as they are, not according to preconceived notions of what they should be: 'Experience spring as spring and autumn as autumn. Accept the beauty and the loneliness of both.'

The appreciation of imperfection has implications beyond aesthetics. Okakura Kakuzo argued that this is the true significance of the Japanese tea ceremony. From the outside it might seem bizarre to treat a humble cup of tea with almost religious devotion, but that is the point. 'Teaism', as he calls the philosophy behind the tradition, 'is essentially a worship of the imperfect, as it is a tender attempt to accomplish something possible in this impossible thing we know as life.'

You might wonder whether the perfect is more deserving of worship, even if it is unattainable. There is sometimes value in setting higher ideals than we can ever meet. Simon Critchley has argued that this is what makes Christian ethics so powerful. Jesus commanded 'Be ye perfect', knowing that no one could follow this command. This defies Kant's idea that '*ought* implies *can*': that it makes sense to say we ought to do something only if it is actually possible for us to do it. Critchley prefers the principle '*ought* implies *cannot*': our moral standards should be higher than we can meet so that we push ourselves to be better than we would if we merely aspired to be good enough.

There is something to this, as long as we accept that perfection is ultimately unattainable. Wittgenstein may be a good example of someone who had perfectionist impulses but did not allow them to get in the way of doing his imperfect best. He wrote of his masterpiece, *Philosophical Investigations*, that he had envisaged a book in which 'the thoughts should proceed from one subject to another in a natural order and without breaks'. But after several unsuccessful attempts, he realised he would never succeed. He concluded, 'I should have

P

265

liked to produce a good book. This has not come about, but the time is past in which I could improve it.' Posterity is pleased both that his pursuit of perfection pushed him to write the best book he could, and that it did not prevent him from accepting imperfection in the end.

One of the most persuasive arguments against holding perfection as an ideal was made by Amartya Sen. He claims that Western political thought has tended to assume that we should first agree on some ideal, such as justice, and then try to get as close to it as possible. The problem is that we can't agree on what those ideals are. But we don't need to know what the perfectly just society would look like in order to be able to spot the worst injustices in the world. The general idea applies more widely: we tend to achieve more when we focus on concrete improvements that are possible, starting from where we are.

What unites Japanese aesthetics, Wittgenstein's attitude and Sen's philosophy is the idea that embracing imperfection does not mean settling for low standards. Quite the opposite – it is only when we are freed from the tyranny of perfection that we can do our best. Our best chance of ascending as high as possible is not to attempt to scale mount impossible.

See also: Achievement, Contentment, Gratitude, Suffering

Reading
Okakura Kakuzo, *The Book of Tea* (1906)

Perseverance

We set great store by perseverance, or 'grit', as we may say nowadays. We admire people who are able to keep their eyes set on long-term goals without being distracted by low-hanging fruit or getting discouraged by setbacks. We don't admire those who lack this quality, and call them butterflies, or quitters.

Perseverance received the backing of Hume, who counted it as a useful quality. But we shouldn't be oblivious to its downsides. The dark side of grit lies in persisting with things after they have ceased to be meaningful, or in a stubbornness that doesn't take other people's opinions into account and refuses to accept evidence that a project may have been misguided. Schopenhauer, who was by all accounts a pretty obstinate chap, wrote that 'When will crowds out knowledge we call the result obstinacy.'

There is something to be said for not always persevering with perseverance. Take a book that you're not getting much out of. (Not this one, we hope.) Maybe you should follow the example of Montaigne, who wrote, 'When I meet with difficulties in my reading, I do not bite my nails over them; after making one or two attempts I give them up. If I were to sit down to them, I should be wasting myself and my time; my mind works at the first leap. What I do not see immediately, I see even less by persisting. Without lightness I achieve nothing; application and over-serious effort confuse, depress, and weary my brain.'

Montaigne may be exaggerating his swiftness to give up, but it's hard to deny that sometimes calling it a day is the right thing to do. According to Aristotle's theory of the mean (*See* **Balance**), we should aim for the appropriate kind of perseverance, avoiding the opposite extremes of giving things up capriciously or rigidly sticking with plans long after their sell-by date. We should neither routinely fail to see things through nor be an obstinate so-and-so who never knows when to stop.

See also: Achievement, Balance, Commitment, Frustration, Perfectionism, Resilience

Reading
Michel de Montaigne, *Essays* (1580)

Pessimism

Pessimists think that they will fail exams or interviews, their relationships won't work out, a sniffle is bound to turn into pneumonia, human nature is warped and the world is doomed. But maybe it's worse than even they feared – the glass is not only half-empty but also poisoned. We are now told that pessimism itself is bad for us, cutting our life expectancy and making us less likely to succeed.

There are various reasons why this might be so. For a start, if we expect things to go wrong anyway we're less likely to do what is needed to look after ourselves – there is no point in having a scan if we already think we're beyond help. Also in some contexts – on a date, for instance– a defeatist attitude might bring about the very outcome that worried us. We might come across as half-hearted, or negative.

But even if we're convinced by this analysis, we should not throw the pessimistic baby out with the half-empty tub of bathwater. Pessimism comes in a variety of forms, and some of them can be very useful indeed.

There are different things we can be pessimistic about: ourselves, the world, the present, the future. Some people's pessimism is global, others' more targeted. Pessimism about ourselves, for instance, might include filtering out all the positives in our life and noticing only the negatives, or expecting the worst in the future. Not only does this mean that we're likely to act in self-destructive ways, it also makes us feel bad.

However, we can separate the *assessment* that things are, or will be, bad from how we feel or behave. So we can be pessimistic without either feeling gloomy or acting in ways that undermine our well-being.

In this, we could follow the example of the Stoics, who made the expectation of disasters one of the pillars of their practice. One of their most famous exercises is known as *premeditatio malorum*, a kind of meditation on future evils. This involves imagining tragedies of various kinds: 'exile, torture, war, shipwreck', suggests Seneca; 'death and exile', echoes Epictetus, 'and everything that seems terrible, but death above all'. The aim was not to produce depression, but to remind students that the anticipated evils are to be expected. This would help them to respond with equanimity to any disaster.

To be truly Stoic, we'd have to believe that none of these things would really be 'evil' anyway, since only vice is evil. But without going so far, we can emulate their trick by splitting our initial assessment – 'I'll probably be ill on holiday', for instance – from the conclusion that this would be a terrible thing. If we could persuade ourselves that it would be OK to be ill on holiday, equanimity rather than gloom would follow. A less demanding version of this might be, 'I may well be ill on holiday, and although I don't like it, I can deal with it.'

While not exactly Stoic, this approach builds on the same disconnect between our assessment of the situation and our response to it. It would stave off gloom, while being more realistic and effective than trying to convince ourselves that the holiday will be perfect and we definitely won't be ill. As Roger Scruton concludes in his eloquent defence of pessimism, our task is not to persuade ourselves that things are good, but to 'look with irony and detachment on our actual condition and to study how to live at peace with what we find'.

This applies equally to pessimism about the world, which again could focus either on the present or the future. The question is whether this is a more rational assessment than a sunnier outlook – isn't it a sound response to what we observe around us and what we know about history and human nature?

Most people, whether they are pessimists or not, would agree that there are lots of bad things going on in the world: war, injustice, torture, exploitation and the destruction of the environment, not to mention everyday injury and infirmity. There is more room for debate about whether the world has improved, how easily any gains could be lost and how bright the future looks.

On the first two questions, there may be less difference between optimists and pessimists than is commonly assumed. Pessimists could accept Steven Pinker's argument that the evidence shows that on a number of measures the human situation has indeed improved; optimists could accept that future events could easily bring about a regression, as Pinker himself does. The march of progress is by no means inexorable.

The real battleground for pessimism is whether things are going to get worse, maybe much, much worse. Pessimists answer in the affirmative, while optimists tend to believe that solutions to the problems that beset us are bound to emerge. John Gray thinks that this reassuring belief is no more than an irrational 'faith in progress', and that 'outside of science, progress is simply a myth'.

There is a case to be made for either set of predictions. But what matters most is that a negative assessment of our prospects doesn't translate into apathy. We don't have to be optimists to do our bit to change the world, or our little corner of it, for the better. All we have to believe is that positive change, even if small and reversible, is possible. In fact, it is arguable that a pinch of pessimism is necessary to arouse the right kind of motivation: we're more likely to succeed in our endeavours if we are realistic about human frailty and the fragility of progress.

See also: Hope, Human Nature, Optimism, Resilience, Worrying

Reading
Roger Scruton, *The Uses of Pessimism* (Atlantic, 2010)

Pets

Not so long ago, the choice of whether to have a pet or not was purely a matter of personal preference. For some time, however, the issue has had an ethical dimension. Now the question you must ask yourself is: as a pet owner, are you more like a slave owner than a carer?

Caged birds went out of fashion in many countries years ago, as many people thought it cruel to keep animals that were born to fly locked up. Now the very word 'pet' has been deemed 'derogatory' by the editors of the *Journal of Animal Ethics*, who argued that 'the word "owners", whilst technically correct in law, harks back to a previous age when animals were regarded as just that: property, machines or things to use without moral constraint.' The rise of ethical veganism has given the issue new impetus: if it is wrong to raise animals for food, is it also wrong to keep them for pleasure?

This moral challenge is serious if our pets are made to suffer either pain or serious deprivation. But our most popular pets – cats and dogs – seem to enjoy our company as much as we enjoy theirs. Both usually have regular opportunities to run away, but choose the comfort of regular feeding, warm beds and petting. Compared to their wild cousins, they are generally healthier, better fed and live longer. It is telling that the leading philosopher-advocate of animal rights today, Peter Singer, says a great deal about the need to reduce animal suffering but very little about pets. (He doesn't have pets himself but says that is partly because he's not an animal lover.)

If we assume that looking after an animal properly is morally acceptable, a more interesting question is how we should relate to them. Some animals are so different from us that no kind of relationship is possible. Thomas Nagel famously asked, 'What is it like to be a bat?', because we haven't got a clue. Anyone who claims to have real empathy with a bat, to know what it is thinking or how it is feeling, is probably only imagining a small flying version of themselves.

But many other creatures are in several respects very much like us. David Hume remarked on this when he argued, way back in the eighteenth century, that animals could reason. That does not mean he thought they could do algebra or make logical deductions. But how much of your reasoning is of that kind? Most of what we call reason is the ability to 'learn many things from experience, and infer, that the same events will always follow from the same causes'. Animals clearly do this too. What distinguishes humans is simply that they can do it more systematically, having the ability to 'carry on a chain of consequences to a greater length than another'.

The animals we most often keep as pets have minds some-where between the bat and the human: similar enough for us to feel some kind of connection but different enough to be alien and somewhat inscrutable. This raises questions about the extent to which animals can be our friends in any mean-ingful sense. Aristotle argued that friendship requires mutual-ity. 'How could one call them friends when they do not know their mutual feelings?' he asked. Friends 'must be mutually recognised as bearing goodwill and wishing well to each other'.

It would be too anthropomorphic to believe that the human-pet relationship is symmetrical. But one of the wondrous things about living with an animal is the experi-ence of encountering a mind that is so very different, yet capable of connecting with us in strange ways. Simon Glendinning captured this beautifully in his description of his interactions with his mother's dog, Sophy: 'My sense of her aliveness to my "state of mind" had seemed to justify breaking with the habitual tendency to confine the scope of "mutual intelligibility" to the forms of intercourse that can go on between humans.' At its best, having a pet is not about ownership or mastery. It is nothing less than a daily reminder of the wonder, mystery and diversity of conscious life.

See also: Empathy, Family, Friendship, Nature, Rationality, Vegetarianism

Reading
Simon Glendinning, 'Human Beings and (Other) Animals', nakedpunch.com

Play *see* Leisure

Pleasure

Pleasure is pleasing. The connection is inherent: the two words are variants of the same root. There is, however, a tendency to be suspicious of putting too much focus on pleasure. We might suspect that it is a shallow foundation for a good life and that it suffers from some serious limitations, such as being short-lived and potentially addictive. According to Seneca, pleasures 'embrace us just to throttle us'. Is this wariness justified or is it just a puritanical refusal to embrace the mortal, fleshy reality of human life?

Hedonists (from the Greek word for pleasure, *hedone*) such as Jeremy Bentham believe that pain and pleasure are our 'sovereign masters', and that it is 'for them alone to point out what we ought to do, as well as to determine what we shall do'. In their view, pleasure is the only thing that is good in itself. Everything else we consider good in life – love, learning, you name it – has value not in itself but only to the extent that it creates pleasure.

Does it matter what kind of pleasure we get? Not for Bentham. What matters is the *quantity* of pleasure, not where it comes from. He claimed that the simple Victorian game of push-pin was the equal of music and poetry. However, his secular godson and fellow utilitarian John Stuart Mill came to believe that pleasures differ in quality, not just quantity. Lower pleasures are based on sense experience; higher ones require more complex – intellectual, moral and aesthetic – abilities. Mill had no doubt that those who have experienced both would choose the higher kind. He clearly hadn't taken into account the numerous libidinous, gluttonous, dipso-maniac intellectuals.

Hedonism is often thought to imply selfishness, but the utilitarianism of Bentham and Mill is rigorously altruistic and ethical. This is because it's the total amount of pleasure in the world that counts, not our own. We should therefore act to create the greatest quantity of pleasure or happiness for the greatest number of people. To help us to do this Bentham came up with the quixotic idea of the hedonic – or 'felicific' – calculus to work out the amount of pleasure produced by an act in terms of intensity, duration, certainty or uncertainty, propinquity or remoteness, fecundity, and purity.

A more common-sense understanding of hedonism is found in the ancient Greek Cyrenaic school, which advocated pursuing our own pleasure, particularly the bodily kind. However, Epicurus, the most famous hedonist of that age, had a more subtle view. He was an acute observer of the problems of overindulgence. 'No pleasure is in itself evil,' he wrote, 'but the things which produce certain pleasures entail annoyances many times greater than the pleasures themselves.'

Proper pleasure for Epicurus turns out to mean something quite different from indulgence. It is rather a simple life that is as free as possible from physical and mental pain. 'When we say that pleasure is the objective, we do not mean the pleas-ures of the profligate or the pleasures of sensuality,' he explains. 'By "pleasure" we mean the absence of pain in the body and of turmoil in the mind. The pleasurable life is not continuous drinking, dancing and sex; nor the enjoyment of fish or other delicacies of an extravagant table. It is sober reasoning which . . . rejects those beliefs which lay open the mind to the greatest disturbance.'

The range of opinion on such a central issue is confusing, but there are some common threads and overlaps. One is that pleasure has to be pursued skilfully or else you end up obese, sick or just feeling empty and exhausted. Epicurus may have been wrong to criticise eating fish and dancing, but he was right to point out that some pleasures create pain in the long run.

Another is that, with the main exception of Bentham, it is generally agreed that not all pleasures are equal. Our best guide to deciding how to distinguish and prioritise them is Aristotle, who argued that there are different kinds of pleasure, ranging from the satisfaction of bodily appetites to the study of philosophy. We are biological beings, so the good life will include enjoyment of bodily pleasures in moderation. But we shouldn't get too attached to them, as a life enslaved to bodily pleasure is 'fit only for cattle'. He thought we are particularly vulnerable in relation to the pleasures of taste and touch, which prey on our intemperate tendencies. We're much more likely to become binge eaters or sex addicts than compulsive listeners to opera or visitors of art galleries.

But perhaps the age-old division between bodily and intellectual pleasures is too crude. Maybe where pleasures come from matters less than *how* we experience them. You can tuck into your food like a pig at a trough or with the attention and consideration of a gourmet; you can go to the opera to revel in your social status or to truly appreciate the performance.

The deepest pleasures are the ones we bring our whole selves to, body and mind. They might also be the ones that do not arise from the direct pursuit of pleasure at all. The best and most long-lasting satisfaction, for Aristotle, comes from being absorbed in an activity that has value in itself, not primarily because of any pleasure that might arise from it.

As is often the case, philosophers don't give us neat answers but they do leave us with some good questions. What kinds of pleasures matter most? How central a place do they have in our life? Does everything boil down to pleasure or are there things that are valuable independently of it? Whatever we conclude, we need to be wary of a simplistic pursuit of pleasure that leaves us hung-over and unsatisfied.

See also: Asceticism, Carpe Diem, Consumerism, Desires, Happiness, Self-Control, Sex

Reading
John Stuart Mill, *Utilitarianism* (1861)

Politics

Not so long ago, it seemed that we knew where we and others stood politically, accepting we did not all stand in the same place. Now, politics across the world has become more fragmented, volatile and unpredictable. Do the old ideological maps need updating or do they need to be completely rewritten?

For centuries, most philosophers argued for the merits of monarchy or aristocracy (meaning rule by the best able, not the richest), denigrating democracy. In the early twentieth century, however, liberal democracy and a new upstart, communism, started to gain ground. Marx argued for a radical egalitarianism in which private wealth was all but outlawed: 'From each according to his abilities, to each according to his needs.' But the states that tried to implement this could do so only by taking enormous power for themselves. The collapse of European communism appeared to confirm the view that freedom was incompatible with such a powerful state. Friedrich Hayek summed up the problem: 'The power which a multiple millionaire, who may be my neighbour and perhaps my employer, has over me is very much less than that which the smallest functionaire possesses who wields the coercive power of the state, and on whose discretion it depends whether and how I am to be allowed to live or to work.'

In democracies, the main question became not what political system was best but what sort of policies a democratic government should implement. It also seemed pretty clear what the political spectrum looked like, with positions set out from left to right.

On the left, democratic socialism distanced itself from state communism, while sharing its desire for greater equality and more public ownership. One of its most potent intellectual challenges came from libertarians such as Robert Nozick, who argued that the right to own the fruits of your own labours was paramount. He argued that 'a minimal state, limited to the narrow functions of protection against force, theft, fraud, enforcement of contracts, and so on, is justified', but that 'any more extensive state will violate persons' rights not to be forced to do certain things, and is unjustified'.

Traditional conservatives objected to socialism on other grounds. Following in the footsteps of Edmund Burke, they argued that society is an evolving ecosystem, not something that can be reconstructed on supposedly rational principles at will. Equality can be imposed only by a tyrannical state. 'Human achievements are rare and precarious,' says Roger Scruton, and 'we have no God-given right to destroy our inheritance, but must always patiently submit to the voice of order, and set an example of orderly living.' Better an imperfect inequality than a ruinous attempt to establish a perfect but impossible equality.

Libertarians (and their close cousins, economic liberals) and Burkean conservatives are both categorised as right-wing because they oppose large state regulation and control of the economy. But they are importantly different. As its name suggests, old-school conservatism seeks to conserve and dislikes abrupt change; libertarians welcome the creative destruction brought about by people and markets unleashed from state control.

Steering a course between the extremes of right and left was a liberalism that sought greater equality without excessively restricting liberty. Most famously, John Rawls argued that the only fair distribution of wealth would be one that we would all agree to if we were placed behind a 'veil of ignorance', not knowing where on the social ladder we would be. He believed that in such a situation, we would tolerate only those inequalities that 'result in compensating benefits for everyone, and in particular for the least advantaged members of society'. (*See* **Justice**.)

At the dawn of the twenty-first century, it seemed to many that liberal democracy was the only game in town. We had reached the 'end of history', as Francis Fukuyama notoriously said. Whereas at the start of the twentieth century there were only a couple of democracies in the world, by 2000 there were nearly ninety, and it seemed only a matter of time before the remaining dictatorships fell. It was simply a question of how right- or left-wing a government should be.

And then something strange happened: voters who had loyally backed the same team for decades started abandoning the old parties, supporting upstarts or switching sides. Class divisions were replaced by cultural ones: metropolitan cosmopolitans who had done well out of globalisation were pitted against dwellers of small towns and villages who felt left behind. The new divide is between 'the people' and out-of-touch elites.

The politicians who claim to stand for the people come from left, right and centre, but all can be characterised as populist. Populism claims that there is a clear 'will of the people' that political elites try to frustrate in order to defend their own selfish interests. Populists tend to offer simple solutions to what are, in fact, complex problems, and ignore the fact that what they see as the will of the people can only ever be the will of a subset of them.

Nietzsche would have had no time for these advocates of popular opinion. For him, popularity means mediocrity. The current best-selling burger, song or book may not be anyone's favourite, let alone 'the nation's' – it's simply the one that has the widest and perhaps also the most shallow appeal. Nietzsche decried the 'herd', who blindly settled for this lowest common denominator, saying that it was engaged in a 'war against everything rare, strange, privileged, the higher man, the higher soul, the higher duty, the higher responsibility, the creative fullness of power and mastery'.

Plato and Aristotle would also have despised populism. But for them this was the natural consequence of democracy, which they thought gave too much power to the majority of people, who were ill-informed and prejudiced. Numerous election results in recent history support the theory that the majority are not always right.

It's easy to dismiss these anti-popular arguments as elitist. Our egalitarian, democratic age rejects any suggestion that some know more or are better judges of quality than others. But this is much more credible than the idea that everyone is equally qualified, no matter what their experience or skills. This does not mean we should replace the opinions of the masses with the judgements of an elite class. The democratic spirit supports neither mob rule nor technocracy, but draws on both popular opinion and specialist expertise.

To save democracy, we have to reject the idea that it is only a matter of following the will of the people. A healthy democracy works when it manages disagreement instead of giving everything to whoever can get across the 50 per cent threshold. In a winner-takes-all democracy, no one wins in the long term because the result is a divided, bitter society.

Politics is a messy, complex process of negotiation and compromise. Anyone who promises anything else is a scoundrel or a fool. Sadly, it is not difficult to find many contemporary politicians who are both.

See also: Authority, Community, Freedom, Justice, Patriotism, Protest, Tolerance, War

Reading
Friedrich Nietzsche, *Beyond Good and Evil* (1886)

Polyamory *see* **Monogamy**

Pornography

If you worry about your own or your partner's use of pornography, you are not alone. However, in many countries, including Britain and the US, you are in a shrinking group – attitudes towards pornography there became much more liberal in the early twenty-first century. In 2011, 32 per cent of Americans thought pornography was morally acceptable. By 2018 45 per cent did, and we can be pretty sure that not all of the remaining 55 per cent lived by their professed standards.

Many see the acceptance of pornography as belonging with a wider liberalisation of attitudes. What people get up to sexually is increasingly seen as their own business. It's a moral issue only if it involves force, coercion, deceit or risking a partner's health. Even many feminists support pro-women porn, as long as women remain in control of its production.

Rae Langton has presented a powerful challenge to this growing consensus. She makes use of J.L. Austin's speech acts theory. Austin's central point is that words are not just utterances: we can actually *do* things with them. We can declare a couple man and wife, belittle people, incite violence, undermine authority and so on. Langton argues that we should think of acts of pornography in a similar way: they do not just *represent* sex acts, they do things, not only to users but to wider society.

Langton's argument builds on the long-standing feminist critique of pornography that it objectifies women. (*See* **Objectification**.) Women in much porn are depicted as dehumanised sexual objects used by men for their own pleasure rather than human beings with their own agency and desires.

You might think this is not a good enough reason to object to pornography – after all, films and novels often present people in negative terms. However, Langton points out that objectification in pornography can have actual effects on women, whether or not they choose to use porn themselves. In a culture that accepts porn, women are constantly being presented as things to be used, and this has the effect of making people think it's OK to treat women in that way. An effect of pornography may be to 'rank women as sex objects, and legitimate discriminatory behaviour towards them'.

Langton also believes that porn can silence women by typically presenting their protestations that they don't want sex as either false or something that can be ignored. A common trope is that women 'really want it', no matter what they say. A pro-porn culture legitimises this, so that when a woman says no to sex, her refusal has less force or none at all, because such refusals are routinely portrayed as valueless.

Whether or not pornography actually has these negative effects depends on whether it is taken to be what Langton calls 'authoritative'. To return to the speech example, a sexist remark by a junior employee is wrong but doesn't necessarily carry much weight. But if that remark is made or even allowed to pass by a senior manager, its effect may be to inhibit women's ability to do their work.

The question of whether pornography is authoritative in this sense is tricky to answer, but there is evidence that it does influence societal norms with harmful consequences. For instance, some have argued that a rise in reported cases of impotence in young men is linked with increased use of pornography. The thesis is that porn creates unrealistic and unachievable norms of sexual performance that in turn drive anxiety. There is also concern that young women in particular feel under pressure to perform sex acts they are not comfortable with because their repeated depiction in porn makes them seem normal. Refusing then appears to be prudery.

Langton is persuaded that pornography changes attitudes and that there is evidence that it is authoritative. 'People's beliefs and desires are changed on exposure to certain kinds of pornography – that's fairly clear empirically,' she says. 'They are more likely to view women as inferiors. They are more likely to think that a rape victim had deserved to be raped. They are more likely to favour a lenient sentence for the rapist.'

Whether or not you fully accept Langton's argument, it presents a challenge and a reminder. The challenge is not to assume that the potential harms of pornography are restricted to those involved in making it, most notably the frequent exploitation of the actors. The reminder is that if we normalise pornography that objectifies, we can't be surprised if object-ification is normalised too.

See also: Character, Consent, Habits, Objectification, Sex

Reading
Interview with Rae Langton in Julian Baggini and Jeremy Stangroom (eds.) *New British Philosophy* (Routledge, 2002)

Potential *see* **Self-Actualisation**

Pride

Is pride something to be proud of? People are often criticised for being too proud, and the old proverb warns us that it comes before a fall. Yet pride has also been celebrated and encouraged, most visibly in the LGBTQ+ festivals of the same name and the Black Pride strand of the civil rights movement.

Whether pride is good or bad depends in part on what we are proud of. In Jane Austen's *Pride and Prejudice*, Miss Lucas says of Mr Darcy that 'His pride does not offend me so much as pride often does, because there is an excuse for it . . . If I may so express it, he has a right to be proud.'

This sounds similar to Aristotle's view that a person is justly proud if they 'think themselves worthy of great things, being worthy of them'. With proper pride, there is a match between the value we place on an attribute or achievement and the value it actually has. Pride was rightly claimed by LGBTQ+ and black rights groups because those oppressed people are entitled to feel good about central aspects of their identity that society has belittled.

Pride goes wrong when it claims more for its possessor than is justified. It then turns into vanity. 'He who thinks himself worthy of great things, being unworthy of them, is vain,' says Aristotle. He also thought you could have too little as well as too much pride. 'The man who thinks himself worthy of less than he is really worthy of is unduly humble.' In contemporary language, we might say that such a person lacks appropriate self-esteem.

For Hume, the line between pride and vanity is thin but critical. 'The world naturally esteems a well-regulated pride,' he says, but only when it 'animates our conduct without breaking out into such indecent expressions of vanity, as may offend the vanity of others'.

Vanity's proximity to virtuous pride made Hume quite tolerant of it. 'Vanity is so closely allied to virtue,' he argued, 'and to love the fame of laudable actions approaches so near the love of laudable actions for their own sake'. If we think something is praiseworthy we will naturally be pleased to be praised for it, and this is a kind of harmless vanity.

But it was perhaps Jane Austen who nailed the critical difference between pride and vanity. 'A person may be proud without being vain,' says Mary Bennet in *Pride and Prejudice*. 'Pride relates more to our opinion of ourselves; vanity, to what we would have others think of us.'

Pride is good when it springs from something you are or have done that you rightly judge to be good or of value. It becomes vanity when you see yourself as better than others, when you are more concerned with praise than what you are being praised for, or when you have no good reason to be proud at all.

See also: Impostor Syndrome, Reputation, Self-Absorption, Self-Love

Reading
Jane Austen, *Pride and Prejudice* (1813)

Problems

Problems come in many shapes and forms: ailments, ageing, interpersonal conflict, unemployment, loneliness, leaking roofs, leaves on the line. All these fall neatly into two of the Buddha's categories for what is unsatisfactory: getting what we don't want or not getting what we want. (*See* **Suffering**.) We could even collapse these into one: the world not cooperating with our wishes. That's hard to accept, even when we know that the world has no reason to do what *we* want.

One of the biggest obstacles to acceptance is the sneaking feeling that, somehow, what we're experiencing shouldn't be happening. There is a sense that with a bit more luck, effort, positive thinking or meditation, it should be possible to sail through life avoiding all these inconveniences.

It isn't, and Seneca does a good job in pointing this out. For any kinds of problems, just head to his letters. In one to a friend, he writes, 'You were troubled by pain in your bladder, you received worrying letters, your losses continued'. He reminds him – and us – that despite how it seems, problems really *should* be happening, because misfortune is a normal and inevitable part of being alive. 'A long life contains them all, just as a long journey contains dust and mud and rain.'

So when we wish for a long life, we must be aware that it brings with it many problems, and that this is not optional. 'All the things that make us groan and get frightened are just life's taxes', says Seneca. It's unreasonable to imagine we're the ones who could get an exemption.

The stark and only choice, according to Seneca, is to take it or leave it. 'We have come into a world where life is lived on such terms: accept them and comply, or reject them and leave by whatever route you like.'

By all means do try to solve your problems, but be aware that the relief is bound to be short-lived, as fresh ones are around the corner. There will be no end to your problems until there is an end of you, so take your difficulties as a sign of life.

See also: Ageing, Contentment, Frustration, Health and Illness, Pain, Resilience, Stress, Suffering, Worrying

Reading
Seneca, Letters

Protest

As a citizen in a democracy, your primary tool for bringing about political change is the ballot box. But are there times when you should go further? Increasing numbers seem to think so. The two largest political demonstrations in the UK have occurred in the twenty-first century (against the Iraq war in 2003 and Brexit in 2019).

If you're thinking of joining a legal demonstration, there's not too much to agonise about. If the cause is just, it is unlikely to be hijacked by people pushing a dubious agenda, and there is at least some chance of success, whether you go or not is a straightforward personal choice.

Matters become more difficult when protest involves breaking the law. That's a serious step. The rule of law is a central plank of democracy. If people simply broke laws every time they disagreed with them, the whole legal system would become meaningless. Aristotle even believed that the rule of law was more important than democracy itself. 'It is more proper that law should govern than any one of the citizens,' he wrote. The law is needed not only to stop a despot tyrannising the majority but to prevent the majority tyrannising a minority.

Nonetheless, many environmental campaigners have argued that all responsible citizens should break the law to try to avert a climate catastrophe. Roger Hallam, one of the founders of Extinction Rebellion, has said, 'The only way to prevent our extinction is through mass participation civil disobedience – thousands of people breaking the laws of our governments until they are forced take action to protect us.' In calling for this he claims to be 'humbly following in the tradition of Gandhi and Martin Luther King'.

The evocation of King and Gandhi is a reminder that we believe that civil disobedience is sometimes called for. The political philosopher John Rawls has come up with a useful list of three tests to check whether or not it is justified. First, it is not enough to strongly disagree – the law or policy you object to has to be a substantial and clear injustice. Second, you should resort to breaking the law only when all legal avenues have been exhausted, or when it is evident that there are no effective legal channels available. Third, your protest has to be public and you must be prepared to suffer the consequences. As Gandhi said at his trial in 1922, 'I am here to . . . submit cheerfully to the highest penalty that can be inflicted upon me for what in law is a deliberate crime and what appears to me to be the highest duty of a citizen.' In this case, Gandhi's faith in the justice of his cause and the democratic system was vindicated, as the jury acquitted him.

These are the questions we should ask when considering taking part in any protest that breaks the law. In the case of the global climate emergency, many activists believe that all three conditions have been met. A climate catastrophe would be a grave injustice to people in the most vulnerable parts of the world and to future generations. The legal, inter-governmental steps to tackle it just aren't enough. And the protestors are standing up, identifiable, willing to be arrested. If they are right, and as long as their actions are peaceful and proportionate, civil disobedience is not only acceptable, it is a duty. Will you join them?

See also: Authority, Courage, Duty, Freedom, Integrity, Justice, Politics, Responsibility, Values

Reading
John Rawls, *A Theory of Justice* (Clarendon Press, 1972)

Purpose

Lots of things in life seem pointless. They leave us feeling dispirited and demotivated. The remedy? Do something else instead. But what if life itself seems pointless? Its opposite is hardly a credible alternative, since it has no purpose whatsoever. So the only positive option is to try to find life's elusive point.

People commonly try to achieve this by throwing in their lot with something bigger than themselves, which can infuse their life with purpose and significance. It could be something like God's will, or the progress of humankind. Thomas Nagel counsels caution about this kind of strategy. He argues that trying to justify our existence by looking for 'a role in some larger enterprise cannot confer significance unless that enterprise is itself significant'. He illustrates this through a thought experiment. Imagine that 'we were being raised to provide food for other creatures fond of human flesh, who planned to turn us into cutlets before we got too stringy'. Would this confer meaning to our lives? The answer is no, because we'd be in the dark about the purpose of *their* lives: it would not be clear how serving their purposes would translate into giving *us* purpose.

Nagel's main point is that a purpose matters only if we believe it serves a cause that is worthwhile in itself. That is why working to advance certain ideals – like scientific progress or human rights – can imbue our lives with a sense of significance.

However, we can get a sense of meaning without there being any end goal. It can be enough to participate in something of ultimate value. Take our connection with 'the richness and diversity of life and the landscapes of free nature', as Arne Næss puts it. 'Part of the joy stems from the consciousness of our intimate relation to something bigger than our ego, something that has endured through millions of years and is worthy of continued life for millions of years.'

Nor does a sense of purpose need to involve having a role or function in something bigger. You get out of bed in the morning with a sense of purpose whenever there is something to do that you think is worthwhile, whether that is tending the plants, feeding the cat or finishing reading a great book. Our actions are justified by the value we see in them, says Nagel, and there is no reason why that should not be found in the ordinary projects of daily life.

Participating in something bigger than ourselves is a natural way of recovering a sense of purpose. But the strategy works only if it connects us with things, people or activities that we appreciate for their own sake. So what matters is purposeful action in line with what we value. This does not have to be towards a goal, like getting married or writing a novel. Once a goal is reached, its purpose is exhausted and it can be ticked off. A value, however, such as being creative or loving, can continue to guide our actions without end.

See also: Achievement, Cosmic Insignificance, Meaning, Midlife Crisis, Motivation, Values

Reading
Thomas Nagel, 'The Absurd', in *Mortal Questions* (Cambridge University Press, 1991)

R

"Were I to live my life over again, I should live it just as I have lived it; I neither complain of the past, nor do I fear the future. I have seen the grass, the blossom, and the fruit, and now see the withering; happily, however, because naturally."
Michel de Montaigne

Rationality

'You're being irrational' is never a compliment. At the same time it is widely believed that many things in life, love in particular, aren't rational, and so it is certainly possible to be *too* rational. But if we think about it, it's less a question of 'how rational should we be?' and more of 'how should we be rational?'.

Rationality (or reason, which is more or less a synonym) has something of an image problem. It is seen as being entirely separate from feelings, as typified by the emotionless Mr Spock in *Star Trek* saying 'That is illogical, captain.' It is also associated with selfish, instrumental thinking. Rational choice theory in economics is the idea that when people act rationally they maximise their own economic benefit.

Both conceptions of rationality are false for the same reason. As David Hume put it, rather hyperbolically, 'Reason is and ought only to be the slave of the passions.' What he meant was that reason by itself is simply a tool to help us to work out what is true, how best to achieve things and whether we are contradicting ourselves. What it cannot do is provide us with primary *motivations* to act. So although Spock was right when he said, 'When there is no emotion, there is no motive for violence,' he should have added that where there is no emotion, there is no motive for kindness or love either.

That's why rational choice theory is misnamed. It is neither rational nor irrational to seek your own maximum financial benefit – it all depends on your goals and motivation. If you believe in fairness and justice, you will be more interested in sharing economic gains than in accumulating them.

Hume might have overstated his case. We can use reason to examine our values and motivations, and they often change as a result. For instance, reflecting on fairness and justice may transform your views about their importance. But he was fundamentally right that, at root, our basic desires are not the result of logical deductions or scientific discoveries. You cannot argue someone into caring for others, or liking something they dislike.

Reason has other important limits too. Sometimes we don't know enough to be able to use it to work out the best thing to do, given our desires. On such occasions we have to go on hunch, subjective preference or maybe even the toss of a coin. That is not irrational. When we have to use something other than reason we are being *non-rational*. We are *irrational* only when we go *against* reason. It's a crucial distinction. If you want a nice meal, it's irrational to pick something off the menu that you don't like, but it's merely non-rational to choose risotto over pizza on the basis of the font it's written in, if you're not able to decide on gastronomic grounds.

Although Hume recognised the limits of reason, the Western tradition as a whole has been bullish about its power. Elsewhere, there is more scepticism. Zen is especially sensitive to the inability of reason to fully capture reality. 'We must accept the fact that the intellect has its limitations,' wrote D.T. Suzuki. For instance, he thought that 'things or facts belonging to our innermost experiences' were 'beyond its domain'. In Zen, you gain a better understanding of experience by carefully attending to something than by trying to reason about it.

Our capacity to reason is a marvellous thing and we should use it whenever we can. But we should not try to use it for more than it is fit to do. Reason has its limits. The most rational people know where they are and do not overstep them.

See also: Argument, Evidence, Faith, Intuition, Knowledge, Superstition, Truth, Wisdom

Reading
Julian Baggini, *The Edge of Reason* (Yale University Press, 2016)

Regret

There are some people who claim they *ne regrettent rien*. Lucky them. Most of us look back on fateful financial decisions, the way we treated a friend or an opportunity we turned down, and feel the rueful pangs all too acutely. We rerun the situation in our minds, changing how we behaved, and it all seems so doable. We are tormented by a feeling that acting differently was within our grasp and we really could have done it.

This sense that we 'could have done otherwise' is a good place to start. What does it really mean to say that? Daniel Dennett borrows an example, originally by J.L. Austin, of a golfer who misses a putt and berates himself because he could have holed it. The golfer does not think he could have holed the putt *if conditions had been different*; he thinks that *in the exact same circumstance*s (which could include his level of skill, physical state, mood, weather conditions, competition and how much sleep he got the previous night) he could have done it. But, Dennett says, if we think a bit harder we'll realise that this can't be right. If we could rewind time to that precise moment, whatever caused us to miss the first time – overconfidence, a freak gust of wind, a twinge of nerves – would cause us to miss again. In imagining a different outcome, we're not looking at '"conditions as they precisely were" but at minor variations on those conditions'.

That is what we are usually doing when we think we could and should have acted differently. So, if we were asked a few searching questions, we would probably acknowledge that we don't mean we could have acted differently in

exactly the same situation. What we mean is that it was within
our general range of abilities to do the desired action. That
may well be true, but for some reason it wasn't possible at that
time. So there's no point in dwelling on the possibility of
having acted otherwise: we couldn't have.

However, it can be useful to reflect on what went wrong,
so long as we don't get stuck in self-blame. What was it that
at that moment stopped us behaving differently? What can we
learn from the experience? What would we like to cultivate in
ourselves to increase the chances that next time we'll act more
in line with who we'd like to be? Maybe this sort of reflection
can help us to avoid similar mistakes in the future.

Another point to bear in mind when we are regretful is
that we simply don't know how things would have turned out
had we done the alternative action that now seems straightforwardly better and superior. In reality, it might have led to
worse outcomes as well as better ones. (*See* **What If**.)

When it comes to regrets about life in general, Nietzsche
provided us with a test to check whether our attitude is life-
affirming. Imagine you were told this:

> This life as you now live it and have lived it you will
> have to live once again and innumerable times again;
> and there will be nothing new in it, but every pain and
> every joy and every thought and sigh and everything
> unspeakably small or great in your life must return to
> you, all in the same succession and sequence – even
> this spider and this moonlight between the trees, and
> even this moment and I myself. The eternal hourglass
> of existence is turned over again and again, and you
> with it, speck of dust!

How would you react? The right answer for Nietzsche is to
fully embrace everything. He calls it *amor fati* (love of fate),
'that one wants nothing to be different, not forward, not

backward, not in all eternity. Not merely to bear what is necessary, still less conceal it . . . but *love* it.'

This is a big ask. It's one thing to say that on balance we accept all the wrong turns and moral slips as part of a life we can on the whole affirm. And of course being generally satisfied with our life so far means accepting the mistakes we made along the way. But *amor fati* demands more than this.

Montaigne seems to rise to the challenge. 'Were I to live my life over again, I should live it just as I have lived it; I neither complain of the past, nor do I fear the future,' he wrote. 'I have seen the grass, the blossom, and the fruit, and now see the withering; happily, however, because naturally.'

But such full-blown affirmation of everything we have done wrong may not be necessary. Acceptance may be enough. There is a lot to accept: ourselves, our imperfections and our limited abilities; that things really did go the way they did; that we couldn't have acted differently at that point; that even if we had done, things could have turned out worse as well as better; and that one of the few absolute truths in life is that we can't change the past, so there's absolutely nothing we can do apart from making amends and trying to behave differently in the future. Acceptance is the most reliable antidote for regret.

See also: Choice, Contentment, Fate, Luck, Uncertainty, What If

Reading
Daniel Dennett, *Freedom Evolves* (Viking, 2003)
Friedrich Nietzsche, *The Gay Science* (1882)

Relationships

According to Nietzsche, 'a married philosopher belongs in comedy'. If Søren Kierkegaard is anything to go by, it wouldn't be a very funny one. He called off an engagement embarrassingly late in the day, treating his fiancée cruelly in the belief that this would make her more willing to accept his decision. He seemed to think that she ought to grieve like a widow for the rest of her life and was positively spiteful about her in his diaries when she eventually married someone else. He continued to tell himself and others that he had broken the engagement for her sake, when it would have been more honest to admit that he felt he had to choose between her and his literary ambitions.

Kierkegaard's love life was particularly tortured, but he is on a very long list of philosophers who were either romantic failures or complete non-starters. (*See* **Parenthood**.) There are, however, two very different exceptions to the rule. Simone de Beauvoir and Jean-Paul Sartre were lifelong partners, whose graves stand side by side in Montparnasse Cemetery in Paris. The key to their relationship's longevity may have been flexibility: they agreed to an open relationship and both took full advantage of the fact. Theirs seems to be an example of this actually working, albeit in a fraught and often messy way.

More conventional were John Stuart Mill and Harriet Taylor Mill. They met when Harriet was still married to her first husband, John Taylor. Their courtship was long and patient, and they waited two years after Taylor's death before marrying. Like Beauvoir and Sartre, their bond was strengthened by mutual respect, especially for the other's mind. Maybe their relationship worked in part because it helped with their vocations rather than distracting from them. Taylor was a talented philosopher herself, who left behind a number of writings. Many scholars believe that several of Mill's works, especially *The Subjection of Women*, were in effect co-authored by her. Such a happy conjunction of interests is rare, so it cannot be used as a formula for a successful relationship, though shared interests do generally strengthen bonds.

Philosophers have always been alert to the fact that knowing what you don't know is the basis of wisdom, and that no one knows everything. There are a handful of insights we can glean from philosophers' love lives. However, we humbly suggest that when it comes to relationships, philosophers aren't the best people to go to for advice.

See also: Commitment, Love, Monogamy, Parenthood, Sex

Reading
Clare Carlisle, *Philosopher of the Heart: The Restless Life of Søren Kierkegaard* (Allen Lane, 2019)

Relaxation *see* Leisure

Religion

These days, asking a philosopher about being religious is a bit like asking a vegan the best way to cook a steak. Professional philosophers are overwhelmingly godless. A large survey of 3,226 philosophers, including 1,803 faculty members, showed that 73 per cent of them accepted or leaned towards atheism, while only 15 per cent felt the same way about theism, belief in a god.

It has not always been thus. Most of the great modern Western philosophers, including Descartes and Locke, were Christians. Almost all philosophers in the Islamic world have been religious, which is why their work is often referred to as 'Islamic philosophy'. Most commentators would agree that all the orthodox schools of Indian philosophy are religious in character.

It should not surprise us that when almost everyone in a society is religious, so are most philosophers. Despite this, the tendency has always been for philosophers to hold less conventional views, which were often seen as heretical. David Hume was known as the 'great infidel' for his sceptical agnosticism. Spinoza's idea of God as being synonymous with nature was a far cry from the traditional Yahweh of Judaism. And the whole classical Chinese philosophical tradition is rooted more in the natural world than the supernatural.

That doesn't mean philosophy is of no use in helping people to think more clearly about their religious beliefs. At the very least, it should convince you that there is no point in trying to provide conclusive rational arguments for religious faith. More interesting are the philosophers who use reason to try to *make room* for faith. Alvin Plantinga points out that all proofs stop somewhere and so there are always some things we have to take as 'properly basic' without demanding arguments for their truth. Evolutionary theorists and physicists have to accept that they are not mad, that nature operates according to constant laws, that they are not living in a virtual reality simulation and so on. Plantinga argues that people who believe they have experienced the reality of God are equally justified in taking that to be properly basic. Such experiences don't *prove* God's existence, of course. But if you have had one yourself, Plantinga argues that it is reasonable to take it as good enough evidence that God exists, in the same way that your perception of having a body, say, is reason enough to think you really do have one.

Plantinga's position has similarities with that of William James. (*See* **Faith**.) They both maintain that while it is impossible to provide conclusive arguments for the existence of God, since it is not possible to provide conclusive arguments against it either, we are justified in using criteria other than rational argument to decide. Religious belief is therefore not irrational, in the sense of being *opposed to* reason. It is rather non-rational, in the sense that it is not *based on* reason.

Another cluster of theories defending religion against the charge of irrationality centres on the question of what we mean when we use religious language. Ludwig Wittgenstein argued that religious language has to be understood as part of a whole form of life in which words do not function as they do in secular discourse. He asked rhetorically, 'If an atheist says there won't be a Judgement Day, and another person says there will, do they mean the same?' According to Wittgenstein, 'In a religious discourse we use such expressions as: "I believe that so and so will happen," and use them differently to the way in which we use them in science.' For example, when Christians say that at communion the bread and wine will turn into the body and blood of Christ, they do not mean that they will literally become human flesh and blood. But nor are they using language merely metaphorically – the bread and wine changes, but not in a way that is scientifically observable. To understand this, you have to understand what it means to live the Christian form of life and to see the divine in the everyday, the infinite in the finite.

Wittgenstein could be seen as belonging to a line of philosophers and theologians who have argued that it is impossible to say what God is. As he wrote, 'If the question arises as to the existence of a god or God, it plays an entirely different role to that of the existence of any person or object I ever heard of.' In this 'apophatic' tradition, we can be clear only about what God is *not*: finite, human, material and imperfect. The positive words we use instead – infinite, supernatural, immaterial, perfect – are terms we can never claim to fully understand. 'God' is our word for a mystery, and we have to accept that our language merely gestures towards his true nature, which can never be grasped.

Most philosophers today are unimpressed by attempts to carve out a space for God that is in some sense beyond reason. But collectively these arguments point to something important about maintaining religious faith in an age of science and reason. You may have heard of scientists who claim that the theory of evolution requires the fine tuning by a creator God, or that the mysteries of quantum physics can be dissolved only with the help of a deity. These arguments are flawed attempts to use the tools of science to prove the existence of a being that has no place in science. If God is not to be dead in the twenty-first century, he must be given life by faith rather than reason.

But perhaps God doesn't need to be real for religion to survive. Another defence of religion is that it is not at its heart a matter of belief at all, but of practice. The rituals and creeds of religion merely give shape and form to a way of life that looks beyond the here and now to the things of ultimate value. Karen Armstrong has defended this view, arguing that religious truth is 'a species of practical knowledge' expressed in the form of myth, not a kind of scientific knowledge. In this view, modern philosophers and theologians have been arguing about the wrong thing: religion is not about what is, but how we ought to live.

See also: Afterlife, Cosmic Insignificance, Faith, Purpose, Risk, Superstition

Reading

Karen Armstrong, *The Lost Art of Scripture* (Bodley Head, 2019)
William James, *The Will to Believe* (1896)
Alvin Plantinga, *Where the Conflict Really Lies: Science, Religion, and Naturalism* (Oxford University Press, 2011)
Ludwig Wittgenstein, *Lectures and Conversations on Aesthetics, Psychology and Religious Belief,* edited by Cyril Barrett (Blackwell, 1966)

Reputation

Some people worry a lot about what others think about them; some believe it's foolish to care so much; and many oscillate between the two camps. There are probably good evolutionary reasons why we find it so hard to shake off this annoying concern. In prehistoric times, being accepted as part of the group was crucial to our ancestors' survival, which could be why the craving for approval has become something of an instinct.

This has not stopped many philosophers arguing that we could and should stop being slaves to this particular impulse. Whether it manifests itself as the desire for reputation, fame or public recognition, it is a false value and we should not waste our time worrying about it.

There are many reasons for this. For a start, reputation is not a reliable measure of worth. Aristotle believed that what he called 'honour' was 'shallow', because it 'appears to depend more on those who honour than on the person honoured'. In other words, how highly people think of us depends on all sorts of factors that are unconnected with merit, such as luck, popular taste and appearance. Whether or not the esteem is truly deserved is rarely the main factor.

Reputation is also fleeting and hollow when measured on the grand scale, and the effort to cultivate it is fuelled by vanity. No one puts it better than Marcus Aurelius, who muses, 'is it your reputation that's bothering you? But look at how soon we're all forgotten. The abyss of endless time that swallows it all. The emptiness of all those applauding hands. The people who praise us – how capricious they are, how arbitrary. And the tiny region in which it all takes place.'

We should also be wary of becoming the kind of people who are so concerned with reputation that their whole lives become attempts to curry favour. Seneca seemed to think that this was the norm for people who achieve high status: 'When you see a man repeatedly taking up the robe of office, or a name well known in public, don't envy him: those trappings are bought at the cost of life.'

In what could stand as a summing up of the philosophical consensus, Montaigne described reputation as 'the most useless, vain and counterfeit coinage in circulation'.

A few dissenting voices have some good things to say about reputation. Despite Aristotle's cautions, he also argued that it is reasonable to be pleased if one has a good reputation that is truly merited. (*See* **Pride**.) Furthermore, reflecting on what makes people genuinely admirable can help us to identify the qualities we need to join their ranks.

Still, we need to make sure we keep our focus on what merits praise rather than the praise itself. As Mencius says, 'If there be honouring and respecting without the reality of them, a superior man may not be retained by such empty demonstrations.' If you waste time worrying about other people, says Marcus Aurelius, 'it will keep you from doing anything useful.' He reminds us, 'It is quite possible to be a good person without anyone realising it. Remember that.' What matters is doing the right thing – if people recognise it, it's a bonus.

See also: Achievement, Guilt and Shame, Pride

Reading
Marcus Aurelius, *Meditations*

Resilience

Resilience has become a much-praised character strength, one that we have been increasingly encouraged to develop. It is essentially the ability to cope with adversity and spring back from it quickly – a very useful skill to have. The question is, how do we achieve it? There are endless courses and books that promise to build our resilience, but the basic principle is simple.

In his 'Consolation to Marcia', Seneca wrote that life entails 'thousands of afflictions of body and mind, wars, robberies, poisons, shipwrecks, climatic and bodily disorders, bitter grief for those dearest to you, and death, which may be

easy or may result from punishment and torture'. It's enough
to test anyone's resilience. Seneca's advice for dealing with it
is simply to accept that adversity is the norm in life – if we
want to live, we must 'live on the terms agreed'.

It sounds brutal: life is hard, so get on with it. We do have
more resources than that to help us. But there is a danger in
always responding to problems by having a sort of seminar
with yourself about what it all means and how you should
best think about it. Sometimes there is value to giving yourself
a metaphorical slap around the face. Life's a bitch. Get used
to it.

See also: Failure, Hope, Loss, Mistakes, Perseverance, Problems,
Stress, Suffering

Reading
Nelson Mandela, *Long Walk to Freedom* (Little, Brown, 1994)

Responsibility

In the 'Hitchhiker's Guide to the Galaxy' series, Douglas
Adams came up with the idea of the 'SEP field', a kind of
protective cloak that the human brain creates to avoid taking
responsibility. It magically appears whenever we decide something is 'Somebody Else's Problem'.

Adams might easily have dubbed it the 'NMR field': 'Not
My Responsibility'. Whatever you call it, shirking responsibility is something human beings seem very keen to do: it's
always the fault of the other driver, the person we got angry
with or 'the system'.

Philosophy takes the possibility of evasion to another level
by asking whether we are ever responsible for anything at all.
The argument starts with extreme cases where everyone
accepts that responsibility is at least diminished. It is clear that
alterations in the brain due to injury, illness or medication can

lead to enormous changes in personality and behaviour. There are some striking examples of this, such as the man who started to show an interest in child pornography as a result of a brain tumour; when the tumour was removed, the new leaning disappeared too. Or the patients with Parkinson's disease who developed a serious gambling habit when they were put on different medication.

But even away from the attention-grabbing pathological end of the spectrum, it is just as true of all of us that the person we grow up to be is determined by the genes we inherit and our life experiences. You don't choose your fundamental personality traits, your gender, your sexuality, your parents or the society you grew up in, all of which shaped you. Ultimately, we did not choose to become who we are.

Does that mean it makes no sense to hold ourselves and others responsible? And should any wrong turn we take be excused as dictated by nature and nurture? Galen Strawson thinks so. He writes that rewarding or punishing people for their actions is just like doing so for the colour of their hair or the shape of their face.

But we shouldn't give up on responsibility too quickly. Even if we are not the *ultimate* authors of our actions, we are still capable of modifying our behaviour and exercising some self-control. Our capacity to guide what we do is never absolute, but there is a difference between someone who has an impulse control disorder and someone who hasn't, for instance.

In Daniel Dennett's words, what we can aspire to can be only 'a modest . . . slightly diminished responsibility'. This modest responsibility, however, is crucial to our social world. By treating people as responsible, we encourage them to do better in the future. This is what we do with children. We are able to respond to praise and blame, and that's enough. Holding people responsible is 'the best game in town', says Dennett.

Although avoiding responsibility is one of the most common human vices, we also need to avoid the opposite evil of taking *too much* responsibility. It's difficult for us to grasp the difference between merely contributing to causing something and being responsible for it. If we think we played a causal role in something bad happening, we almost automatically feel a sense of responsibility and even guilt.

Take a fictitious example from the British-made television sitcom *Father Ted*. The eponymous priest phones Father Larry Duff, who answers his mobile phone while he is skiing down a slope, which leads to him tumbling down the mountain and ending up on crutches. There is no doubt that if Ted had not phoned him at that moment, he would not have crashed. However, while Ted partly caused the crash, that does not mean he is responsible it. To attribute responsibility, there has to be an element of intention, or culpable negligence.

Some kind of negative feeling might still be in order in such situations. (*See* **Dilemmas**.) Bernard Williams mentions the more serious case of someone who runs over a child, through no fault of their own. It would be inhuman for the driver not to feel bad. But this kind of negative emotion should have no link with blame. Guilt and remorse are not appropriate when we have done no wrong. Perhaps we might feel a kind of regret, if by this we mean feeling sorry about a situation rather than taking responsibility for a wrong we have committed. (*See* **Regret**.)

Aristotle is surely right to say that we can't be praised or blamed for things 'that happen by force or through ignorance', as these are involuntary. But this needs to be qualified. Sometimes, he says, we are responsible for our own ignorance, such as when we get drunk and behave badly while under the influence, or when we toss aside an unread safety manual with the result that someone gets hurt.

We should neither evade nor exaggerate our responsibility. Of course we don't have *ultimate* responsibility, but whoever believed we did? We only need to have *enough* responsibility to make us responsive to praise, blame, reward and punishment, which we clearly are. It is hard to see how human beings could even function without holding each other to account.

See also: Dilemmas, Duty, Free Will, Guilt and Shame, Regret, Self-Control, Self-Deception, What If?

Reading
Daniel Dennett, *Elbow Room: The Varieties of Free Will Worth Wanting* (MIT Press, 1984)

Retirement

Some dread it, some spend their whole lives looking forward to it. Many used to get it early, many now wonder whether they'll ever get it. Should we see retirement as a goal to achieve or a fate to avoid? Should we bother to think about it at all?

The answers to these questions depend on what stage of life you are at. One potentially useful way of thinking about this is to adopt David Lewis's concept of a person – unlikely though this might at first seem. Normally we think of ourselves as three-dimensional entities that are fully present at every moment. These selves move forward in time, always occupying the position perceived as 'the present'. This sounds like common sense, but Lewis argues it is wrong. We are actually four-dimensional objects that exist *across* time. Think of yourself at any given moment as simply a 'time-slice' of a person that exists in the three dimensions of space but also across the fourth dimension of time. What we normally think of as the future you is really just a future time-slice, or 'person-stage', of you.

When we look ahead to our potential retirement, we are not imagining our *present selves at a future time* – we are imagining *future parts of ourselves*, which are as real as the present time-slice that we are currently conscious of. This seems weird, as we have no awareness of our future parts. But that is merely an effect of distance in time. Just as Tierra del Fuego and Alaska are both parts of the same American land mass, just thousands of miles apart, so your younger and older selves are part of the same person, just many years apart.

There is something head-spinning about this thought, but it brings a fresh perspective to our thinking about retirement. First, take the question of how much we should be concerned about our future retired selves. On the one hand, because we are four-dimensional creatures, our past, present and future person-stages are all equally real, so it is a kind of self-neglect not to plan for the future. On the other hand, we don't know what these future time-slices will be like or what they will want. We might think a house in the country would suit them brilliantly, but it's more than possible that they will prefer the city. More gravely, we don't know how long into the future our four-dimensional self will extend – it might not reach as far as retirement.

The only sensible strategy is to try to give your future time-slices options, without second-guessing what they will want or even if they'll be there. No one knows enough to justify making retirement plans the focus of their lives, but for the same reason it is foolish to make no plans at all. Perhaps the most realistic way to think about this is that all preparations for retirement are contingency plans for something that may or may not happen, but for which you need to be ready in case it does.

Thinking of yourself as a four-dimensional being also brings home the obvious truth that you never completely change overnight: your retired self is a continuant of your working self. So, if you build your life completely around your work, you're going to have a shock if and when you give it up. There are times in life when complete devotion to work can be rewarding, but you should start thinking beyond work as soon as retirement is on the horizon. The best way to prepare for retirement is to avoid getting trapped in just one or two of your many identities, such as 'manager' or 'breadwinner'. (*See* **Identity**.) Remember that you are also an aficionado of this, an enthusiast of that, a seeker of the other.

Should you actually find yourself as a retired time-slice, consider yourself lucky. The 'problem' of what to do in retirement is a very modern one – the first country to introduce a state pension was Germany, in the 1880s.

The downside is that, as a pensioner, you have fewer person-stages ahead of you and a lot more time-slices behind you. But this can be a comfort. If you see your self as a lifelong whole, all the things you have already done belong to you just as much as the things that you see around you now. This includes failures, disappointments and heartbreaks, for sure. But it also includes your working life and experiences as an adult. Rather than thinking of these things as having been left behind in the past, imagine them as parts of who you still are. The younger self you see in photos is not someone who has vanished but is still a part of you, distant in time but intimately connected. In retirement it is easier than at any other time to see that you are your whole life, not just the person-stage you are now.

See also: Ageing, Career, Carpe Diem, Identity, Inner Life, Leisure, Memory, Midlife Crisis, Work

Reading
David Lewis, 'Survival and Identity' in *Personal Identity*, edited by Raymond Martin and John Barresi (Blackwell, 2003)

Right and Wrong

Do you know the difference between right and wrong? Most people like to think they do. At the same time, many have become unwilling to make moral judgements, saying, 'who am I to judge?' or 'what's right for me may not be what's right for you.' So what is the right way to think about right and wrong?

Nietzsche might look like an unlikely saviour for our confusion. In the popular imagination he is the man who went 'beyond good and evil', destroyed morality and replaced it with the crude assertion of the 'will to power'. In reality, he was much more interesting than this.

He argued that the distinction between good and evil is fundamentally different from that between good and bad. For most of human history, when people said things are 'good' or 'bad', they simply meant that they were pleasant or unpleasant, helpful or harmful, life-enhancing or life-diminishing. So health, medicine, music and delicious food are all good while disease, poisons, muzak and pop-tarts are all bad. Sometimes things are good in some ways and bad in others, like tasty but unhealthy triple-chocolate muffins. So although there are sometimes disputes about what is good or bad, there is nothing mysterious about what we mean by these terms.

The distinction between good and evil is different. Nietzsche believed that it developed in the Christian tradition to appeal to oppressed people who had bad lives and no ready means of improving them. Because they were unable to become good – in the sense of being flourishing and free – the meaning of good was changed so that it could apply to the meek and the weak, while the powerful and rich could be branded as 'evil'. In this way, good and evil became God's prerogative, detached from what matters for human well-being. So things like sex and pleasure became morally wrong, while suffering became virtuous.

We don't have to agree with the specific details of the story Nietzsche told and the conclusions he drew from it to accept the key point: you can ground your morality in religious terms as the rules set by God to ensure that people behave according to the divine will; or you can understand morality in purely human terms, as what is or isn't life-enhancing. In Hume's view, for instance, to say that something was morally right simply meant that it was pleasing or useful, to ourselves or others. Today one of his heirs, the neuro-philosopher Patricia Churchland, defines morality as 'the set of shared attitudes and practices that regulate individual behaviour to facilitate cohesion and well-being among individuals in a group'.

When religion is not a major factor in a moral debate, we find that people agree more often than not. It is no coincidence that the greatest moral disagreements today are between the religious and the non-religious. Without religious doctrine, issues around contraception, assisted dying, abortion and same-sex relationships would be much less controversial.

If we set aside the issues affected by religious belief, we almost all agree that it is good when people keep their promises, are of good character, are educated, healthy, free from poverty, able to work, living in peace and so on, and bad when the opposite is true. We can then agree that right actions promote what is good and wrong ones work against it. The major disagreements in moral theory are really about the relative priority of the good outcomes that we wish to promote.

So we shouldn't be shy about speaking the language of right and wrong. But if you say that something is wrong, you should be able to explain how it is causing some kind of harm, making things worse for people, breaking an important rule of social interaction or eroding character. For example, failing to tackle climate change is wrong because it will damage the lives of future generations – it's that simple.

When we accept that good and bad mean nothing more than what is good or bad for people, animals and perhaps even the planet, judgements of right and wrong make much more sense. To refuse to talk about right and wrong might seem virtuously 'non-judgemental', but in effect it means pretending that nothing is good or bad.

See also: Altruism, Character, Dilemmas, Duty, Empathy, Justice, Selfishness

Reading
Friedrich Nietzsche, *On the Genealogy of Morals* (1887)
Patricia Churchland, *Conscience* (W.W. Norton, 2019)

Risk

How often have you held back from doing something you wanted to do because you thought it was too great a risk? Failing to take just one momentous decision can leave us feeling timid. Should we simply be prepared to take more risks?

One way to think about this is to consider a famous argument about the risk of missing out on eternal salvation because you do not believe in God. Blaise Pascal argued that 'God is, or He is not', but that 'according to reason, you can defend neither of the propositions'. You have to wager on which is true.

Let's say you place your bet on God existing. Pascal says, 'If you gain, you gain all; if you lose, you lose nothing.' In other words, if God does exist, heaven's doors open; if he does not, you die a mortal as you would have done anyway. If, on the other hand, you place your bet on God not existing, and you're right, you gain nothing and you die a mortal; if you're wrong, you miss out on eternal life, and you might just end up in eternal damnation instead. Clearly then you ought to bet on God, as it is the only possible way to gain, and betting against him is the only way to lose.

This clever and ludicrous argument teaches us several important lessons, positive and negative, about dealing with risk. Most notably, Pascal makes some basic mistakes. His argument rests on the claim that the stakes are so high that the length of the odds is irrelevant – no matter how unlikely it is that God exists, the rewards of belief in him are infinite and those of non-belief are non-existent. Pascal is invoking the old gambler's maxim that you should never stake what you are not prepared to lose. No bet should be made on the assumption that you'll win it, so make sure you can live with losing.

But the likelihood of such a God existing has to be a factor. Many believe that a deity who demands belief in return for salvation is so absurdly improbable that it needn't be taken seriously. When risks and potential gains are extremely unlikely, we have to discount them.

Also, Pascal clearly does not take every possibility into account. For example, he doesn't consider what would happen if God preferred sincere unbelief to purely self-interested belief, or punished people who took a bet on the wrong deity.

More positively, we can take from Pascal the insight that decisions concerning our future fortunes are made in a position of uncertainty. Often we can't even be sure of the probabilities. Will that job work out? What will happen to house prices? Will I like my new life in the countryside or will I find the isolation intolerable? You can think about it endlessly but a lot of the time, if you're honest, you just don't know. Accepting this state of fundamental ignorance is key to rational risk-taking: to take a risk in good faith is to act knowing that the outcome is undetermined and be willing to face the consequences.

Remember that the next time someone trots out the tired old line that we regret only the things we didn't do, not those we did. Tell that to the person who is in jail for the crime they committed, or the couple whose house was repossessed because they were too optimistic about their ability to pay the mortgage.

Accepting our incomplete knowledge, however, should not mean taking every possibility as equally likely, as Pascal did. Not knowing for sure isn't the same as having no relevant information. We can and should weigh up the probabilities, no matter how rough they are.

To do this well, we have to challenge some common distortions of thinking. One is 'loss aversion', which makes us keener to avoid losing what we have than we are to get what we don't. That's sensible enough when you have a bird in the hand and might eat nothing if you go after the two in the bush. But it's foolish if you are so attached to what you've got that you don't walk through an open door to something better.

Another is the 'gambler's fallacy', the belief that future probabilities are affected by past events that are unconnected to them. So, for example, if a fair coin has come up heads three times in a row, many assume it is more likely it will come up tails next time. This isn't true – however unlikely the prior sequence is, the next toss is 50/50, like any other. This fallacy can convince us that something is less of a risk than it is: 'surely this time it will work out in my favour,' we tell ourselves.

In the PR battle between risk-takers and risk-avoiders, those who dare generally win. Risk-takers are seen as romantic seizers of the day, risk-avoiders as dull plodders who let their lives pass them by. That is, until a risk goes spectacularly wrong, when suddenly the brave and the bold become rash and reckless. Taking risks is cool only when it pays off or costs little when it doesn't. Many of us are too cautious, but the antidote is not indiscriminate risk-taking.

See also: Boredom, Carpe Diem, Choice, Commitment, Courage, Dilemmas, Fear, Indecision, Optimism, Pessimism, Regret, Uncertainty, What If

Reading
Blaise Pascal, *Pensées* (1670) §233

Routine

Routine is often perceived as oppressing and stultifying, something we need to free ourselves of if we want to allow in the new and creative. There is, of course, a comforting, reassuring side to our routines, which is why it can be so hard to let go of established ones to make room for change.

Many philosophers (as well as writers and artists), however, led the most routine lives imaginable. Kant, for instance, from the age of 40 stuck faithfully to this timetable: he rose at five o'clock, had tea and smoked his pipe, prepared his lectures and did some writing; between seven and eleven o'clock he delivered his lectures before going out for lunch; then he went for a walk and visited his closest friend, before returning home for more work and reading, and went to bed at ten.

Schopenhauer followed what seems like an even stricter daily routine for 27 years while living in Frankfurt. He rose at seven o'clock and had a bath and coffee, before writing until noon; practised the flute for half an hour; lunch at the Englisher Hof, after which he read until four o'clock; then a two-hour walk whatever the weather, after which he read *The Times* in the library; theatre or concert; dinner out; home between nine and ten o'clock; bed.

It's not only male German philosophers who had structured lives. Simone de Beauvoir's routine regularly included having tea, working alone, lunching out with friends and then working alongside Sartre in silence for a few hours, before the day turned more sociable.

We could go on. The point is that for these philosophers, routine was precisely what *enabled* their creativity – freeing their minds of trivial daily matters allowed them to focus all their attention on what mattered, which was their philosophy.

William James, who found routine difficult while appreciating its value, wrote about the importance of forming 'habits of order':

> The more of the details of our daily life we can hand over to the effortless custody of automatism, the more our higher powers of mind will be set free for their own proper work. There is no more miserable human being than one in whom nothing is habitual but indecision, and for whom the lighting of every cigar, the drinking of every cup, the time of rising and going to bed every day, and the beginning of every bit of work, are subjects of express volitional deliberation.

That seems to be the reason why, according to John Maynard Keynes, Wittgenstein 'declared that it did not much matter to him what he ate, so long as it always remained the same'.

When thinking about whether we need to shake up our own routines, we should work out whether they are playing an enabling or a disabling role in our life: whether they are stifling us, sucking our energy and vitality, or providing the necessary scaffolding for our creative activities. If we conclude that some shaking up is in order, it doesn't necessarily mean that routine should completely give way to spontaneity. It might simply be a matter of playing around with the jigsaw pieces of the day to find a routine that is more conducive to a fulfilling life.

See also: Boredom, Busyness, Change, Character, Habits

Reading
Mason Currey, *Daily Rituals* (Picador, 2013)

S

> 'A weak-willed person is one who is easily distracted or disheartened, apt to convince himself that another time will be more suitable or that the reasons for undertaking the task were not after all very strong.' Gilbert Ryle

Sadness *see* **Melancholy**

Security *see* **Insecurity**

Self-Absorption

It's easy to get wrapped up in ourselves – after all, we are in our own company 24 hours a day. Whether it's negative rumination about what's wrong with us or positive efforts to find fulfilment, too much of ourselves can not only make us self-centred, it can also be boring and wearying. Don't you sometimes get tired of yourself?

Looking outwards rather than inwards seems to be the antidote. Bertrand Russell wrote that the increasing happiness he found in older age was largely due to a 'diminishing preoccupation' with himself. In his view, cultivating impersonal interests such as science, nature or literature is one of the keys to a happy life.

According to Viktor Frankl, the more we forget ourselves – by directing our energy and attention outwards – the more human we become. 'Self-actualisation is possible only as a side effect of self-transcendence', he wrote.

Of course, a certain amount of self-reflection is necessary to work out how to become a better person. But being our own constant focus of attention is something to guard against. Paradoxically, the more we focus on our own needs and wants, the less likely we are to find what we're looking for.

See also: Inner Life, Self-Love, Selfishness

Reading
Stephen Hawking, *A Brief History of Time* (Bantam, 1988)

Self-Actualisation

If you lived your life to its fullest potential, what would that mean? Many people would answer with a version of the model proposed by the psychologist Abraham Maslow. He described a 'hierarchy of needs' in which our basic requirements come first, followed by the needs for security, belonging and then esteem. At the top of the pyramid is the highest of all human needs: to fulfil our potential and 'self-actualise'.

While Maslow's theory is not universally accepted, it is certainly true that the desire for something like self-actualisation is often very strong. But what does it actually mean? In the broadest sense, to self-actualise is to become your most complete or truest self. That is a reasonable aspiration, but one that risks making two misguided assumptions. One is that this self is already latent within you, as a potential that simply has to be made actual. But no such self exists. (*See* **Authenticity**.) The second is that the project of self-actualisation is essentially self-centred – critics may even say narcissistic.

Fortunately, there is a way of thinking about self-actualisation that avoids these pitfalls. In Confucian philosophy, the key injunction is 'Cultivate your person'. It is understood that becoming the best person you can be requires constant work to cultivate the right virtues and habits. (*See* **Character**.) There are three features that distinguish Confucian self-cultivation from the ways of thinking about self-actualisation that are dominant in the West.

First, self-cultivation is an inherently ethical project. It does involve developing skills, six of which – etiquette, music, archery, riding, calligraphy and mathematics – are core in traditional Confucian society. But it also involves being a good person: benevolent, just, wise, fair. It can be argued that true self-actualisation requires this too. You might climb

Everest or become a top CEO, but if you are a selfish bully, you haven't reached your full potential.

Second, self-cultivation does not assume that your 'true self' is in some sense already there inside you, waiting to be discovered: self has to be created. The Confucian philosopher Roger Ames suggests that we should think of ourselves as 'human becomings' rather than 'human beings', because we are never the finished article.

Third, self-cultivation cannot be done alone. To achieve your full potential, you need to acquire skills and wisdom from outside yourself, not just build on what you have. Who we are, says Ames, is 'expressed through those family, community, and cosmic roles and relations that one lives'. A Confucian understands that 'we need each other. If there is only one person, there are no persons.' The world's best cricketer plays a sport with others, invented by others and that makes no sense without others. A great book is nothing without readers. Anyone who becomes great in any field stands on the shoulders of other people, not only the giants among them.

The word 'potential' has its root in *potentia*, the Latin word for power. The Confucian lesson is that when we think about fulfilling our potential, we must not think that it is a power that solely resides in ourselves. We are social creatures who have more power together than we do alone. Self-actualisation is less about the self than you might think.

See also: Achievement, Character, Community, Identity, Needs, Self-Absorption, Self-Care

Reading
Roger Ames, *Confucian Role Ethics: A Vocabulary* (University of Hawai'i Press, 2011)

Self-Care

Self-care has become a fashionable preoccupation, the subject of many books and blogs. How could that not be good? Surely we could all do with caring for ourselves a little more. The question is, what would that look like? If you ask a doctor, they may encourage you to take more responsibility for your health. Looking for an answer on social media might leave you with the belief that it's all about looking and feeling good.

A more challenging interpretation is found in two Socratic dialogues attributed to Plato. In the *Alcibiades* (which Plato might not have actually written), Socrates argues that taking care of oneself is not the same as taking care of one's body or belongings, and concludes that caring for ourselves means cultivating our soul. In the *Apology* (which Plato did write), he reiterates the advice 'not to care for your bodies or for your wealth so intensely as for the greatest possible well-being of your souls'. What matters is not whether we feel good but whether our 'actions are just or unjust, the deeds of a good [person] or a bad one'. Plato gives an ethical dimension to self-care, to add to the 'indulgent' and the medical ones.

Understanding self-care as a process of ethical development counters any concerns that it could slide into self-centredness or even selfishness. In fact, taking care of oneself in this way could help people to become *less* self-centred and more connected with the world.

Plato's emphasis on the soul may sound a little rarefied, but the core of his message does not require it. The ethical dimension of self-care makes just as much sense if we see ourselves not as split between body and mind, but as complex organisms in which the physical and the mental are finely intertwined.

For most of the ancient Greek philosophical schools, self-care was rooted in practical exercises that were relatively independent of theory and therefore usable by anyone. Self-monitoring and self-examination were central practices, particularly for the Stoics. Seneca, for instance, says that 'the mind must be called to account every day.' To this end, he recommended a practice he had adopted from Sextius, another Stoic philosopher. This involved setting aside some time every evening to review what he'd said and done, being brutally honest about any mistakes he'd made, with the aim of improving himself.

This kind of practice could benefit most of us. Other elements of a self-care routine might include edifying reading, keeping a journal or meditation. But as Aristotle recognised, we are rational animals, so it is right and proper to care for our bodies. We are holistic beings, so we need holistic self-care. Our ethical development may be our primary task, but a healthy diet, rest and physical activity are also important. (*See* **Balance**, **Pleasure**.)

Peter Goldie suggests that 'a person's overall character or personality is best understood on the analogy of an ecological unit – a garden perhaps.' Just as in an ecological system, everything in us – values, emotions, character traits, habits – is linked to everything else. We need to be aware that any change we make in one area will have knock-on effects elsewhere. Self-care can be seen as a kind of gardening for the soul, requiring attention as well as effort.

See also: Balance, Character, Education, Inner Life, Leisure, Pleasure, Self-Love, Selfishness

Reading
Plato, *Apology*

Self-Confidence

Believe in yourself and you can achieve any goal. Or so we are told. However, watch the first episodes of any talent show and you'll see dozens of people in tears as their wishful thinking collides with reality. Still, if you don't believe in yourself, surely you'll never get anywhere. Isn't self-delusion the price we have to pay for the confidence to give our best?

The lives of philosophers suggest it ain't necessarily so. Wittgenstein was often wracked with self-doubt. When he first tried to work his 'Brown Book' notes into a proper book, he wrote that 'the whole attempt at a revision . . . is worthless'. Describing thinking, he said, 'when it's most important it's just disagreeable, that is when it threatens to rob one of one's pet notions and to leave one all bewildered and with a feeling of worthlessness.' Philippa Foot, one of the twentieth century's greatest philosophers, once said, 'I'm not clever, I don't find complicated arguments easy to follow.'

Of course, some philosophers have self-confidence in abundance. Nietzsche's philosophical autobiography contains chapters with titles such as 'Why I Am So Wise', 'Why I Am So Clever' and 'Why I Write Such Good Books'. Socrates may have said that he knew nothing, but he also boasted that this was precisely what made him the wisest person in Athens, as certified by the Oracle of Delphi.

The lives of philosophers, like those of artists, entrepreneurs or anyone else, suggest that achieving your best has no correlation with how self-confident you feel. The only common denominators among people who have fulfilled their potential is that they believed that what they were doing was worthwhile and were fully committed to doing it. At some level they must have believed that success was *possible*, but they didn't need to think it was *inevitable*.

This does require a kind of self-confidence, but not about your abilities. It is rather the conviction that what you judge to be most worthwhile really is, regardless of your doubts or those of others. That is all the confidence your self needs to do the best it can.

See also: Achievement, Commitment, Hope, Impostor Syndrome, Motivation, Optimism, Resilience, Values

Reading
Julian Baggini and Jeremy Stangroom (eds), *What More Philosophers Think* (Continuum, 2007)

Self-Control

I must cut down on my drinking. I will quit my job. I'm setting my alarm earlier to do some yoga before work. Many people make such declarations in full sincerity. And then what happens? We thoughtlessly pour the next glass of wine, we never write the letter of resignation, we reach for the snooze button.

Whether we call it weakness of will or lack of self-control, at times like these our judgement about what's best and our motivation to do it come apart. Be it a temptation, a habit we find hard to change or a problematic emotion that keeps us stuck, most of us have been there.

Although this is a common human experience, philosophers have often found it puzzling, even impossible. Plato was one of them. In the *Protagoras* Socrates says, 'no one who either knows or believes that there is another possible course of action, better than the one he is following, will ever continue on his present course.' In the end, Plato explains the fact that people evidently do act against their better judgement by suggesting that there is an appetitive part of the soul, represented as an unruly horse, which strains away from reason.

Aristotle agreed that a strong desire can cloud judgement, but he also believed that the part of us producing the wayward motivation was not completely irrational and could be made to listen to reason.

It is striking that both philosophers talk of 'parts of the self'. Any puzzlement about how we can both want and not want something is lessened if we think of the self not as a singular and unified agent but as made up of different parts, with different interests. (*See* **Identity**.) Some are more concerned with immediate gratification, others with future considerations, and these can clash.

Al Mele helps to dissolve another seeming paradox: how a weak-willed action can be both rational and irrational. It's rational in the sense that it's done for a reason. It need not be a weighty one, and could be nothing but the lure of sensual gratification. Whatever it is, it's not the reason that we ourselves had judged the most persuasive and conclusive, and it is in this sense that our action is irrational.

Mele suggests that a number of factors can contribute to our acting against our better judgement. A crucial one is how near we are to the source of reward. We tend to value closer rewards more than distant ones. For example, the rewards of sticking to a diet are in the dim future and uncertain, while those of devouring a brownie are immediate and certain. In this competition, the immediate often wins, even though we realise that the longer-term gains are more valuable.

We can often rationalise this by telling ourselves (and others) that it's not that we lacked self-control, we just changed our mind: I genuinely did want to go on a diet, but then genuinely wanted to eat cake instead. But weakness of will is different from changing our minds. A useful question to ask is whether the weak-willed option is chosen only when we are close to it. If we wouldn't choose it at a distance, it's probably a case of weakness of will.

So what can we do if we find ourselves lacking self-control in some area of our life? What we shouldn't do is to rely on willpower. That would imply there is a thing called 'willpower' that we either do or don't have. For Gilbert Ryle, the concept of will, like that of mind itself, is an illegitimate and unhelpful way of confusing a capacity with a thing. 'A weak-willed person,' he says, 'is one who is easily distracted or disheartened, apt to convince himself that another time will be more suitable or that the reasons for undertaking the task were not after all very strong.' A strong-willed person, conversely, is more able to stick to tasks without being deterred or diverted. What we need to do, then, is to facilitate our ability to do this.

The first thing to do is to check that the decision to do or stop doing something is sound, and takes all relevant factors into consideration. Is leaving our job really the best thing for us, if we look at the situation in the round?

Then we need to understand the particular motivation that is leading us astray. What is it exactly? It could be fear, for instance. Is it appropriate? When does it show up, and how does it affect our actions?

Finally we should commit to the option we have judged best, at a time when we are not being influenced by the wayward motivation. We need to think ahead, identify situations of potential backsliding and take concrete steps to stop ourselves acting against our better judgement. In social science these are called precommitment strategies. For instance, not having unhealthy foods in the house removes temptation. We can up the stakes by making failure to meet our commitment costly. Making a public promise, for example, provides us with the motivation not to lose face.

The most effective strategy is to make failure to stick with our resolution impossible. A paradigmatic example of this comes from the *Odyssey*. On his travels, Ulysses is warned by the sorceress Circe about the danger of sailing near the Sirens' island. The Sirens 'bewitch any mortal who approaches them' with their song, leaving corpses 'heaped up all round them, mouldering upon the bones as the skin decays'.

Ulysses wants to hear this magical music but knows he will not be able to rely on willpower to stop himself being lured to the island. His solution is to physically prevent himself and his crew from being bewitched. He is told, 'you must stop the ears of all your crew with sweet wax that you have kneaded, so that none of the rest may hear the song.' He himself must be bound 'hand and foot as you stand upright against the mast-stay, with the rope-ends tied to the mast itself'. Next time you feel in danger of backsliding, think of Ulysses.

See also: Ambivalence, Carpe Diem, Commitment, Free Will, Motivation, Perseverance, Self-Deception, Virtue

Reading
Alfred Mele, *Backsliding: Understanding Weakness of Will* (Oxford University Press, 2012)

Self-Deception

There are lots of things in life we wish weren't true: perhaps our partner is being unfaithful, we're not good enough to become a professional singer or we don't have enough money to get through the year. We are remarkably good at convincing ourselves that such inconvenient truths aren't really true, though when we later look back with a clearer head, we often admit that we were kidding ourselves.

Self-deception often becomes allied with weakness of will. (*See* **Self-Control**.) Say we're trying to lose weight, or cut down on our drinking. When faced with the effort and discomfort of changing well-worn habits, we can easily convince ourselves that a little top up of sauvignon blanc is OK on this occasion, or that the ice-cream is literally irresistible.

If you think about it, this is a puzzling phenomenon, as Sartre, one of the main theorists of self-deception, makes plain. There is an asymmetry, he says, between lying to oneself and lying to others. The ordinary liar lies in full knowledge of the facts, which they hide from another person. But hiding the truth from oneself is not so straightforward, as 'I must know in my capacity as deceiver the truth which is hidden from me in my capacity as the one deceived.' How is this possible?

It might be our unconscious playing tricks on us, as Freud suggested. According to Sartre, however, thinking about it in these terms does not solve the problem, it simply shifts it back one level. This is because the censor, whose job it is to decide what to allow and what not to allow into consciousness, still has to know something in order to 'unknow' it.

So how do we fool ourselves? For Al Mele, the answer is to see self-deception as a kind of magnified wishful thinking. Not only do we lack evidence for a certain belief, there is actually evidence against it, which we would see if we took the time to look. For example, it's not only that we have no good reason to think the object of our desires has feelings for us, it's quite clear they find us a bit irritating. So why don't we see this? The culprit is motivation. We so want something to be true that we attend only to the evidence in favour of it, ignoring anything that could count against it. We don't do it intentionally, it's just that our desire warps our attention.

Sartre proposes another mechanism through which we avoid taking responsibility. When we are self-deceived, or in bad faith (*mauvaise foi*), we deny our fundamental freedom and treat ourselves as if we were objects without agency, rather than as human beings capable of choice. We show clear signs of this when we cling to a fixed view of ourselves and say things like 'it's just the way I am,' or 'there's nothing I can do about it.'

If the fog of self-deception cleared, Sartre thought, we'd realise that we're responsible for how we act, even if we did not choose to be in a situation in the first place. 'You can always make something out of what you've been made into,' he says.

It might still seem puzzling how we can pull the wool over our own eyes. We can make sense of this if we think of ourselves as made up of a number of sub-selves, each with different desires and motivations. (*See* **Identity**.) Some of them may prioritise knowing the truth over believing a comforting untruth. But they may be slumbering, and we may need to wake them up. To do this, it would help to get into the habit of asking ourselves why we believe what we believe, considering whether it's reasonable and systematically seeking evidence that challenges it. Self-deception is an automatic, unconscious response to uncomfortable facts and it takes deliberate and conscious effort to overcome it.

See also: Ambivalence, Authenticity, Identity, Responsibility, Self-Control, Self-Knowledge, Unconscious

Reading
Alfred Mele, *Self-Deception Unmasked* (Princeton University Press, 2000)

Self-Esteem *see* Self-Love

Self-Knowledge

'Know thyself,' read the famous inscription on the Temple of Apollo at Delphi. Philosophers have tried to heed the call and were for a long time optimistic about succeeding – surely we have a special relationship with the contents of our minds, a kind of 'privileged access'? It was thought that our thoughts and feelings were transparent to ourselves and that we couldn't be mistaken about them. For instance, I may be wrong in thinking you're upset when in fact you're just tired, but I can't make the same mistake about myself.

Numerous philosophers have expressed versions of this view. According to Descartes, sensations, emotions and appetites 'may be clearly perceived provided we take great care in our judgements concerning them to include no more than what is strictly contained in our perception'. And in Locke's view, it is 'impossible for any one to perceive, without perceiving that he does perceive. When we see, hear, smell, taste, feel, meditate, or will any thing, we know that we do so.' This self-knowledge is attained by looking inside ourselves through what Kant called 'inner sense', which is comparable to the ordinary senses with which we perceive external objects.

Alas, a lot of this optimism has gone. Our attempts to know ourselves come up against the fundamental obstacle that most of our mental processing happens outside of our awareness and is not available for conscious scrutiny. (*See* **Unconscious**.) Our deeper motives will probably remain forever hidden from view, as Kant already knew. 'We can never, even by the strictest examination, get completely behind the secret springs of action,' he wrote.

However, there is a sense in which we do have privileged access to our own mental states. We know when we're in pain, angry or sad, more directly than we would know the same of other people. True, we can sometimes be wrong. We might think we're sad and on reflection realise that we're angry, for instance. But we can sharpen our self-awareness by paying closer attention to our experience.

So we are not wasting time and money when we sit on therapists' couches and meditation mats in the attempt to learn more about who we are, what inspires us and what upsets us. But we need to widen the methods we use to acquire self-knowledge beyond introspection. Gilbert Ryle questioned the idea that getting to know ourselves involves taking 'a peep into a windowless chamber, illuminated by a very peculiar sort of light, and one to which only [we have] access'. Instead, both our own and other people's motives are discovered by observing things like our 'conduct, remarks, demeanour, and tones of voice'. Observing ourselves as if from the outside, as others see us, can be more revealing than peering 'within'. As Heidegger argued, self-knowledge is not a matter of 'perceptually tracking down and inspecting a point called the Self', but of considering how we are in the middle of daily living.

To get to know ourselves better, we need to look at ourselves from every available perspective, not simply by attending to how things seem to us. Our ambitions in our quest for self-knowledge should certainly be modest. Complete self-awareness is beyond even the wisest sage. But that does not mean we should not try.

See also: Authenticity, Self-Deception, Unconscious

Reading
Quassim Cassam, *Self-Knowledge for Humans* (Oxford University Press, 2015)

Self-Love

People who love themselves too little and those who love themselves too much both have a problem. The trouble is that only those in the first camp realise it. Perhaps we should start with the assumption that getting the balance right is so difficult that we could all do with questioning whether we love ourselves in the right way.

Today's digital and online culture makes this difficult to do, pushing us to construct and present ourselves to look impressive to others and stand out from the crowd. As our sense of self becomes enmeshed with our public persona, we tend to identify with our flashier qualities and lose touch with who we are in the round. Furthermore, if our self-esteem is based mainly on others' approval, we are vulnerable when that validation is withdrawn.

Rousseau's distinction between two forms of self-love helps to illuminate what's going on. The first kind, *amour de soi*, is a natural and positive concern for one's self-preservation and well-being. This self-love requires only that our true needs are satisfied. *Amour-propre*, on the other hand, is not so benevolent, involving an artificial sense of self-worth that relies on doing better than others. In the online age, our attention is constantly directed to the needy, competitive *amour-propre* rather than the necessary and healthy *amour de soi*.

It's not that we should never view ourselves through the eyes of others. We are after all social animals, so the opinions of our peers should count for something. But Rousseau argues that *amour-propre* can never be content. 'This sentiment, preferring ourselves to others, also demands others to prefer us to themselves, which is impossible,' he writes.

This kind of self-love, which is sometimes translated as vanity, must be managed. It is connected with other excessive and inappropriate forms of self-love, such as conceit and self-centredness. (*See* **Pride**.) Bertrand Russell gives us a pragmatic reason to avoid these more inflated forms of self-love. In his view, if we underestimate ourselves we'll frequently be surprised by success, whereas overestimating ourselves leads to being surprised by failure. 'The former kind of surprise is pleasant, the latter unpleasant. It is therefore wise to be not unduly conceited, though also not too modest to be enterprising.'

Although our image-focused online culture seems to encourage narcissistic tendencies, it can equally fuel the other extreme. It is all too easy to feel inadequate when we compare the messiness of our own lives with the perfectly curated profiles of virtual friends and contacts. This can eat away at positive forms of self-regard such as self-worth, self-esteem and self-respect, which in the right amounts are necessary and useful. We need to remember that 'our own self-esteem should be formed without regard to the achievements of others,' as Peter Goldie puts it.

Rousseau shows that it is not only how much we love ourselves that matters, it's *how* we do so. Aristotle has more to say about the appropriate forms of self-love, arguing that a proper concern for ourselves requires clear ideas about what our well-being consists in, namely being the best people we can be – 'virtuous', in his terminology. Unlike the more vulgar forms of self-love in which we want stuff and status, this need not involve competition. Aristotle believes that if we are not virtuous, we tend to love ourselves by wanting for ourselves 'the larger share of money, honours and bodily pleasures'.

The importance of virtue is relevant to the question of how unconditional self-love should be. The right form of unconditionality is not thinking we are great and can do no wrong, but never giving up on ourselves and always seeing the possibility for improvement.

Aristotle compares self-love to a good friendship. Just as friendships involve good will, like-mindedness and pleasure in spending time together, a friendly attitude towards oneself will include benevolence towards oneself, a degree of inner harmony and enjoying one's own company. This seems like good advice, and it chimes with the practice that Buddhists call 'loving kindness', which traditionally begins by wishing oneself happiness and freedom from suffering.

Aristotle's conclusion was that 'we ought to be self-lovers. But not in the way that the masses are.' We need to make sure we love ourselves in the right way, with a concern for our genuine well-being and not for shallow things like popularity or power. We should guard against the vanity and self-centredness that often accompany what we commonly regard as self-love. Instead, we should aspire to be the best person we can be and kindly encourage ourselves to become it.

See also: Competition, Friendship, Self-Care, Selfishness

Reading

Aristotle, *Nicomachean Ethics*

Selfishness

Selfishness is a flaw that we find easier to spot in others than in ourselves, which is somewhat ironic, given that it implies being more interested in ourselves than others. Selfishness is good at hiding itself from self. If we were to look more carefully, might we conclude that we are all selfish really?

This was the cynical view of Glaucon, one of Socrates' interlocutors in Plato's *Republic*. He retold the myth of Gyges, a shepherd who found a ring that enabled him to become invisible. Did he use these powers to serve others? Not exactly: 'He seduced the queen, and with her help conspired against the king and slew him, and took the kingdom.' Glaucon argued that anyone who had such a ring would behave similarly and that the apparently just would be no different from the unjust. 'No man would keep his hands off what was not his own when he could safely take what he liked out of the market, or go into houses and lie with any one at his pleasure, or kill or release from prison whom he would, and in all respects be like a God among men.' Indeed, anyone who didn't take advantage of these powers 'would be thought by the lookers-on to be a most wretched idiot'.

Glaucon is advocating psychological egoism, the view that as a matter of fact people only ever act in what they believe to be their own interest. Apparent counter-examples are just that: kindness wins favours and admiration, and even the ultimate sacrifice can result in posthumous fame, a form of immortality.

One reason why many are persuaded by this idea is that they have noticed, as Hume put it, that 'every act of virtue or friendship was attended with a secret pleasure'. Doing good makes people feel good, so it is easy to jump to the conclusion that they do good only *because* it makes them feel good. Hume argued that this confuses cause and effect. 'I feel a pleasure in doing good to my friend, because I love him; but do not love

S

him for the sake of that pleasure.' It is only because we care about more than ourselves that it pleases us to care for others.

Psychological egoism is a theory of human nature. Ethical egoism, in contrast, argues that it is right to act in our own best interest. This position is more often attributed to others than used as a self-description, though Ayn Rand was one of the few to proudly claim it. She argued that 'man must live for his own sake, neither sacrificing himself to others nor sacrificing others to himself; he must work for his rational self-interest, with the achievement of his own happiness as the highest moral purpose of his life.'

Put starkly, this sounds brutally selfish. But there are moral arguments in favour of egoism. The most common is what you might call the 'airline oxygen mask principle': secure your own before helping others. It is better for everyone if we all look after ourselves first because we know our own needs, are best-placed to meet them and can never be sure what is in others' interest.

There are grains of truth in both psychological and ethical egoism. We can concede that the person I am best able to help is often myself, and that we are more use to others when we are at our strongest. But to reduce all human motivation and morality to selfishness is too simplistic. The moral of the Ring of Gyges is not that everyone would behave as the shepherd did if given a chance, but that the temptation to selfishness is strong.

None of this licenses pure selfishness. To think only of yourself is to shrink your world to an insular ego, separated from open and caring connection with others. This is a form of life that no sensible person would desire. To act in our own best interest therefore actually requires us not to be selfish: we do not best care for ourselves by thinking only of ourselves.

See also: Altruism, Empathy, Self-Absorption, Self-Care, Self-Love

Reading

Plato, *Republic*, Book 2

Ayn Rand, 'Introducing Objectivism' from *The Voice of Reason: Essays in Objectivist Thought* (1962)

Sex

Are you having too much or too little sex? Are you thinking about it too much or too little? Are you doing it with the right people? Is the way you like doing it normal? There are lots of people making a living trying to help others to think through these issues. Philosophers are not usually among them.

There is no reason to believe that philosophers think or care about sex less than other people, but you wouldn't know that from their writings. In pretty much every philosophical tradition, surprisingly little has been said about it.

One noble exception is Daoism. Its philosophy is based on an understanding of nature as a dynamic system in which everything is in ever-changing, active interrelation. Some of its main concepts like *qi*, *yin* and *yang* may sound like spooky forces that have no place in our modern scientific understanding. But they are better seen as helpful ways of framing how we see the world, drawing our attention to the constant flows and tensions of energies. Robin Wang, a leading contemporary Daoist philosopher, sees *yinyang* as 'a strategy or technique that enables one to function effectively in any given circumstance'.

Sex provides a perhaps surprising example of this. Sex is rooted in sensations and desires that ebb and flow in and between (typically) two people. Skilful sex is a response to this that allows our sexual desires to run their course as effectively as possible. In the language of *yinyang*, the penis is *yangjiu*, or 'yang equipment', and the vagina is *yinhu*, or 'yin house'. Good (heterosexual) sex requires each to pick up the energy of the other without extinguishing its own too slowly or too quickly.

Hence good sex is sometimes called *caiyinshu*, 'the art of picking yin'.

To see just how naturally sex is a part of the *yinyang* way of thinking, consider the seventh century BCE classic the *Guanzi*, which asks the question 'What is *yinyang*?'. The answer is 'timing' – which may also be a pretty good answer to the question 'what is good sex?'

Daoism treats sex as a serious topic because it is a philosophy of the natural world in which mind and body, humanity and nature are not separated. In traditions where the idea that our highest nature is essentially mind or spirit has prevailed, sex is an embarrassing reminder of our inferior animal nature, regarded as a force to be kept in its place.

In the West, the lowly role of sex in human life and society was for centuries taken for granted and not considered in need of philosophical analysis. More recently it has been assumed that, as Peter Singer put it, 'Decisions about sex may involve considerations of honesty, concern for others, prudence, and so on, but there is nothing special about sex in this respect, for the same could be said of decisions about driving a car.' Indeed, he adds, 'the moral issues raised by driving a car, both from an environmental and from a safety point of view, are much more serious than those raised by sex.'

It's not surprising that philosophers tend to steer clear of sex. They like to be logical and analytic, but how can you be rational about something so palpably irrational? Sex and logic look like mutually exclusive categories. Bertrand Russell lived as if this were true. Married four times and a frequent philanderer, he seemed to put his romantic life in a different compartment from his philosophy and label it unamenable to reason. Russell 'assumes that affairs of the heart are essentially and irretrievably irrational,' says Ray Monk, his biographer. 'Russell felt, I think, that anything that couldn't be satisfied by a valid deductive argument was just settled by the whim of feeling . . . So if he wakes up one morning and discovers that he's not in love with Alys [his first wife], that's it.'

Nonetheless, Russell did try to philosophise about sex in his book *Marriage and Morals*, though he did not count such popular 'shilling shockers' among his serious philosophical works. Much of the book is a rejection of religion-based sexual morality, in which he argues against the idea that sex is somehow disgusting or dirty and in favour of open sex education. Many of the battles he fought have since been largely won: he argued for divorce, especially when children are not involved, and in favour of premarital sex. 'It seems absurd to ask people to enter upon a relation intended to be lifelong, without any previous knowledge as to their sexual compatibility,' he wrote.

Russell did not take the view that sex is just sex and that we should give up all restraint completely. 'I do not think that the new system any more than the old should involve an unbridled yielding to impulse,' he wrote, 'but I think the occasions for restraining impulse and the motives for doing so will have to be different from what they have been in the past.'

Russell argued that 'civilised people cannot fully satisfy their sexual instinct without love', and was quite alarmed at what would happen if this fact was ignored. 'When people no longer feel any moral barrier against sexual intercourse on every occasion when even a trivial impulse inclines to it, they get into the habit of dissociating sex from serious emotion and from feelings of affection; they may even come to associate it with feelings of hatred.' Another bad habit, he thought, was regular 'association with prostitutes', which 'is likely to have a bad psychological effect upon a man. He will get into the habit of feeling that it is not necessary to please in order to have sexual intercourse.'

The general thrust of Russell's argument is in tune with the virtue ethics of Aristotle and Confucius. Religious morality was concerned with distinguishing sexual acts into the right and – more often – the wrong; virtue ethics asks us to think about what sorts of sexual habits are better or worse for our flourishing. There are very few absolutes in this way of thinking. Just as people argue that there are no bad foods, only bad diets, we could also say that there are few bad sexual acts, but many bad sexual lifestyles and attitudes. For example, sex without love is not bad in itself, but when it becomes the norm an important dimension of the sexual experience is lost.

Russell's writings suggest a way in which sexual ethics remains important even if we reject traditional sexual morality. Sex is a significant dimension of human life, so how we conduct ourselves sexually matters both for the flourishing of our lives and the lives of those we have sex with.

See also: Consent, Jealousy, Love, Monogamy, Objectification, Relationships

Reading
Robin R. Wang, *Yinyang* (Cambridge University Press, 2012)
Bertrand Russell, *Marriage and Morals* (George Allen & Unwin, 1929)

Shame *see* Guilt and Shame

Silence

We live in a noisy, chatty world, made even chattier by the arrival of the Internet. We are constantly being urged to 'join in the conversation', and feel left out if we don't. Silence has become so rare that some people are actually scared of it and switch on the radio to drown it out.

We don't need telling that too much noise can be irritating and stressful. However, the kind of silence that most interests philosophers is not the absence of sound but of *words*. Western thinking is often said to be 'logocentric', meaning word-focused. This has become even more prominent in modern, urban settings. We are surrounded by screens, signs, headphones, loudspeakers and chatter. Estimates vary wildly, but claims that on average we speak 7,000 words a day and read 30,000 are widespread and credible.

In non-Western traditions, however, there is a common belief that much of what is important in life cannot be expressed in language. In Daoism, for example, 'the Way' (or *Dao*) can never be adequately described in words. 'Those who know do not talk about it,' says the *Daodejing*, 'those who talk about it do not know.' Similarly, the orthodox Indian schools of philosophy see ultimate reality, *Brahman*, as indescribable. This is captured neatly in the characterisation of it as *neti neti*: 'not this, not that'. Both Daoism and the orthodox Indian schools maintain that it is still possible to have some knowledge of the *Dao* or *Brahman*, but this comes in the form of direct experience and cannot be put into words.

A related idea, common in Buddhist philosophy and the schools inspired by it, is that language distorts reality by placing it in a linguistic mould that can never conform to its true features. 'Meanings and judgements are an abstracted part of the original experience, and compared with the actual experiences they are meagre in content,' said the twentieth-century Japanese philosopher Nishida. This has the paradoxical-sounding consequence that it is only when we put things into words that we become capable of making mistakes. 'If I would make any proposition whatever, then by that I would have a logical error,' wrote the third-century BCE philosopher Nagarjuna. 'But I do not make a proposition; therefore I am not in error.'

Such views raise many questions, most notably whether it is possible to have a non-verbal experience of ultimate reality. Kant thought we could not. We are trapped in the 'phenomenal' world of perceptions, and the 'noumenal' world of things-in-themselves is unknowable.

Whatever we conclude about this massive metaphysical question, there is surely some truth in the more modest idea that language can sometimes get in the way of experience. When we retreat from conversation and turn down the volume of our inner monologue, we begin to notice things that all those words have crowded out, from the colours of the leaves to how we are really feeling. Whether we are able to put what we find into words or not, it is only by setting words aside that such moments of awareness and sensitivity can arise.

See also: Busyness, Gossip, Inner Life, Mindfulness, Noise, Slowing Down, Solitude

Reading
Julian Baggini, *How the World Thinks* (Granta, 2018)

Simplicity

Maybe because of the complexity of modern life, there has in recent years been a growing yearning for simplicity. We've seen the rise of decluttering, downshifting, upcycling, even Scandinavian death cleaning. The clean eating and living trend seems to be part of this ideal. Few people will end up giving away all their possessions and going to live in a cave, but many are sufficiently inspired to attempt some serious stripping back.

Minimalism has reinvented itself, turning from an art movement to a lifestyle choice. The new minimalists encourage us to simplify our life and create more space for the things that really matter: relationships, personal interests, self-cultivation, making a contribution.

A famous precursor of this trend was Henry David Thoreau, who in 1845 retreated to a cabin in the woods near his hometown of Concord, Massachusetts. He lived a simple life for just over two years, recording his thoughts and experiences in *Walden*. It is widely recognised that his description of the experience was somewhat airbrushed. For instance, his mother, who lived in the town, helped out with his laundry and cooking. Nonetheless, his writings have proved consistently inspiring to subsequent generations seeking simplicity.

His advice does indeed strike a very modern note: 'Simplicity, simplicity, simplicity! I say, let your affairs be as two or three, and not a hundred or a thousand; instead of a million count half a dozen, and keep your accounts on your thumb nail.'

Thoreau is realistic and does not believe that his model of the simple life would suit everyone. 'I would not have anyone adopt my mode of living on my account,' he wrote. Instead he thought that each person should find their own way of living 'simply and wisely'.

But what does that mean in practice? The concept of simplicity in this sense is not at all simple and includes different strands, such as living as cheaply and self-sufficiently as possible, giving up unnecessary items and activities, being close to nature and enjoying small everyday pleasures. Another way of thinking about simplicity is not as a reduction to the minimum elements but as getting to the core of something: a good 'simple' thing like a cup of coffee requires not the fewest ingredients but the right, good-quality ones, prepared with skill and care.

In our technological and connected world, it is not straightforward to boil things down to the essential. Emrys Westacott reminds us of this by asking, 'Which is simpler, washing all your clothes and sheets by hand, or using a washing machine?' Similar questions apply to cooking over a fire with wood we've collected and chopped instead of turning on the cooker, or delivering messages by hand instead of making phone calls. 'Reducing our dependence on infrastructure and technology may bring us closer to simple living in one sense – we are more self-sufficient – but takes us away from it in other ways since it makes basic tasks much more difficult, arduous and time-consuming.'

Westacott points out that the world today is a different place from previous eras when philosophers recommended a simple life. (*See* **Needs**.) There is a lot more to give up if we want to go back to basics. It's much easier to choose a simple life in a world that is quite simple anyway, something else altogether to opt out of a complex one.

Once you factor money into the equation, things become even more complicated. An ironic indication of the complex relationship between simplicity and money is that the beautifully designed magazines advocating the simple life cost in excess of £5, while a holiday to a secluded off-grid hut or yurt will probably cost you four figures. The cabin in the woods – or the land to build it on – does not come cheap.

Even if you were prepared to leave all mod cons behind and go back to basics, you'd still need somewhere to pitch your tent and some money to live on. Instead of simplifying your life, maintaining this lifestyle could end up becoming an all-consuming effort. After his experience in the woods, Thoreau chose to compromise and earned a living by working as a part-time land surveyor, which left him enough time to pursue his interests and his writing.

Thoreau later acknowledged that simplicity was complicated in yet another way: 'There are two kinds of simplicity, one that is akin to foolishness, the other to wisdom. The philosopher's style of living is outwardly simple, but inwardly complex.' We can try as best we can to simplify our lifestyle, but our *inner* life should remain complex.

Living simply is not easy. Our best chance of doing so requires working out what is essential in life and keeping it at the front of our mind so it can guide our choices. The cabin in the woods is optional.

See also: Asceticism, Consumerism, Desires, Needs, Slowing Down

Reading
Henry David Thoreau, *Walden* (1854)

Sleep

We've recently been bombarded by warnings about the dire health consequences of not getting enough sleep. But while it's good to encourage people to establish good 'sleep hygiene', telling them how bad it will be if they don't get the required number of hours will surely only keep them awake at night even more.

We could try to reassure ourselves that sleep is overrated. 'When a man is asleep he is no better than if he were dead,' wrote Plato. 'He who loves life and wisdom will take no more sleep than is necessary for health.' Plenty of very successful and productive people have struggled to get enough sleep, including Isaac Newton, Benjamin Franklin, Groucho Marx and Bill Clinton.

More helpful is the Stoic advice about remembering what is and what is not in our control. Unlike the other two pillars of health – diet and exercise – sleep is not completely in our control. Sure, we can create the right conditions in our bedrooms, refrain from looking at our screens after a certain time, avoid eating and drinking in excess, do yoga or meditation. But none of that can ensure that sleep will come, and worrying about it will make this less rather than more likely. It would be much better to relax and accept that how well we sleep is not in our power. Paradoxically, this might help us to sleep better.

See also: Anxiety, Contentment, Control, Frustration, Worrying

Reading
Darian Leader, *Why Can't We Sleep?* (Penguin, 2019)

Slowing Down

The speed of light is a physical constant. The speed of *life*, however, is a cultural variable that appears to be increasing with each ever more rapidly passing year. In response there has been a flourishing of slow movements advocating slow food, slow journalism, slow radio, slow travel – pretty much anything that usually *isn't* slow.

This is one of those rare occasions when, by being so far behind the times, philosophy actually ends up ahead of the curve. Philosophy has always been proudly slow. Seventeenth-century philosophers are still called 'early modern', and 'recent' might mean any time in the last fifty years.

Philosophy as a discipline moves slowly because it is concerned with perennial issues rather than the headlines of the day. Journalists discuss particular injustices, philosophers discuss the nature of justice itself. Philosophy requires us to stand back, not just from specific cases but from the present moment. Whether or not it can meet Spinoza's lofty aim of achieving understanding *sub specie aeternitatis* ('from the perspective of the eternal'), it seeks at least to break free from the narrow perspective of particular times and places.

Philosophy as a practice also requires time and patience. It is a compliment rather than an insult to point out that great philosophical texts are not generally page-turners, but require careful attention and active engagement. 'I should not like my writing to spare other people the trouble of thinking,' wrote Wittgenstein.

Philosophers have increasingly engaged with society's short attention span. The excellent *Philosophy Bites* podcast, for example, features short interviews with leading thinkers. But philosophical snacks like this are mere hors d'oeuvres, not main courses. Like the entries in this book, they are not intended to be consumed in a few minutes and just as quickly forgotten. They are spurs to slower thinking and invitations to longer reading. Time is our most precious currency – sometimes we get the best value by spending it slowly.

See also: Everything

Reading
The complete works of David Hume, Aristotle, Plato, René Descartes . . .

Social media *see* **Virtual Life**

Solitude

Judging from media reports, modern life has created a chronic and deadly loneliness epidemic. Millions report suffering from unpleasant feelings of being alone that are said to have catastrophic consequences for our health. Some might find it reassuring to discover they are not alone in their loneliness. Others, who were until now happy enough by themselves, might be stressed to learn that their situation is so bad that it is likely to cause their premature death.

But aloneness and loneliness are not the same thing. Aloneness is a simple description of an environmental state, while loneliness refers to feelings of isolation and a longing for connection. The two don't necessarily go hand in hand, and it is loneliness that is the source of psychological and health problems. Feelings of loneliness don't always occur when people are on their own, and it is not uncommon to feel alone in a crowd. Many people who report feeling lonely have as much human contact as those who don't.

Existential philosophers have written about a fundamental sense of isolation that is inseparable from being human. As Paul Tillich puts it, 'Being alive means being in a body, and being in a body means being separated from all other bodies. And being separated means being alone.' Nor can we ever fully get inside the thoughts and feelings of another. There is a gap between ourselves and others that can never be completely bridged. A certain amount of loneliness therefore has to be accepted as part of the human condition.

One way of dealing with loneliness is to reclaim solitude as a positive state that is worth seeking out. The lives of many illustrious philosophers, including Descartes, Newton, Locke, Pascal, Spinoza, Kant, Leibniz, Schopenhauer, Nietzsche, Kierkegaard and Wittgenstein, have been largely solitary. Many philosophers have also recommended cultivating solitude.

Montaigne writes that we should make 'our happiness depend on ourselves' and be content with being 'really and truly alone'. However, he also advises making preparations for being alone: 'It would be madness to entrust yourself to yourself, if you did not know how to govern yourself.'

It's not that we should all become hermits. Even those who advocate solitude rarely recommend an exclusive diet of it, and most philosophers advise combining it with company. Seneca writes, 'Solitude and company must be blended and alternated. The first will bring on a longing for people, the second for ourselves, and each condition will be the cure for the other; solitude will heal loathing for the crowd and the crowd one's weariness of solitude.'

So if you're feeling lonely, a dual strategy is advisable. One prong is to reach out and connect, as we're advised to do. Join a club or a class, get out more. This is great advice, although since we can feel lonely in company it might not be a sufficient remedy by itself. The other prong is to adjust our expectations about how much connection we really need. If a degree of loneliness is natural, then it would be useful, alongside practical steps to seek company, to develop our ability to be alone. We should acknowledge that the experience of being alone depends on our attitude towards it – as Lars Svendsen argues, we need to take responsibility for our own loneliness.

Above all, this requires forging the kind of relationship with ourselves that allows us to have a more positive experience of solitude. Montaigne writes that the soul 'can keep herself company', and advises setting aside a space where our 'conversation should be of ourselves, with ourselves, so privy that no commerce or communication with the outside world should find a place there'. Everyone needs an Instagram-free zone.

Our capacity for solitude is built on an ongoing inner dialogue with ourselves. (*See* **Inner Life**.) This is undermined by the ready availability of distractions and constant technological connectedness, but it can be developed through reflection, meditation, reading or walking. 'Perhaps our era's greatest problem,' says Svendsen, 'is not excessive loneliness, but rather too little solitude.' Strengthening our relationship with ourselves could help to transmute crippling loneliness into contented solitude.

See also: Community, Friendship, Inner Life, Relationships, Self-Love

Reading
Lars Svendsen, *A Philosophy of Loneliness* (Reaktion Books, 2017)

Stress

Bereavement, divorce, moving house, major illness, job loss. You'll probably recognise these as being at the top of the league table of stressful life events. They are followed by many others, including pending deadlines, conflicts with colleagues or neighbours and excessive work demands.

And yet the concept of stress is vague and potentially unhelpful. Have you stopped to ask yourself what you really mean when you say you're 'under stress'? How is it different from having a problem that is hard to solve or being unhappy about an aspect of your life?

It's not too surprising if we're confused, as the term has a tortuous history. It began life as a concept in physics and was later applied to animal and human behaviour, shifting in meaning. It is now a multi-purpose word that is used to refer to, among other things: a situation that we perceive as a threat to our well-being; an experience of feeling over-whelmed or unable to cope; a physiological response of the fight-or-flight kind; and even to the health consequences that this response might lead to.

It's worth taking a step back and considering the original meaning of stress. In physics it occurs when an external force is applied to an object, which resists. The object can withstand a certain amount of stress but it will eventually break.

One of the problems with the way we commonly talk about stress is that we do so with this metaphor in the background. We say we are 'under pressure', 'ready to snap' or 'at breaking point'. This implies that there are certain things that are inevitably stressful, and we are passive before them.

In their classic *Metaphors We Live By*, George Lakoff and Mark Johnson argue that our thought processes are largely metaphorical, and that by focusing 'on one aspect of a concept . . . a metaphorical concept can keep us from focusing on other aspects of the concept that are inconsistent with that metaphor'. For instance, focusing on the conflictual aspects of a discussion can conceal its cooperative aspects. In the same way, talking about being under stress as though we were objects subject to a physical force will bring to the fore our passivity and obscure our resourcefulness.

Nothing is objectively stressful – not even moving house. Unlike a car being flattened by a crusher, for us stress is all to do with perception. Whether we find something stressful or not is very much a matter of how we relate to it. That is why one of the most useful definitions of stress highlights not just the stimulus or the response, but the gap between them. On this account, stress is the result of a disconnect between the perceived threat and our perceived ability to respond to it. This suggests that there is some leeway for changing our perceptions, our response, or both. Perhaps the threat can be reframed as a challenge, or the stressful situation viewed simply as a problem to be dealt with. Maybe you are or can become more resourceful than you give yourself credit for.

A few words of caution are needed here. First, we have to be careful not to rationalise the situation, kidding ourselves that our difficulties are more manageable than they are – trying to convince yourself that you are fine when you're not won't help in the long run. Second, some situations in life are so challenging that only exceptionally wise or placid individuals could manage not to be adversely affected by them.

We have to be realistic. Life will always throw challenges at us and we will sometimes feel the pressure. Whatever else we do, changing the way we look at things might make a big difference.

See also: Anxiety, Fear, Frustration, Mental Health, Problems, Resilience

Reading
George Lakoff and Mark Johnson, *Metaphors We Live By*
(University of Chicago Press, 1980)

Success *see* Achievement

Suffering

In our youth, says Schopenhauer, 'we sit before the life that lies ahead of us like children sitting before the curtain in a theatre, in happy and tense anticipation of whatever is going to appear. Luckily we do not know what really will appear.' What's in store for us is toil and strife, infirmity, old age and death.

Schopenhauer was influenced by Indian religions. Among these, Buddhism has suffering at its core. The Buddha says, 'Now this, monks, is the noble truth of suffering: birth is suffering, ageing is suffering, illness is suffering, death is suffering; union with what is displeasing is suffering; separation from what is pleasing is suffering; not to get what one wants is suffering.'

The word translated here as 'suffering' is *dukkha*. A better translation is 'unsatisfactoriness', which doesn't misleadingly suggest that we are always in some kind of pain. It's just that everything is constantly changing and will eventually come to an end, so the things we normally believe will make us happy will never give us lasting satisfaction.

This seems accurate. We suffer because of some inescapable facts about our existence. Our bodies get old, ill and die. While we're alive we regularly face experiences we don't care for and lose or fail to secure things we love and cherish. There can be no argument that for much of the time we are beset by losses, disappointments and bodily malfunction.

According to David Benatar, 'we must continually work at keeping suffering (including tedium) at bay, and we can do so only imperfectly. Dissatisfaction does and must pervade life. There are moments, perhaps even periods, of satisfaction, but they occur against a background of dissatisfied striving.'

The question is, what follows from this realisation? The advice of Buddhism and Schopenhauer is to let go of our desires rather than strive to fulfil them: if we are less concerned with how things turn out for us in this world, we are likely to suffer much less.

Disengaging from most of the things that give our life meaning and pleasure might be a step too far. A more achievable ambition is to learn that life is fundamentally imperfect and throw ourselves into what it has to offer while we can, taking suffering on the chin.

Schopenhauer also suggests that despite life being miserable, the experience of living can be momentarily transformed by appreciating art, music and nature. At those times, our will stops striving and we become absorbed in the beauty of what is before us. That is the good news; the bad news is that those moments are only fleeting.

Nietzsche takes a different approach to suffering, believing that while it is inevitable, the key is to take it as an opportunity for self-improvement. He says, 'Examine the lives of the best and the most fruitful people and peoples and ask yourselves whether a tree which is supposed to grow to a proud height could do without bad weather and storms: whether misfortune and external resistance, whether any kinds of hatred, jealousy, stubbornness, mistrust, hardness, greed, and violence do not belong to the favourable conditions without which any great growth even of virtue is scarcely possible?'

There is some truth in this. Some people even say they are glad for their misfortunes because they helped them to develop. However, we don't have to wish for suffering or glorify it in order to realise that it is part of every life and we can try to use it as a chance to grow.

See also: Health and Illness, Melancholy, Mental Health, Pain, Problems, Resilience, Vulnerability

Reading
Arthur Schopenhauer, *The World as Will and Representation* (1859)

Suicide

'There is only one truly serious philosophical problem,' wrote Albert Camus, 'and that is suicide.' What could be more important than 'judging whether life is or is not worth living'? None of the so-called major problems of philosophy even approaches the gravity of this one. 'I have never seen anyone die for the ontological argument,' Camus said of the unending debate about whether God's existence is necessary.

Camus, however, did not provide as ringing an endorsement of existence as you might have wished. For Camus, life is absurd. He compares the human condition to that of Sisyphus in Greek mythology. 'The gods had condemned Sisyphus to ceaselessly rolling a rock to the top of a mountain, whence the stone would fall back of its own weight.' Sisyphus is able to be happy by embracing his fate rather than railing at its injustice and futility. We should be like him: 'The struggle itself towards the heights is enough to fill a man's heart.' In this worldview, the pointlessness of life is the point. Life has to be its own answer, as the enlightened aliens in Ray Bradbury's *The Martian Chronicles* put it.

Camus's yes to life, however, is not an argument against those who find themselves saying no to it. To decide that life is not worth living is not a sign of irrationality – indeed, some-times it is all too rational. The philosopher Walter Benjamin fled Nazi Germany in 1932. In 1940 he was in the Catalan town of Portbou when the nationalist Spanish government of General Franco ordered that all Jewish refugees must be returned to France. Seeing his fate as helpless, he deliberately took a fatal overdose of morphine.

It is difficult to deny that Benjamin's decision was a reasonable and courageous response to the horror of his situation, especially when we consider that his brother Georg was killed at the Mauthausen-Gusen concentration camp in 1942. Benjamin's grave in Portbou carries words from a completed manuscript that his friend Hannah Arendt was able to pass on to his colleague Theodor Adorno: 'There is no document of culture which is not at the same time a document of barbarism.' Who can blame anyone who rejects such a world?

David Hume believed that suicide was a perfectly reasonable choice when 'age, sickness, or misfortune may render life a burthen, and make it worse even than annihilation'. In many religious traditions, however – including Christianity, Islam, Judaism and Hinduism – suicide has been considered a sin, and cultures dominated by these religions have frowned on it and often made it illegal. Hume argued that these prohibitions made no sense. The idea that suicide defied God's will was incoherent because we are always making choices that change what happens. Why is the choice of suicide any more a defiance of God's will than taking an aspirin? After all, according to believers, everything happens only because God allows it, so 'When I fall upon my own sword ... I receive my death equally from the hands of the deity, as if it had proceeded from a lion, a precipice, or a fever.' Such views were so radical that Hume felt unable to publish this essay in his lifetime.

There is, however, an extremely important point to make about suicide, one that Hume missed. He wrote, 'I believe that no man ever threw away life, while it was worth keeping. For such is our natural horror of death, that small motives will never be able to reconcile us to it.' The evidence suggests that this is tragically false. Most suicides are not the result of a settled, rational judgement that life is not worth living, but take place in bouts of depression or despair. Between one third and four-fifths of all suicide attempts are impulsive. One study found that 90 per cent of people who survive a suicide attempt do not go on to die by suicide, suggesting that suicidal intent usually passes, if it is given a chance to do so.

There is a time and a place for philosophical debates about the ethics of suicide. The window ledge is not one of them. If you or someone you know is contemplating suicide, the most important thing you can do is try to delay the irreversible decision to go ahead. If someone remains convinced that life isn't worth living, they'll get the chance to act on that conviction later; if not, acting now would be a tragic mistake. Either way, pull back from the edge and save the philosophising for later.

See also: Afterlife, Assisted Dying, Bereavement, Cosmic Insignificance, Hope, Love of Life, Meaning, Purpose

Reading
Albert Camus, *The Myth of Sisyphus* (1942)
David Hume, 'Of Suicide' (1777)

Supernatural *see* Nature

Superstition

There are many rational and intelligent people who touch wood, cross their fingers and avoid walking under ladders or booking a table for thirteen. Should we be embarrassed by our inability to shake off all superstition, or do we actually have nothing to be embarrassed about?

David Hume helps to resolve this tension. Superstitions are generally false ideas about one thing causing another. Believing that stepping on a crack in the pavement will make something bad happen or that wishing upon a star will cause something good seems crazy. But Hume put forward the sceptical argument that neither reason nor experience ever really justifies our beliefs about what causes what, even 'reasonable' beliefs like that the sun causes skin to burn or water helps plants to grow.

We never see one thing *causing* another. All we observe is one thing *following* another. Nor can we justify the leap from 'A then B' to 'A causes B' with a rational argument. Children don't conclude that water quenches thirst by logical deduction; they learn, as Hume said, by habit and instinct. Nature has made us attribute causal effects when we observe the 'constant conjunction' of one thing reliably following another. We believe there is a 'necessary connection', but the necessity is something we project rather than observe. The link is forged in our heads: one idea becomes causally associated with another.

The idea that belief in causation is based in neither observation nor reason seems shocking. Shouldn't we give up any belief that is so groundless? The problem is that we can't – the assumption of cause and effect is essential to how we make sense of the world.

This not only makes space for superstition to wriggle its way in, it makes it virtually inevitable. Because there is no straightforward rational principle that we can use to identify genuine causal relations, whenever we see one thing following another it is always possible that we will mistakenly see a causal link.

For example, if you wore your lucky hat and your team won, it is natural to at least wonder if the first thing caused the second. The mind is hypothesising causal connections all the time. Of course you didn't *see* the causal link between the two, but you don't see the causal link between taking paracetamol and your headache going either. Similarly, we rely on the testimony of others. After all, the only reason we have to follow all sorts of medical advice is that experts tell us it works. When millions of people believe that walking under ladders will bring bad luck, it is tempting to believe there must be some truth in it.

There are, of course, answers to these defences of superstition. We do have fallible but rational ways of testing whether supposed causal links are real. Experiments show that paracetamol relieves headaches and biology helps us to understand how that happens. The same can't be said for black cats crossing your path and good or bad things happening. So rational people should be able to distinguish between real causes and superstitions.

The problem, as Hume pointed out, is that this kind of rational analysis is exactly what we are not doing moment to moment, day to day. We rely on imperfect habits and instincts to make sense of our experience. Cooler scientific analysis requires more time and thought than everyday life allows.

That's why even intelligent people can't shake off every superstitious thought. What they can do is to avoid acting on them, at least when important things are at stake. Crossing your fingers might be a harmless habit, but refusing to get on a plane because you forgot your lucky charm is disruptive and expensive. Understanding how the charm casts its spell won't make your fear go away, but it could give you the reassurance you need to ignore it.

Phobias are harder to overrule, even though they are rooted in the same psychological mechanisms. A phobia is a visceral belief that something harmless has a necessary connection with something terrible. In Hume's terminology, one idea has become associated with another and we project that association onto the world. The link was not forged by reason, and reason has little power to break it.

Superstitions can also play a social role that might have nothing to do with belief in causal powers. For example, Confucianism advocates the importance of performing rituals, some of which sound hocus pocus, but the third-century BCE Confucian Xunzi suggests that many people didn't really believe that these rituals had any magical effects. 'One performs the rain sacrifice and it rains. Why?' he asks. 'I say: There is no special reason why. It is the same as when one does not perform the rain sacrifice and it rains anyway.' So why then perform rituals before deciding on important affairs? 'Not for the sake of getting what one seeks, but rather to give things proper form.'

Rituals that appear to have a superstitious dimension are often no more than shared practices that help to create a sense of community and history. When you blow out the candles on a cake and make a wish, or nail a horseshoe to your front door, you are not necessarily foolishly believing that these actions will have any effects – you might simply be doing what people do in order to affirm your membership of a community and a tradition.

All superstitions are in some sense silly and irrational, but so are human beings. We can't wish them away, but we can make sure they don't have a disruptive influence on our lives.

See also: Afterlife, Evidence, Faith, Fear, Rationality, Religion

Reading
David Hume, *An Enquiry concerning Human Understanding* (1748)
Xunzi

T

> 'Due to extreme delusion produced on account of a partial viewpoint, the immature deny one aspect and try to establish another.' Mallisena

Temptation *see* **Self-Control**

Tolerance

Many of us value openness and acceptance of people who are different from ourselves. At the same time we get riled when people express views we find abhorrent or act in ways we strongly disapprove of. So how tolerant should we be?

Philosophy has generally treated the issue of toleration as a political one. Liberal democracies in particular face the challenge of how far they should tolerate intolerance. If someone believes homosexuality is a sin, for example, should they be bound by laws that prohibit discrimination on grounds of sexuality?

The political issues also play out at the personal level. If you pride yourself on your liberal, tolerant values, are you obliged to respect the views of people whose beliefs you find bigoted? If, on the other hand, your views are more traditional and conservative, should you accommodate those that are more permissive?

Some of the most useful texts to help us to think this through were carved in stone in the north of the Indian subcontinent in the third century BCE. The Edicts of Ashoka were an attempt to spread the eponymous emperor's interpretation of Buddhist social philosophy. One of the most famous of them stated that 'all sects should reside everywhere, for all of them desire self-control and purity of heart.' Ashoka knew that people in his kingdom followed various religions and that peace and harmony required mutual respect. Everything he said about religion applies to any kind of belief or value system.

This does not mean that anything goes. First, there were some core principles that everyone had to sign up to in order to enjoy this respect and freedom. For Ashoka, these included not just the requirement that they were tolerant themselves, but also that they obeyed the command that 'In my domain no living beings are to be slaughtered or offered in sacrifice.'

Ashoka's specific bottom lines are idiosyncratic, but the fact that there were any at all points to the importance of some shared values if toleration of difference is to work. When we object to people ignoring or rejecting these core values, we are not necessarily being intolerant; we are rather insisting on what is necessary for true toleration to be possible.

This links with the second key feature of Ashokan tolerance, which is that it works only if it is mutual. That means we have to be aware of our own role in maintaining harmonious relations. Ashoka believed that for this we need 'restraint in speech, that is, not praising one's own religion, or condemning the religion of others without good cause. And if there is cause for criticism, it should be done in a mild way.'

Too often we think that toleration means that everyone has the right to say what they think without self-censorship. But thinking about how our words affect others should be second nature in a genuinely tolerant society, office, club or home.

A third aspect of Ashokan tolerance is the plea to go beyond mere tolerance. Toleration has the implicit connotation of putting up with something that we find vexatious. Ashoka believed we should try to do more than this and seek to understand, even love, those who are different from us. 'One should listen to and respect the doctrines professed by others.' That doesn't mean we will always agree with them, and if they go against the shared values of our society we may need to resist them. But if people with different beliefs try to see the best rather than the worst in each other, they often find they are able to not only tolerate but appreciate each other's existence.

Ashoka had the important insight that our own values are best served by opening them up to challenge. If we praise them without question, we end up becoming dogmatic, rigid and blind to any weak spots we might have. This is why he said, 'Whoever praises his own religion, due to excessive devotion, and condemns others with the thought "Let me glorify my own religion," only harms his own religion.'

John Stuart Mill had a similar thought two millennia later. He argued that a person has justified confidence in their beliefs only when 'he has kept his mind open to criticism of his opinions and conduct' and when 'it has been his practice to listen to all that could be said against him; to profit by as much of it as was just'.

Collectively, the Edicts of Ashoka give us three pillars for successful toleration. First, try to sympathetically understand difference rather than merely put up with it. Second, think about how you should behave before being too judgemental about the acts of others. Third, remember that not everything should be tolerated and that upholding core common values is the precondition for harmony, not a threat to it.

See also: Community, Duty, Empathy, Freedom, Office Politics, Politics, Protest, Religion

Reading
John Stuart Mill, *On Liberty* (1859)
Edicts of Ashoka

Travel

So many places, so little time and – for most of us – not enough money. The world is presented to us as a smorgasbord of varied delights, more accessible than ever before, but the list of places we want to see is always longer than those we have seen. As aviation becomes a guilty accomplice of climate change, we might stop to wonder whether our wanderlust has got out of control.

If we ask why we travel, we might be tempted to give the worthy answer that it broadens the mind. It certainly worked for Descartes: 'In my travelling,' he wrote, 'I learned that those who have views very different from our own are not therefore barbarians or savages, but that several use as much reason as we do, or more.' He realised that a Frenchman such as himself 'would become different from what he would have been if he had always lived among the Chinese or the cannibals', and concluded that 'we are clearly persuaded more by custom and example than by any certain knowledge.'

What is most striking about this today is why an intelligent man like Descartes needed to travel to learn these lessons. In our hyperconnected world, you don't need to go anywhere to realise that people are people across the globe and that cultures make us different.

Travel can also confirm stereotypes as much as it challenges them. David Hume loved Paris but it seemed to harden his negative view of Londoners. In a letter he wrote, 'The Taste for Literature is neither decayd nor depravd here, as with the Barbarians who inhabit the Banks of the Thames.'

The benefits of a change of scenery and the chance to relax are not to be underestimated. Perhaps this, as well as the desire to see as many of the wonders of the world as possible, is reason enough to travel. But if we are honest, very few places leave a deep and lasting impression on us. It would be good to enjoy holidays when we can, without this escalating into an insatiable desire to tick more and more places off our bucket list. Being bothered by where we haven't been only detracts from the pleasure of where we have.

Travel is not the only thing that provokes this fear of missing out, or 'FOMO' as it is now known. FOMO is an unsettling feeling that leaves us constantly unsatisfied, our eyes always on the next thing rather than the present one. If we can accept that it is better to do less properly than more in a rush, we might even embrace what the Danish psychologist

Svend Brinkmann calls 'JOMO', the joy of missing out. *Acceptance* of missing out would do, but unfortunately it doesn't have a nice acronym.

If we are to worry less about the quantity of our experiences and focus more on their quality, a good model is the seventeenth-century Japanese philosopher-poet Basho, whose short book *Narrow Road to the Interior* is a classic of travel writing. Basho called his journey a pilgrimage, but that does not mean he was focused on a sacred destination. Although he did spend time performing rituals and visiting shrines, what made it a pilgrimage was the spirit of the journey rather than any particular goal or act. It was an opportunity to reflect, meditate and marvel at the world.

Basho's trip had several hallmarks of a normal holiday. He saw famous sights, like the reeds of Tamae in bloom, the pines of Shiogoshi and the bay at Kisakata. But travel is not all fun. At one point 'a heavy storm pounded the shack with wind and rain for three miserable days' and at another he was invited to stay a week by someone who 'knew from his own many travels ... the trials of the road'. Nonetheless, the rewards were at times immense. At one point he comes across a derelict monument that is nearly a thousand years old. Reading the inscriptions covered by moss, he is touched by his connection to a past that 'remains hidden in clouds of memory'. Such a moment, he says, 'is the reason for pilgrimage: infirmities forgotten, the ancients remembered, joyous tears trembled in my eyes.'

Travel is most valuable when it is done in the spirit of Basho. It is an opportunity to empty our minds of our usual thoughts and concerns and to pay attention to new surroundings, engaging with them in ways that enable us to truly connect: with nature, culture, people and history. When we do this, we free ourselves from the ceaseless desire to do more, feeling truly grateful for the wonderful moments that emerge and accepting of the discomforts they sometimes require. We become pilgrims in the world, blessed and in awe of its sacred wonder.

See also: Carpe Diem, Consumerism, Gratitude, Home, Leisure, Love of Life, Routine, Slowing Down

Reading
Matsuo Basho, *Narrow Road to the Interior*, trans. Sam Hamill (Shambhala, 1991)

Trust

Who do you trust? The chances are your answer won't be a long one. People who trust too easily are quickly bitten, although a remarkable number of us don't learn the lesson. But those who trust too little often find that they have problems developing intimate relationships or making any kind of commitment that involves a risk. Negotiating the middle path generally leaves us trusting very few people completely and others only partially.

Why is it so difficult to gauge the appropriate level of trust correctly? Onora O'Neill has a lot to offer us here. She points out that trust is not and cannot be the same as a guarantee. Indeed, it is only when we lack guarantees that we need trust. You don't ask a friend for a legally binding contract when they say they'll do something for you. A guarantee is offered by companies that you don't trust to do the right thing without one.

Demanding a guarantee can actually undermine trust. A pre-nuptial agreement, for example, signals that one or more party does not trust the other to behave honourably in the event of a divorce, something that this signal only reinforces.

Another thing that we sometimes look for when seeking trust is transparency. If everything is out in the open we can be confident that we will not be deceived. But this can also

T

work against trust: to demand that nothing is hidden from you shows how little you trust the other person. If you trust your business or life partner, you don't need to put a tracking app on their phone or read their emails. Real trust requires that we are not obliged to give a full account of everything we do.

O'Neill's central point is that because trust is inherently risky, it is 'inevitably sometimes misplaced'. If you've never been let down, you are very lucky, a brilliant judge of character or haven't done much trusting in your life. And if you haven't trusted, you haven't really loved, at least not in full openness and reciprocity.

To demand guarantees and transparency is to give up on trust and choose something more transactional and formal instead. But without trust life would be intolerable. It is one of the things that bind us, which is why so many businesses do clichéd trust exercises, as if catching a falling colleague on an away day were proof that you can be trusted when the eyes of all your colleagues aren't on you.

There is one other aspect of trust that is easily overlooked. We always ask who we should trust. But should people trust you? O'Neill begins her book about trust by citing Confucius, who said it is one of the three things a ruler needs, along with weapons and food. If you couldn't have all three, you would give up the weapons first and then the food. Trustworthiness is one of the most admirable virtues and also one of the most socially essential. Without it, we soon find ourselves alone; with it, we are rarely short of friends and colleagues.

See also: Betrayal, Character, Consent, Forgiveness, Friendship, Jealousy, Relationships, Risk, Vulnerability

Reading
Onora O'Neill, *A Question of Trust* (Cambridge University Press, 2002)

Truth

Do you care about the truth? For all the talk of a 'post-truth' world, most people would answer yes. We hate being lied to and get cross when politicians, businesses or scientists deceive us. At the same time, there is a widespread view that there is no such thing as 'the Truth', only what is 'true for me' or 'true for you'. The right to our own truth seems fundamental. So what is the truth about truth?

The answer is suggested by a parable that first appeared in an ancient Buddhist text, the *Udana*. A group of blind men are brought before the king and each is shown a part of an elephant – the head, ears, tusk, trunk, body, leg, thigh, top of the tail and tip of the tail – before each is asked to describe what an elephant is like. Each of them gives a different answer: it is like a pot, a winnowing fan, a ploughshare, a plough pole, a store house, a pillar, a mortar, a pestle and a broom.

Their contradictory claims lead them to start punching each other. The king is pleased by this because it demonstrates an important point: 'They dispute like people who see only one side.'

The moral of the story is that it is not enough to know something that is true – you need to know how it fits together with other truths to create the most truthful overall picture. To have only part of the truth is often as misleading as having none of it at all, which is the point of the saying 'a little knowledge is a dangerous thing'.

This explains why we are often right to be sceptical when people claim to know 'the truth'. Usually people have only a part of the truth, which they mistake for the whole. Even when we have several parts we easily believe that we have all of them, or at least all the ones we need.

It is important, however, to remember that the parable makes sense only if there are real truths rather than just opinions. If one of the blind men had felt the tusk and said it was like a broom, he would have been either mistaken or lying. We do not have a right to assert any old 'truth' as our own. A claim that something is true has to be answerable to reality, not just to our own will.

The Jains picked up the parable and ran with it, using it to illustrate their concept of *anekantavada* (or 'many-sidedness'). Truth and reality are complex and have many sides. No single statement can therefore entirely capture the full truth, and so any claim should be considered as partial and incomplete. This is why the thirteenth-century Jain Mallisena says, 'Due to extreme delusion produced on account of a partial view-point, the immature deny one aspect and try to establish another. This is the maxim of the blind men and the elephant.'

At first sight, the view that no single perspective captures the complete truth might seem to be indistinguishable from what Jean-François Lyotard called the postmodernist 'incredulity towards metanarratives': a rejection of single, overarching explanatory accounts. However, postmodernism led to a celebration and validation of partial perspectives rather than an attempt to piece them together. Where we should have a mosaic, we have only innumerable fragments.

We don't need to buy into *anekantavada* completely to agree that, in practice at least, no one ever has the whole truth. This is a kind of prophylactic against dogmatism and unjustified certainty. It is not, however, a reason to shrug our shoulders and be sceptical about the possibility of truth al-together. It is one thing to have an incomplete grasp of the truth, quite another to wilfully misrepresent it or claim as true something that is no more than an opinion. The parable of the blind men and the elephant should increase our respect for truth as something that it is important to strive towards but difficult to fully attain.

In practice, this means that when you are not sure whether to believe someone, it's not always a matter of deciding whether what they're saying is neatly true or false. Better questions to ask are, 'Is this the whole truth?' or 'What is this person *not* saying?' The truth is out there, but in pieces that we need to work hard to put together.

See also: Argument, Evidence, Intuition, Knowledge, Lying, Rationality

Reading
Udana translated by Anandajoti Bhikkhu, 6.4
Julian Baggini, *A Short History of Truth* (Quercus, 2017)

U

'Our conscious awareness is the mere tip of the iceberg of nonconscious processing.'
Michael Gazzaniga

Uncertainty

In the business news, we're often told that 'markets don't like uncertainty'. If so, that has to be the way in which markets are most human. Uncertainty is unsettling, certainty reassuring. But uncertainty is the norm rather than the exception. Our knowledge about the world is limited, there are normally arguments for and against a point of view, and we can't know how things will turn out in the future. Can we learn to embrace uncertainty rather than get distressed by it?

The Sceptics thought so. The school started in the fourth century BCE with Pyrrho of Elis. He wrote nothing, but patchy accounts of his life and thought have reached us through other sources. He is reported to have travelled to India with Alexander the Great and spent time with Indian sages. Diogenes Laertius tells us that through them he was inspired to adopt a philosophy of 'suspension of judgement, upon which freedom from anxiety follows like a shadow'. After Pyrrho, Scepticism underwent various makeovers, not always in keeping with his original teachings.

The basic idea is that we can't know how truthful our sensations and opinions are, so we should avoid relying on them and suspend judgement about pretty much everything. Pyrrho advocates remaining 'unopinionated' and 'uncommitted', which has the added advantage of leading to calm and tranquillity. This is because if we suspend judgement about what is truly good or bad we will get less stressed about getting the former and avoiding the latter.

Hume had a lot of sympathy for Pyrrho's position. He sounds quite Pyrrhonian, for instance, when he writes that the 'manifold contradictions and imperfections in human reason has so wrought upon me, and heated my brain, that I am ready to reject all belief and reasoning, and can look upon no opinion even as more probable or likely than another.'

But Hume recognised that it's not really possible to *live* by Sceptic principles, so he advocated a 'mitigated scepticism' with only 'a small tincture of Pyrrhonism'. This is needed because most people tend to display excessive certainty and dogmatism in their opinions. Reflecting on 'the imperfection of those faculties which they employ, their narrow reach, and their inaccurate operations' would 'inspire them with more modesty and reserve, and diminish their fond opinion of themselves, and their prejudice against antagonists'.

Hume was surely right that we ought to be modest about our own capacity to understand and form sound judgements. Often we are so keen to avert uncertainty that we cling too tightly to definite opinions. If asked for our views on a current political issue, for instance, we may feel embarrassed to reply that we just don't have any. But uncertainty is often a fitting response to what we know about the world, so we could all do with being a bit more provisional with our beliefs. If the way forward is unclear, that is the nature of things. If we think we've made a mistake, or something good or bad has happened, let's try to suspend judgement: we don't really know.

Hume's moderate scepticism might seem very different from the Pyrrhonian version. There are stories about Pyrrho practising what he preached, 'neither avoiding anything nor watching out for anything, taking everything as it came, whether it be wagons or precipices or dogs, and all such things, relying on his senses for nothing'. But these are probably colourful confabulations. If that was indeed his lifestyle he would have been unlikely to have lived until he was nearly ninety, as he is reported to have done.

The more prosaic reality is that Pyrrhonian Sceptics were not silly. Of course they acknowledged 'that it is daytime, that we are alive, and many other appearances'. They adopted a common-sense approach to daily life, acting on the basis of how things appear, while avoiding taking this as a guide to how things really are. 'That honey is sweet I do not posit; that it appears so I concede,' says Pyrrho's pupil Timon.

To bring a little scepticism into our lives, we simply need to counter our tendency towards excessive certainty. A Daoist story perfectly illustrates this spirit of suspending judgement. A Chinese peasant owned a horse, which he used for transport and for ploughing the fields. When the horse ran away, all the neighbours expressed sympathy, but the peasant just said, 'Maybe.' After a few days the horse came back, bringing two wild horses, and when the neighbours offered congratulations, the peasant just said, 'Maybe.' Then the peasant's son tried to ride one of the wild horses, but he was thrown off and broke his leg. The neighbours again commiserated, but the peasant again said, 'Maybe.' A week later, conscription officers came to the village to take young men for the army, but the peasant's son was rejected because of his broken leg. When the neighbours rejoiced, the peasant said, 'Maybe.'

'To know that one does not know is best; not to know but to believe that one knows is a disease,' says the *Daodejing*. But the acceptance of uncertainty does not require a foolish refusal to believe anything – it simply requires proper modesty about the extent of our knowledge. Be less certain, more questioning, suspend judgement a little more. Scepticism is a powerful medicine against dogmatism, so you only need a small tincture of it.

See also: Ambivalence, Regret, What If

Reading
David Hume, *An Enquiry concerning Human Understanding* (1748)

Unconscious

'Why did you do that?' is a question you will have asked or been asked, possibly in a tone of curiosity, anger or disbelief. Usually the answer would explain why we did what we did: we switched on the light because it was getting dark or we put on a jumper because we were cold.

But we have become increasingly suspicious of the idea that it is possible to access our true reasons for doing things. Instead, the new common sense is that we are largely driven by unconscious motives. The challenge has come from different quarters: psychoanalysis, social psychology and neuroscience. Scores of studies show that we lack insight into our own personality traits, our motives, how we're likely to feel and behave, how others perceive us – you name it. The consensus among neuroscientists, as Michael Gazzaniga puts it, is that 'Our conscious awareness is the mere tip of the iceberg of nonconscious processing.'

We're right to be sceptical about how far we can know ourselves. But we shouldn't rely too heavily on unconscious mechanisms to explain our behaviour. Wittgenstein believed that Freud had made this very error by confusing *reasons* and *causes*, which in Wittgenstein's view are 'two different orders of things': 'Causes may be discovered by experiments, but experiments do not produce reasons.'

To postulate a cause is to put forward a hypothesis, which is properly settled by empirical investigation. For example, to say that a fracture in a bridge caused it to collapse would be verified – or not – by a structural engineer. The causes of actions and states of mind, in contrast, are usually hidden away and often a matter of speculation. Maybe your dislike of your stepfather is caused by Oedipal issues – but then again, maybe not. Your anger might have been caused by low blood sugar but perhaps it was the brain parasite *Toxoplasma gondii*, or something completely different.

Accepting that there are hidden causes of our actions and states of mind doesn't eliminate the need to provide reasons to make sense of why we did, felt, thought or said something. Reasons are often implicit rather than immediately obvious. For instance, it might take some reflection to identify your reasons for disliking your stepfather – maybe some jealousy in you, some fault in him or some combination of these and other reasons. This kind of reflection demands care and honesty. It is easy to rationalise our behaviour or confabulate bogus reasons for action. Indeed we can never know for sure that the reasons we believe we've identified were really those at work. However, if we do not believe that there are such things as genuine reasons, we are in effect saying that we are automata in which beliefs and desires play no role.

A useful concept in this respect is Daniel Dennett's 'intentional stance', which in a nutshell is the strategy of treating people *as if* they were rational agents whose behaviour is governed by beliefs and desires. Yes, we are largely ignorant of what is happening in our own and other people's skulls, and have no idea what role – if any – beliefs and desires really play in generating action. But the intentional stance allows us to reliably predict and make sense of each other's behaviour. It is hard to imagine how we could function if we gave it up.

Wittgenstein completely understood the appeal of taking a complex phenomenon and explaining it on the basis of something simpler. He described the attraction of being able to say, 'This is really only this' as 'overwhelming'. One of the examples he mentions with disapproval is Freud's interpretation of a dream about beautiful flowers as being 'really' about sex.

The unconscious undeniably plays a huge role in our lives. It would be hubristic madness to imagine that reasons can explain everything about why we do what we do. But they do have an indispensable role in explaining both our actions and those of others. Without reasons for action, human behaviour would simply make no sense.

See also: Free Will, Intuition, Self-Deception, Self-Knowledge

Reading
Daniel Dennett, *Intuition Pumps and Other Tools for Thinking* (W.W. Norton, 2013)
Ludwig Wittgenstein, *Wittgenstein's Lectures: Cambridge, 1932–35,* edited by Alice Ambrose (Blackwell, 1980)

Unemployment

Unemployment is primarily a practical problem, since it is difficult to make ends meet without a job. For many, however, it is also an existential issue: even if our material needs are being met, not being able to work can make us feel inadequate.

Strangely enough, such profound discontent can have two opposite causes. The first relates to what Marx called 'alienation'. For most of human history, productive activity has been part of what it means to be human, integral to our 'species-being'. In a capitalist economy, however, 'labour is *external* to the worker' and 'belongs to another' – the employer. Work is 'therefore not the satisfaction of a need; it is merely a *means* to satisfy needs external to it'. Work, which should be an intrinsic part of ourselves, becomes instrumental. Hence we feel 'self-estrangement' or 'alienation', a loss of self.

One objection to Marx's theory is that many people seem happy enough doing their supposedly alienating work, as long as it is sufficiently rewarding. Arguably, alienation becomes more of a problem when we're *not* able to work. Our lack of control over our productive lives becomes starkly apparent when we can't even engage in them.

In Marxist terms then, unemployment underscores the separation between our productive selves and our work. Sartre, however, suggests that sometimes the problem is that we identify with our jobs too much. He describes a waiter who 'bends forward a little too eagerly; his voice, his eyes express an interest a little too solicitous for the order of the customer'. The waiter is playing a kind of social game of being nothing but a waiter to his customers, but he takes it too far. He is trying too hard to be a waiter because his identity has become fused with his job. He has become so attached to how others view him that he treats himself as others treat him: as a waiter, and nothing more.

It's easy to imagine how traumatic it would be for this waiter to lose his job. Suddenly he would no longer be able to be what he essentially believes himself to be. This is how many feel when they become unemployed: their identity has become so wrapped up in their job that losing it is like losing themselves.

The connection between Marx's and Sartre's very different accounts of our relationship with work is that both describe a kind of loss of self. Whether we identify with our jobs or feel alienated from them, we are attaching our sense of ourselves as productive beings to our work. This means that our self is no longer wholly ours, but is determined by a job.

This suggests that one way to live with unemployment is to remember that our nature as productive selves is not entirely invested in paid work: we do not need the validation of a pay cheque to reassure us that we are fully human. The financial aspects of unemployment are problematic enough without the extra burden of allowing it to undermine our self-esteem. Being productive does not necessarily mean being paid. We depend on work to live, but we don't need it to give us a sense of self.

See also: Career, Identity, Insecurity, Leisure, Needs, Self-Love, Wealth, Work

Reading

Karl Marx, *Economic & Philosophic Manuscripts of 1844*, marxists. org
Jean-Paul Sartre, *Being and Nothingness* (1943)

V

'Our sense of the reality of things and people and our ability to interact effectively with them depend on the way our body works silently in the background.' Hubert Dreyfus

Values

If you are reading this book, you are probably the kind of person who takes their self-development seriously. If so, you may have developed an awareness of your personality traits, key character strengths, core skills and long-term goals, as well as your psychological and emotional weaknesses and vulnerabilities. Yet there is something important that is often left out of this work: a thorough examination of your values.

Values drive all we do. 'It is hard to imagine a human life going on at all without an implicit awareness of some values of some kinds,' says Simon Blackburn. And yet many people spend their whole lives without ever properly examining them.

So what are values? Attaching value to something means judging it as good or bad, important or otherwise. This entails judging certain other things negatively: if you value freedom, for example, it follows that the lack of it is bad.

All the big decisions we face in life depend to some degree – often a very large one – on our values. A new job, for instance, might force you to decide which you value more: money and career progression or quality of daily life. Two people in equally problematic marriages might make very different decisions if one places more value on family integrity and the other on personal happiness. Friendship might test the relative importance of loyalty and honesty.

There is some resistance these days to calling things good or bad, right or wrong, as it is considered 'being judgemental'. But a life without any such judgements is impossible. 'If we are condemned to act in the human world,' writes Blackburn, 'we are compelled to rank situations and actions as better or worse.'

One of the central things to bear in mind about values is that they are not the same as facts. Take moral values. Hume argued that morality 'consists not in any matter of fact, which can be discover'd by the understanding'. You can't prove that murder is wrong in the same way that you can prove one plus one equals two, or that cyanide is a poison. To place supreme value on life is to make a judgement, not to demonstrate a fact. 'Valuing something,' says Blackburn, 'is not to be understood as *describing* it'.

Does this mean that values are no more than matters of opinion, which cannot be questioned? Not quite. Values should not be indifferent to reality. Often our values are misguided because they are based on false assumptions about what is true. People value money because they think it will make them happy, or undervalue women in the workplace because they think they are not as smart as men. Our values are informed by facts, and when we understand things better, our values often change. To take an everyday example, you may value your almond milk because you think it is environmentally friendly, but you would stop valuing it if you realised it was made from water-hungry, heavily pesticide-sprayed plants in California.

Interrogating our values is therefore a serious and time-consuming task. We need to start by asking ourselves what we most value and why, before checking whether those reasons are good ones. The rewards of such a 'value audit' can be enormous. When we have clarity of values we have clarity of purpose and a sound basis on which to make life-defining decisions. What could be more valuable?

See also: Ambivalence, Authenticity, Character, Dilemmas, Integrity, Motivation

Reading
Simon Blackburn, *Ruling Passions* (Oxford University Press, 1998)

Vanity *see* **Pride**

Vegetarianism

In many parts of the world, vegetarians had become used to being treated as idealistic eccentrics, vegans as virtual nutcases. In recent years, however, plant-based diets have become mainstream. Some people adopt them for health reasons, but many have a moral motivation. Those who still devour steaks and fried chicken need to confront that challenge. Does meat mean murder and milk misery?

It seems extraordinary that in many times and places people did not consider the welfare of animals at all. René Descartes was convinced that animals were mere automata who lacked rationality or language and therefore also the immaterial souls that give human beings consciousness. 'My opinion is not so much cruel to animals as indulgent to men,' he wrote, 'since it absolves them from the suspicion of crime when they eat or kill animals.'

But Descartes did not deny life or sensation to animals. For Jeremy Bentham, this was enough to require us to consider their welfare. In what could have been a direct rebuttal of Descartes, he wrote of animals, 'the question is not, Can they *reason*? nor, Can they *talk*? but, Can they *suffer*?' Bentham was way ahead of his time. 'The French have already discovered that the blackness of the skin is no reason why a human being should be abandoned without redress to the caprice of a tormentor. It may come one day to be recognised, that the number of the legs, the villosity of the skin, or the termination of the *os sacrum*, are reasons equally insufficient for abandoning a sensitive being to the same fate.'

Bentham was making a clear comparison between racism and our treatment of animals. In the twentieth century, Richard D. Ryder coined the term 'speciesism' to make this explicit. We are 'speciesist' whenever we treat living creatures differently purely on the grounds of what species they belong to. That does not mean we are always obliged to treat all species the same, but different treatment must be justified by some morally relevant difference. For example, to allow pigs to be killed for meat when we do not slaughter dogs would be speciesist if there were no morally relevant differences between dogs and pigs to justify these different standards.

In broad terms, Bentham's once radical ideas are now mainstream common sense. Most people believe that animals can suffer and we ought to consider their welfare. The reason we're not all vegetarian is that many remain convinced that it is possible to raise meat and dairy animals in ways that do not involve suffering.

To clinch the ethical case for vegetarianism you therefore have to show why killing animals is in itself morally wrong. This is difficult to do. You might argue that no one has the right to take another creature's life, but that would make all of nature a violation of justice. The planet is filled with omnivores and carnivores, and the cycle of life depends on this.

If we accept that killing for food is not itself morally wrong, farming animals is permissible as long as welfare is good and slaughter is humane. Some utilitarian arguments make animal husbandry almost obligatory. The great advocate of animal liberation, Peter Singer, argues that the more satisfied creatures there are in the world, the better. So, for example, it would be better to have lots of happy sheep leaping around fields before swiftly getting the chop than it would be if those fields were full of joyless wheat. If animals live in the moment, all that matters is that there are as many such moments as possible. The length of individual animal lives is irrelevant.

If welfare really is the issue, however, most of us need to tighten up our standards. The principle that it is morally acceptable to eat well-reared, humanely slaughtered meat clashes with the reality of most industrial farming, where animals often lead miserable lives. Conditions are often particularly bad for egg-laying birds and dairy animals, so vegetarians who are not choosy about where they get their animal products are contributing more to animal suffering than omnivores who buy only from high-welfare producers.

Vegans might feel that they are off the hook in this debate. But it is not obvious that abolishing farms is better for animal welfare. Nature is cruel and provides no vets. As Mark Bryant Budolfson argues, 'humanely [reared and] slaughtered animals lead a dramatically better life than they could expect to live in the wild.'

It's not even true that a vegan diet requires no animal killing. Modern arable farming kills a vast number of animals every year with its machinery and chemicals – 7.3 billion according to one estimate. Bob Fischer and Andy Lamey have argued that it is difficult to take any such figure as reliable, but the number is certainly large, and so almost every vegan meal involves the killing of animals.

Some people are ethical vegans or vegetarians on environmental rather than welfare grounds. It is widely accepted that a sustainable global diet requires much less meat than is the norm in developed countries. However, the most efficient use of land would involve some animal farming – pigs and chickens can be fed otherwise inedible byproducts, and ruminants can graze on land that is unsuitable for crops. Methods of farming are also important. Pasture-reared cows emit methane, for instance, but grassland is a carbon sink, to which the broken-down methane returns. Many nut milks, in contrast, come at the cost of huge amounts of irrigation and pesticides. Some plant-based foods could have bigger carbon footprints than some farm animals.

The argument that we have a moral obligation to think about the welfare of animals and the planet when we eat is now unanswerable. But what that requires of us is far from clear. Vegans and vegetarians do not automatically occupy the moral high ground, but at least they are trying to reach it. Are you?

See also: Nature, Pets

Reading

Julian Baggini, *The Virtues of the Table* (Granta, 2014)

Jeremy Bentham, *An Introduction to the Principles of Morals and Legislation* (1789)

Ben Bramble and Bob Fischer (editors), *The Moral Complexities of Eating Meat* (Oxford University Press, 2015)

Virtual Life

It's rare to hear someone complain that they don't spend enough time online or glued to their smartphones, and many of us worry about our increased fixation with small screens. A report by the UK government regulator Ofcom in 2018 found that the average Briton spends more than a day a week online, a figure that could well have risen by the time you read this. Should we be concerned, or is this just the latest moral panic that accompanies any societal shift?

Psychologists have produced conflicting reports on how good for our well-being all this virtual living is. (Spoiler alert: it's not the amount of time on your devices that matters most, but how you use them.) From a philosophical point of view, however, the most pressing question is whether it is causing us to lose touch with reality.

At the dawn of the millennium, as the Internet was beginning to become widely used, Hubert Dreyfus wrote an influential book in which he warned about the limits of online living. His central point was that human beings are essentially embodied creatures: 'Our sense of the reality of things and people and our ability to interact effectively with them depend on the way our body works silently in the background.'

One consequence of this is that whenever we interact with people in ways that eliminate the body, we interact incompletely. For instance, when we leave our bodies behind we feel less vulnerable. This may sound good, but it is only by making ourselves vulnerable that we can truly open ourselves up to deep friendships. (*See* **Vulnerability**.) There is therefore a dehumanising aspect to virtual relationships, which is most evident in the incivility that is rife online, aided and abetted by the anonymity of the trolls and the physical absence of those they attack.

There are other benefits of leaving our bodies behind. Many find it easier to be open and honest when not face to face, and we might also be liberated from prejudices if we can't see the skin colour, age, gender or body shape of the person we are interacting with. It's not as though we bring our full selves to all social interactions anyway. Many of us have a work persona that is different from our home one.

Although there is no arguing with Dreyfus's basic premise, he did not anticipate how typical it is to use online as an adjunct to offline life, rather than as a substitute for it. Most strikingly, over two-thirds of couples now meet online. Our ability to shift seamlessly from off- to online seems to be much better than Dreyfus anticipated. Cyberspace works best not as an alternative to physical space, but as an extension of it.

To his credit, Dreyfus was no doom-monger. The value of his work is that it warns us of the perils of spending more time online and so helps us to avoid them. His conclusion is as pertinent today as it was in 2001: 'As long as we continue to affirm our bodies, the Net can be useful to us in spite of its tendency to offer the worst of asymmetric trade-offs: economy over efficacy in education, the virtual over the real in our relation to things and other people, and anonymity over commitment in our lives.' Virtual life is full of potential, as long as we return to our bodies to keep it real.

See also: The Body, Dating, Friendship, Relationships, Trust, Vulnerability

Reading
Hubert L. Dreyfus, *On the Internet* (2nd edition, Routledge, 2008)

Virtue

For a long time, 'virtue' was deeply unfashionable and associated with pious goody-goodies. The revival of 'virtue ethics' in philosophy has done something to rehabilitate the notion, but becoming more virtuous was and probably still is on very few people's lists of New Year's resolutions. But it should be, and would be, if we better understood what virtue actually meant.

The fundamental idea about virtue is quite straightforward: there are human qualities and character traits that are conducive to a flourishing life, so naturally if we want such a life, we need to cultivate them. Without these virtues, we simply cannot thrive. But what are they?

Thinkers have offered different lists. For Plato, the main virtues were courage, temperance, justice and prudence. These were adopted by the early Christian tradition and became known as the 'cardinal' virtues, which were then combined with faith, hope and charity to form the seven primary Christian virtues.

Aristotle distinguished between virtues of character and virtues of thought. The main virtue of thought was practical wisdom, the ability to make wise decisions in concrete situations. (*See* **Indecision**, **Wisdom**.) The key virtues of character were courage, temperance, generosity, magnificence, greatness of soul, even temper, friendliness, truthfulness, wit, justice, friendship. Most of these are still relevant today, although the odd one – notably 'greatness of soul' – sounds distinctly alien. Cultivating these virtues involves training ourselves to develop the relevant habits and inclinations. (*See* **Balance**, **Habits**.)

Being virtuous therefore requires us to cultivate the character traits that incline us to act well and the skills of judgement that allow us to tailor our reactions to the precise needs of any given situation. We need to harness both habitual responses and conscious reflection. To do this we have to be motivated to pursue virtue, which we should be once we realise that flourishing depends on it.

The ultimate list of essential virtues has yet to be compiled, but even if we had one, their application would still vary according to context. Hume gave an example of this when he remarked that 'It is not surprising that during a period of war and disorder, the military virtues should be more celebrated than the pacific, and attract more the admiration and attention of mankind.'

Virtues are also culturally variable, since societies differ in time, place and circumstance. Patricia Churchland observes that honesty is a much more important virtue in Inuit than in Polynesian culture, because the harsh environment of the frozen north makes trust and cooperation imperative for survival. 'Starvation is always just a seal away. So when someone deceives them about something and the whole group undertakes an activity as a result, they waste precious energy and resources.'

That does not mean that there can't be a more-or-less universal basic set of virtues, which may carry different weight or be expressed differently in different times and places. A human society in which courage, honesty, kindness and generosity are considered vices is barely conceivable, and no one could flourish if greed, deceit and cruelty were counted as virtues. Hume argued that a good case could be made for the naturalness of moral sentiments, precisely because 'there never was any nation of the world, nor any single person in any nation, who was utterly depriv'd of them'.

As Martha Nussbaum explains, the question of virtue concerns everyone because it relates to issues that we all have to grapple with, 'areas in which human choice is both non-optional and somewhat problematic'. These are things like death, the body, pleasure and pain, allocating limited resources, dealing with danger and social interactions.

Virtue is, of course, a matter of degree: few lack it entirely and no one is completely virtuous. This means there is always room for improvement, not for the sake of feeling virtuous in the 'worthy' sense, but for the sake of living life to the full. Virtue is something we should always resolve to cultivate, not just at New Year.

See also: Balance, Character, Habit, Indecision, Intuition, Self-Control, Wisdom

Reading
Aristotle, *Nicomachean Ethics*

Vulnerability

At the time of writing, Brené Brown's TED talk on 'The Power of Vulnerability' had been viewed over 45 million times. It's clearly a topic that strongly resonates with people. Generally we don't like being vulnerable, which for Brown means showing our weaknesses and imperfections, leaving ourselves open to people's judgement and rejection. She believes that in order to really connect with people, we need to be prepared to do all this and let others see us in our entirety.

Historically, many thinkers have been more keen to reduce vulnerability than to celebrate it. Stoics and Buddhists thought we could do this by curbing desires and attachments. Marcus Aurelius tells himself, 'The mind without passions is a fortress. No place is more secure. Once we take refuge there we are safe forever.'

But as Epicurus said, there are limits to self-protection: 'one can attain security against other things, but when it comes to death, all men live in a city without walls.' Even if invulnerability *is* possible, it is definitely not cost-free – we pay for it in terms of humanity and richness of human experience. Todd May has written in praise of what he calls 'vulnerabilism'. For him, the ideal of invulnerability is 'too disengaged emotionally from the world' and narrows 'the range of human emotion and reaction'. If we care for people and projects, we will inevitably get attached to them, and if we're attached, we're vulnerable to suffering. We need to accept 'the idea that we can be shaken to our very foundations'.

You might say that we can act with compassion while retaining some kind of distance, as Buddhism commends. But that is not the same as caring, which requires an emotional investment. Caring, says May, 'is a package deal. Either we care and expose ourselves to suffering, or we are serenely compassionate and do not.'

May acknowledges that the ideal of invulnerability might work for some. And there are practices we can borrow from invulnerabilism, such as keeping things in perspective, avoiding worrying about remote possibilities and focusing on what Pierre Hadot has described as 'the minuscule present moment, which, in its exiguity, is always bearable and controllable'. But May believes that for most people, these are best used to serve the less extreme goal of achieving some kind of balance and peace with the world, which is both more attainable and more desirable.

The key to this is to accept that we can't control what happens and that we are therefore vulnerable to bad things affecting us. If these occur, we'll feel sad and upset. Acceptance of this situation does not remove the pain, but it might reduce it, whereas kicking against reality will definitely increase it. (*See* **Contentment**, **Suffering**.)

Being vulnerable is our natural state. It is not invulnerability we should seek, but what May calls 'a slightly less lacerating vulnerability'.

See also: Calm, Contentment, Control, Failure, Health and Illness, Loss, Mortality, Suffering

Reading
Todd May, *A Fragile Life: Accepting Our Vulnerability* (University of Chicago Press, 2017)

W

" 'Money never made anyone
rich: all it does is infect
everyone who touches it with a
lust for more of itself.' Seneca

War

Only a few generations ago, most people in the developed world had either fought in a war or knew someone who had. Now war is something that many of us have never had to experience at all. But our governments have not stopped waging it. Depending on how you count, the USA has been involved in something between fourteen and thirty-eight armed conflicts since the Second World War, while the UK has participated in around thirty. As citizens, we have to ask ourselves: when should we support such military ventures and when should we do all we can to stop them?

Absolute pacifism provides a simple answer, but few are willing to say that a world without any killing at all is possible. Even Gandhi, who promoted *ahimsa* (non-violence), accepted that pure pacifism was an ideal to be strived towards and not something that could ever be fully achieved: 'Man cannot for a moment live without consciously or unconsciously committing outward *himsa*' (violence).

Most people see war as a regrettable necessity. Although the principles governing the ethics of war are contested, there has been remarkable agreement over the centuries about what has come to be called Just War Theory. Although this has its origins way back in the Christian ethics of St Augustine (354–430 CE), its modern versions are mostly secular.

Just War Theory is divided into two parts. One concerns conduct in war (*jus in bello*), which in broad terms requires all warring parties to use proportionate force and to discriminate between combatants and civilians. Most agree with these principles in theory, although they are often ignored in practice.

More fundamental is the ethics of going to war in the first place (*jus ad bellum*). Again the list of criteria is widely endorsed: the war must be waged for a just cause, it must be a last resort, it has to be declared by a proper authority, it has to have the right intention, it has to have a reasonable chance of success, and the scale of the fighting must be proportionate.

It's easy enough to identify flagrant exceptions to both sets of principles. When Saddam Hussein invaded Kuwait in 1990, for instance, it was simply a land-and-resources grab, without any just cause. The widespread use of Agent Orange and napalm in Vietnam was disproportionate and indiscriminate in its effects.

However, the clarity of the principles turns into obscurity when you try to put them into practice. 'Last resort' sounds simple, but how long do you refrain from taking action if people are suffering at the hands of a cruel regime? Avoiding civilian casualties is obviously right, but what do you do if an enemy is operating from residential areas?

Just War Theory does not provide an easy algorithm for determining whether conflict is justified, but it is useful as a set of tests and questions to help us to make the difficult judgements of war and peace. The next time you are considering joining a protest march against a war or calling for a military intervention, check your own reasons for doing so against Just War criteria.

See also: Authority, Dilemmas, Patriotism, Politics, Protest

Reading
Richard Norman, *Ethics, Killing and War* (Cambridge University Press, 2011)
Michael Walzer, *Arguing About War* (Yale University Press, 2004)

Weakness of Will *see* Self-Control

Wealth

Philosophers and sages can be boringly predictable when it comes to money. Seneca wrote that 'Money never made anyone rich: all it does is infect everyone who touches it with a lust for more of itself.' Musonius argued that 'one man and one man only is truly wealthy – he who learns to want nothing in every circumstance.' Tell us something we don't know. Even young Liverpudlian pop stars in the 1960s knew that money can't buy you love. It's revealing, however, that the Beatles still sang in protest against the taxman when they got rich. Is the lure of money so strong that we never fully learn our lesson, or is the 'money doesn't matter' mantra too simplistic?

If you look at what philosophers do as well as what they say, few have acted as though money were of no importance. Take some apparent paradigms of the wealth-renouncing thinker. Wittgenstein was born rich and is widely admired for having given all his money away. Socrates wandered the marketplace talking to all and sundry, never charging for his services, unlike the sophist teachers he mocked. Rousseau abandoned the corrupt city for the pure simplicity of country life, refusing pensions that would have given him financial security because he didn't want to be indebted to anybody.

Look more closely, however, and none of these tales is what they seem. Wittgenstein did not give his money away, he left his share with his siblings. Like many rich people who embrace self-imposed 'poverty', he knew there would be a safety net if he needed it.

Socrates had one of the biggest insurance policies of them all: as a free man of Athens, he had slaves at his disposal and didn't have to work. He also had wealthy friends who were prepared to indulge him. He no more renounced wealth than a person renounces smoking when they stop buying cigarettes but constantly scrounge them from friends.

Rousseau was perhaps the most disingenuous of the three. He made a great display of being offended by offers of pensions, arranged by friends who were concerned for his welfare. But for many decades he was dependent on people helping him out, as long as they weren't so vulgar as to shove cash directly into his hands. He coped without wealth by relying on others who were prepared to share theirs.

One of Rousseau's benefactors, Hume, was more honest about the value of wealth. He was never poor, but for a person of his social class he was for a long time not particularly rich either. He never made the pursuit of wealth his goal and abandoned potentially lucrative careers in law and trade. But he was always aware of how much easier life would be if he could find financial security, and he was very pleased when he finally did.

One of the most interesting arguments for wealth comes from the effective altruism movement. It consists mostly of utilitarians, who argue that we ought to do whatever does the most to increase the well-being of as many people as possible. But that doesn't necessarily mean working as a doctor, teacher or social worker. As William MacAskill argues, there are plenty of people who are equally able and willing to do these jobs, but there are not many bankers who earn lots of money with the goal of philanthropy. So if you want to help others, first get rich and then give your money away instead of spending it on Gucci handbags and Beluga caviar. As Peter Singer points out, 'Although it is possible to earn an average income and still donate enough to do a lot of good, it remains true that the more you earn, the more you can donate.'

In one of his essays, Hume approvingly quotes from Agur's Prayer, which pleads, 'Give me neither Poverty nor Riches.' No one needs to be filthy rich, and having too much money can distort and corrupt our values. But even though it is possible to have a good life with very little, let's not pretend it's better to be poor. The sages are right that wealth should not be our central aim, but money is often useful for helping us to achieve our worthier goals.

See also: Altruism, Asceticism, Charity, Consumerism, Envy, Needs, Selfishness, Simplicity, Work

Reading
Peter Singer, *The Most Good You Can Do* (Yale University Press, 2015)
David Hume, 'Of the Middle Station of Life', davidhume.org

What If

What would life have been like if we'd chosen a different career, married someone else or gone travelling? How would it compare with the one we actually lived? Often these questions are laced with regret. (*See* **Regret**.) It's because we're not entirely happy with how things turned out that we wonder about how they might have been.

What can we do with the tantalising thought that our lives might have been different? One perspective comes from the philosophy of possible worlds. The expression comes from Leibniz, who believed that our world was chosen by God from an infinite number of possible worlds. The contemporary debate, started by Saul Kripke, involves heavy-duty metaphysics. David Lewis even put forward the idea that every possible world is in fact real.

The concept becomes of practical use if we borrow it as a way of thinking about alternative scenarios. The kinds of possible worlds that are most useful here are those that were exactly like the actual world until something set them on a diverging course. When we say that we might have left our job and gone travelling, we can express this thought by saying there is a possible world in which we did just that.

It can be instructive to reflect on how close the world we are daydreaming about is to the actual one. It might be reassuring to realise, for instance, that the alternative scenario we are fondly nurturing in our mind could take place only in a possible world that is very far from the actual one. Maybe it would require us to have a completely different personality or to have been raised in utterly altered circumstances. There's little point in dwelling on such remote possibilities.

It's trickier if the possible world seems quite close to the actual one. Maybe it could have come to pass if we had made one different decision. Perhaps we even contemplated that choice and very nearly made it, before settling on something else. The apparent closeness of such a different outcome can be tormenting.

What we need to remember is that we are far more ignorant of what that world would really have been like than we might think. We imagine that if only we'd done something differently our life would be more or less as it is except that one key element in it would be transformed. But little changes can be momentous, and we just don't know whether we would have liked the overall outcome more than what we got. Consider Ray Bradbury's story 'A Sound of Thunder', about a time travel expedition to the era of the dinosaurs. A careless step on a small butterfly alters future outcomes beyond recognition.

It can be fun to speculate about possible worlds, but not so much to live in their shadow. There is no way of knowing how things would have been different as a result of even a simple alteration of the past, let alone a major one. The best cure for thinking that we should have done something else is to remind ourselves that we don't know what would have happened if we had.

See also: Envy, Failure, Fate, Loss, Midlife Crisis, Mistakes, Regret, Resilience, Uncertainty

Reading

Ray Bradbury, 'A Sound of Thunder' in *The Golden Apples of the Sun* (1953)

Willpower *see* Self-Control

Wisdom

When the Western philosophical tradition began to develop, in ancient Greece, philosophers were interested in many things, including logic and the physical world around them. The question of how to live wisely, however, was always central.

After centuries of philosophical neglect, wisdom almost became a dirty word in twentieth-century Anglophone philosophy. But wisdom has fought back. The question of how to live is back on the agenda, and books on some of the ancient philosophers who pondered it, such as the Stoics, are popular.

Aristotle distinguished between two kinds of wisdom: *sophia* and *phronesis*. *Sophia* referred to the application of fundamental principles to the workings of the natural world, while *phronesis* was a practical wisdom that guided our conduct. It is the latter that is closest to our current understanding of wisdom.

Phronesis involves consistently listening to the counsel of reason and taking the appropriate steps towards the most flourishing life available to us. It does not guarantee we'll achieve our goals, but most of the time it gives us more of a chance. In any case, living with practical wisdom fulfils the most important goal of acting in accordance with the core of being human, and is therefore its own reward.

Practical wisdom requires various skills. One is to be clear about what truly matters. (*See* **Values**.) Another is the ability to translate general principles into our own particular situation, as Aristotle tells us to do. Wisdom is not something that can be captured by a neat aphorism that is applicable to everyone equally. We have to be able to work out what being kind, courageous or accepting means in our particular situation. In daily life this isn't always easy, mystified as we often are by limited knowledge and clashing values and priorities. But then if wisdom were simple, you really could capture it in a tweet.

See also: Indecision, Intuition, Knowledge, Rationality, Virtue

Reading
Barry Schwartz and Kenneth Sharpe, *Practical Wisdom: The Right Way to Do the Right Thing* (Riverhead Books, 2010)

Work

In many countries, one of the first questions a new acquaintance will be asked is 'what do you do?' People don't typically answer with 'I go walking at weekends', 'I like cooking new dishes' or 'I read a lot' – they say what their job is, and if they don't have one, they often give a somewhat apologetic explanation as to why not. Work is a key part of what defines who we are. Some people constantly feel they're not working hard enough, as if it is only through hard work that they can justify their existence. Many take a lot of pride in their 'work ethic', whether or not it is working for them; others might recognise they are too work-focused, 'workaholic' even.

It's understandable why work looms so large in our lives – for a typical person, nothing takes up more of their waking life. The World Health Organization found that, on average, a little more than a third of your adult life is spent working, slightly more time than we spend sleeping.

However, the fact that these figures don't include unpaid work, including that of stay-at-home parents, is a clue to where we might have gone wrong. 'Work' has come to mean *paid* work, whether employment or self-employment. If work is not paid it needs the qualifier 'voluntary' to make this clear, since 'work' by itself would suggest income.

Earning a living is a necessity for most of us, which makes it valuable as a means to an end. According to Bertrand Russell, this is how most working people see their jobs. 'They consider work, as it should be considered, as a necessary means to a livelihood, and it is from their leisure hours that they derive whatever happiness they may enjoy.' If that is the case, then the workers are on the side of Aristotle, who said that 'we work to have leisure, on which happiness depends.' (*See* **Leisure**.)

However, we live in a culture that makes a virtue of work in itself. How did this happen? Max Weber rooted it in what he called the 'Protestant work ethic', which he linked with 'the spirit of capitalism'. How far the latter is based on religion is contentious, but Weber was surely right to say that in modern capitalist economies 'people are oriented to acquisition as the purpose of life; acquisition is no longer viewed as a means to the end of satisfying the substantive needs of life.'

To fuel this consumption we need to be constantly working and earning, even if the work is onerous and unrewarding. 'Capitalism as such is not interested in quality of life,' says Gary Gutting. 'It is essentially a system for producing things to sell at a profit, the greater the better.'

As a child, Russell was taught the inherent value of work as though it were a spiritual truth, being told that 'Satan finds some mischief for idle hands to do.' Over time he changed his mind and came to believe that 'there is far too much work done in the world, [and] that immense harm is caused by the belief that work is virtuous.' He advocated reduced working hours to allow for more leisure time.

However, we should be careful not to demonise work. Today we have an acute awareness that it is unhealthy to work too hard and that we should make time for other things. But the expression 'work-life balance' unhelpfully cuts work off from the rest of life. Although for some people work is only toil, surveys consistently show that a clear majority derives some satisfaction from at least part of their work, and a sizeable minority is lucky enough to love it. So it might be better to think in terms of what Hume called the 'mixed kind of life', which involves balancing instrumental activities, such as working to earn a living, with things we enjoy for their own sake, such as learning and engaging with active pursuits.

Theodore Roosevelt said, 'Nothing in the world is worth having or worth doing unless it means effort, pain, difficulty.' 'Nothing' might be an overstatement, but it is true that little of value comes free or easy. The mistake of modern capitalist society is to confuse the value of *effort* with that of *paid work*. Give life your all, but do not give all your life to your employer.

See also: Career, Leisure, Office Politics, Retirement, Unemployment, Wealth

Reading
Max Weber, *The Protestant Ethic and the Spirit of Capitalism* (1905)

Work-Life Balance *see* **Leisure**

Worrying

In Roger Hargreaves's children's book *Mr Worry*, the eponymous hero gradually learns that none of the things that bother him are genuine causes for concern. So is he happy at the end of the book? No: he's worried that he has nothing to worry about.

It's an exceptionally astute psychological truth to teach infants. We are capable of worrying about anything, although some areas – finances, careers, relationships, appearance and people's opinions of us – tend to feature most prominently. Can we do better than Mr Worry?

Worry is a kind of fear, one that can make our lives miserable. Thoughts about what might happen and worst case scenarios run around like wild animals in our heads. According to Bertrand Russell, the problem is that people 'cannot cease to think about worrying topics at times when no action can be taken in regard to them'.

What are the philosophical remedies? Russell's primary recommendation borrows from the Stoics. (*See* **Pessimism**.) He writes that if some kind of potential misfortune appears on the horizon, what we need to do is 'consider seriously and deliberately what is the very worst that could possibly happen. Having looked this possible misfortune in the face, give yourself sound reasons for thinking that after all it would be no such very terrible disaster.' For best results, he advises going through this process a few times.

According to Russell, we can always find reasons to believe that something isn't terrible, even in the case of very bad scenarios, 'since at the worst nothing that happens to oneself has any cosmic importance'. Not everyone would find this a consolation.

This isn't a simple, doom-laden, 'expect-the-worst' approach, which may well be counterproductive. It involves accepting that the worst *might* happen and reassuring ourselves that we'd be able to cope with it. Having done that, we might realise that the worst scenario is by no means the most likely one anyway.

Although Russell was very confident about the effectiveness of this method, we should acknowledge that it doesn't always work. Sometimes the worrying thoughts have too much of a hold on us. In those cases, we could try a remedy that Russell recommends for times when things have already gone wrong: distraction. He mentions chess, detective stories or becoming interested in astronomy or archaeology. But anything that can settle our mind on something other than the worrisome topic will be beneficial.

Hume had a similar strategy for easing his philosophical worries. 'I dine, I play a game of back-gammon, I converse, and am merry with my friends; and when after three or four hour's amusement, I wou'd return to these speculations, they appear so cold, and strain'd, and ridiculous, that I cannot find in my heart to enter into them any farther.' Philosophy helps to understand life, but even philosophers need to stop thinking from time to time. You can't live life with the user's manual always in one hand – having studied it, you have to put it down and just live.

See also: Anxiety, Calm, Contentment, Cosmic Insignificance, Fear, Pessimism, Stress, Uncertainty, Vulnerability

Reading
Roger Hargreaves, *Mr Worry* (Penguin, 1978)

Zest *see* **Love of Life**

Philosophy: Where to Start

There are specific suggestions for further reading after each entry in this book, but the following are good places to start if you are interested in exploring the practical side of philosophy more generally.

Philip J. Ivanhoe and Bryan W. Van Norden (eds), *Readings in Classical Chinese Philosophy* (2nd edition, Hackett, 2005)

Until recently, Western readers were drawn to classical Chinese philosophy mainly for its promise of mystical divination (*I Ching*) or for business guidance (*The Art of War*). Now people are waking up to the enduring interest of Confucian, Daoist and Legalist thought. These schools pull in different directions. Confucianism advocates a social and inner harmony that comes from personal virtue, Daoism the need to live in harmony with the natural order, and Legalism a somewhat cynical belief that only strong laws can hold society together.

This excellent anthology contains core writings from them all.

Deepak Sarma (ed.), *Classical Indian Philosophy: A Reader* (Columbia University Press, 2011)

At first blush, classical Indian philosophy can look more like theology than philosophy. In fact, the distinction can barely be made, such is the intermingling of the two on the subcontinent. But there is plenty of interest to the non-religious, particularly in the materialist Charvaka school, the analysis of argumentation in Nyaya, and the rich Buddhist tradition. This anthology contains helpful notes and introductions, as well as a good selection of core texts.

Bhikkhu Bodhi, *In the Buddha's Words: An Anthology of Discourses from the Pali Canon* (Wisdom Publications, 2005)

People debate whether Buddhism is a philosophy or a religion, but this is a false choice: it is clearly both. One of the most important aspects of its philosophy is the idea that nothing has a fixed, abiding essence and that everything, including the self, is a temporary collection of parts. This anthology collects some the earliest texts.

Aristotle, *Nicomachean Ethics* (various editions)

Aristotle is our philosophical hero. He was much more grounded than his teacher Plato, who sometimes seemed more interested in a perfect world of ultimate reality than the one we live in. None of Aristotle's actual books survive and the *Ethics*, like all his other extant writings, is a collection of lecture notes. Aristotle is appropriately modest about how far philosophy can go. We never tire of his adage: 'It is the mark of an educated mind to rest satisfied with the degree of precision which the nature of the subject admits and not to seek exactness where only an approximation is possible.'

Marcus Aurelius, *Meditations* (various editions)

The Stoics and the Epicureans bequeathed innumerable eminently quotable gems that often thrive nowadays as online memes. Modern readers tend to ignore the more demanding or counterintuitive aspects of their teachings. But a book like Marcus Aurelius' *Meditations* can be read as a source of insight without the reader having to buy into the whole system. You don't have to be Stoic to see that 'The things you think about determine the quality of your mind. Your soul takes on the colour of your thoughts.'

David Hume, *An Enquiry Concerning the Principles of Morals* (various editions)

Hume is the philosophers' philosopher, coming top of a poll of professional academics who were asked which dead thinker they most identified with. The heir of Aristotle, he had even less time for abstract reasoning or obtuse metaphysical speculation. Hume has not achieved wide popularity outside academia, partly because the practical application of his ideas isn't always obvious and partly because his long, eighteenth-century sentences can be a little difficult to tune into. Give it time though, and it becomes clear why he was considered not only a philosophical genius but a great prose stylist.

Arthur Schopenhauer, *Essays and Aphorisms* (Penguin, 1976)

Schopenhauer presents a grand system, in the manner of much modern German philosophy. However, we would suggest that he is best read not as an engineer of a fantastical metaphysical system but as a poet, whose piecemeal insights are much more than the sum of their parts. It is easier to do this in his essays and aphorisms, which can be read independently for the gems they contain. Be prepared to be disturbed: Schopenhauer looks the struggle of life in the face with unremitting persistence.

Søren Kierkegaard, *The Living Thoughts of Kierkegaard*, edited by W.H. Auden (New York Review Books, 2009)

Kierkegaard is a poet-philosopher with an acute and analytic intellect. His vast output is impressive, given his short life – he died at the age of 42. It is also bewildering, since he wrote from the point of view of various pseudonymous authors, each analysing a philosophical outlook from the inside. At the heart of his philosophy is the idea that human life contains contradictions that cannot be reconciled by reason, and that we need to take a leap of faith which embraces the paradox of the human condition. This collection, edited by the poet W.H. Auden, is a good entry point.

Viktor Frankl, *Man's Search for Meaning* (1946)

Existentialism claims that we can create our own meaning in a universe without purpose. The writing of the psychiatrist Viktor Frankl, who survived Auschwitz, provides remarkable evidence that this is possible. Frankl was the founder of logotherapy, a modality of psychotherapy based on the idea that our primary motivation is to find meaning in life.

Simone de Beauvoir, *The Ethics of Ambiguity* (1947)

For decades, Beauvoir was cast as Sartre's disciple and lover. Belatedly, many scholars now argue that she was not only his equal but in many ways his superior. Sartre never managed to articulate an ethics based on his existential philosophy. In *The Ethics of Ambiguity*, Beauvoir does a better job of articulating the ethical dimension of the existentialist philosophy of freedom. If it is too dense for your taste, Kate Kirkpatrick's biography *Becoming Beauvoir* (Bloomsbury, 2019) is eminently readable.

Bernard Williams, *Moral Luck* (Cambridge University Press, 1981)

Philosophers are often known for the positions they take. Bernard Williams was different. A brilliant analyst of the puzzles and problems of human life, he refused to provide neat answers. To read him is to accompany an exceptional intellect in his thinking. *Moral Luck* is a collection of essays published in academic journals, but you would never know that from their lucidity and elegance.

Thomas Nagel, *Mortal Questions* (Cambridge University Press, 1991)

Death, war, equality, sex, personal identity – Nagel's book deals with the big questions of life and value with sensitivity and intellectual rigour. This collection of essays also includes the classic 'What Is It Like to Be a Bat?', which gets to the heart of why consciousness seems so mysterious. Nagel is in

no hurry to offer solutions, knowing that our first priority is
to be clear about the shape of the problem.

Martha Nussbaum, *The Therapy of Desire* (Princeton University Press, 1994)

It has become commonplace to champion the Hellenistic
philosophies of the Stoics, Epicureans and Sceptics as ther-
apies for our time. Nussbaum did this earlier and with
more subtlety and insight than most contemporary cheer-
leaders. She also includes the philosopher without whom
these later schools would never have existed: Aristotle. The
book uses the fictional device of a young woman working
her way through the various schools. It's accessible, wise
and engaging.

Pierre Hadot, *Philosophy as a Way of Life* (Blackwell, 1995)

Hadot championed the idea that ancient philosophy was a
practical system for flourishing, not just an attempt to describe
reality. *Philosophy as a Way of Life* attempts to describe the 'spiritual practices' that were as essential as the theories they were
based on. He finds them in philosophers from Socrates to
Michel Foucault.

Daniel Dennett, *Intuition Pumps and Other Tools for Thinking* (W.W. Norton, 2013)

Philosophy is often championed as a way of learning critical
thinking. There are few better arguments for this than
Dennett's *Intuition Pumps*. He covers some classic principles
and methods of reasoning such as Occam's razor ('do not
postulate more entities than are needed for an explanation')
and *reductio ad absurdum* (showing that a position is absurd by

taking it to its logical conclusions). It is also packed with his own inventions, such as 'skyhooks' (groundless nothings on which people hang treasured beliefs) and 'deepities' (profound-sounding but empty pronouncements). A master-class in how to reason better.

Index